PENGUIN BOOKS

THE CRETAN RUNNER

George Psychoundakis was born in Crete in 1920. After a brief period of schooling he lived as a shepherd until the beginning of the German occupation in 1941, when he joined the Cretan Resistance as a runner. He was later awarded the BEM.

Patrick Leigh Fermor was born in 1915 of English and Irish descent. After a 'stormy' school career and his year-and-a-half journey on foot to Constantinople, he lived and travelled in the Balkans and the Greek Archipelago. During that time he acquired a deep interest in languages and a love of remote places. He joined the Irish Guards in 1939 and the 'I' Corps in 1941, became liaison officer in Albania and fought in Greece and Crete, to which he returned three times during the German occupation. He lived for over two years in the mountains, organizing the resistance and the capture and evacuation of the German Commander, General Kreipe. He was awarded the DSO in 1944 and the OBE in 1943, and was made Honorary Citizen of Herakleion, Crete. Partick Leigh Fermor has written a number of books, including *The Traveller's Tree*, winner of the 1950 Heinemann Foundation Prize for Literature and the 1951 Kemsley Prize; *Mani*, winner of the Duff Cooper Memorial Prize and a Book Society Choice; its companion volume *Roumeli; A Time of Gifts*, winner of the 1978 W. H. Smith & Son Annual Literature Award and the 1992 Prix Audiberti de la Ville d'Antibes; and its sequel, *Between the Woods and the Water*, winner of the 1987 Thomas Cook Travel Book Award and the Silver Pen Award. Many of his books are published by Penguin. Patrick Leigh Fermor now lives in Greece in a house he designed and built. He is a visiting member of the Athens Academy, has been awarded the Gold Medal of Honour of the Municipality of Athens, and is a Hon. D.Litt. at the University of Kent.

THE CRETAN RUNNER

His story of the German Occupation

GEORGE PSYCHOUNDAKIS

Translation and Introduction by
PATRICK LEIGH FERMOR

Annotated by the translator and
XAN FIELDING

PENGUIN BOOKS

PENGUIN BOOKS

Published by the Penguin Group
Penguin Books Ltd, 27 Wrights Lane, London w8 5tz, England
Penguin Putnam Inc., 375 Hudson Street, New York, New York 10014, USA
Penguin Books Australia Ltd, Ringwood, Victoria, Australia
Penguin Books Canada Ltd, 10 Alcorn Avenue, Toronto, Ontario, Canada m4v 3b2
Penguin Books (NZ) Ltd, 182–190 Wairau Road, Auckland 10, New Zealand

Penguin Books Ltd, Registered Offices: Harmondsworth, Middlesex, England

First published by John Murray 1955
Published in Penguin Books 1998
1 3 5 7 9 10 8 6 4 2

Set in 10.75/11.75pt Monotype Bembo
Typeset by Rowland Phototypesetting Ltd, Bury St Edmunds, Suffolk
Printed in England by Clays Ltd, St Ives plc

Contents

Contents

Contents

List of Illustrations

by Joan Eyres Monsell* and from contemporary photographs

Photograph 4 ('Aleko') reproduced by permission of Mrs Xan Fielding and 20 ('Mikhalaki') by permission of Ralph Stockbridge.

Additional illustrations by Patrick Leigh Fermor appear following page 33

Cover-names of non-Cretans

in order of their appearance

YANNI
Captain (later Major) Jack Smith-Hughes, OBE

MICHALAKI, *later* **SIPHI**
Sergeant (later Captain) Ralph Stockbridge, MC and bar

ALEKO
Captain (later Major) Xan Fielding, DSO

MONTY
Captain (later Colonel) the Hon. C. M. Woodhouse, DSO, OBE

YANNI *or* **O TOM**
Captain (later Lieutenant-Colonel) Tom Dunbabin, DSO

MICHALI *or* **'PHILEDEM'**
Captain (later Major) Patrick Leigh Fermor, DSO, OBE

SIPHI
Flight-Sergeant Jo Bradley, DFM, MM

LEVTHERI
Captain (later Major) Arthur Reade

LITTLE ALEKO *or* **'KALAÏDZIS'**
('THE TINKER')
Corporal (later Sergeant-Major) Alec Tarves, MM

MATTHAIOS
Corporal (later Captain) Matthew White

LEVTHERI
Lieutenant (later Captain) Hugh Fraser

YANNI
Lieutenant (later Captain) John Stanley

ALEXIS
Captain (later Major) Sandy Rendel

VASILI *or* **KIWI**
Sergeant-Major D. C. Perkins, NZ Forces

PAVLO
Captain (later Major) Dick Barnes

CHARIS
Sergeant (later Sergeant-Major) Harry Brooke,
DCM

DIONYSIOS
Captain (later Major) Denis Ciclitira

MITSOS
Major Bruce Mitford

THEOPHILOS
Major-General Heinrich Kreipe (Knight's Cross of
the Iron Cross)

STEPHANOS
Lieutenant (later Captain) Stephen Verney, MBE

MANOLI
Lieutenant Geoffrey Barkham

Dedication

To the Greeks and their brave allies and brothers-in-arms who fell fighting in the Cretan Mountains in 1941, and to Cretan and British friends who worked for freedom during the dark years that followed.

Γ.Ψ.

E.G.Morton

EAN SEA

DIA

Panormo

HERAKLEION

Veni Gave

Knossos

MO

enoi

Kare
Veni

Anoyeia

Pestos Asipopoulo
Apostoloi

na Karines
Meronas
Elenes
Vistayi Asomaloi Amari
Neys Amari Vizari
Smiles Phourphoura

My Vasili
Nerakari
Dryes Ano Meros
Akhtounda
Ay Yanni Nithavri
1920

Krya Vryssi Ay Pareskevi Apodoulon
Melabes
Kamares

Sakhtouria
Grigoria Katous
Margarikari
Zaro

Ayia Galini
Klima

Timbaki
Galia

Gulf of
Messara

Moires

TA PAXIMADIA

C. Lithinos

Vasiliki Anoyia
Kapetaniana

TURKEY

GREECE

CRETE
Mediterranean Sea

LIBYA

MERSA
MATRUH
ALEXANDRIA

EGYPT

YAN SEA

Introduction

by Patrick Leigh Fermor

Back in Crete three years ago I soon found my way to Asi Gonia, travelling by bus from Canea to the little town of Episkopi on the main Retimo-Herakleion road, and then inland to Argyroupolis, where mules were waiting: strong mountain animals with cumbrous wooden saddles commodiously padded with scarlet blankets.

We followed the river bed for an hour or so, picking our way among the boulders under the plane trees, the gorge leading us ever deeper into the complex of mountains. We climbed at last to the village of Asi Gonia, where the mountains rise on three sides in forbidding crags, the southernmost joining the ragged *cordilleras* of Sphakia. These are dead, barren ranges, gashed with landslides, with a solitary shepherd's hut here and there and a scattered herd of goats only to be discerned by locating the far-away clink of their bells. Even on this second return to the island since the war, it seemed incredible to be moving about these regions freely.

The first of our old Asi Gonia friends to greet this little cavalcade was George Psychoundakis. He came leaping down the cobbled lane as nimbly as ever, flourishing his tortuous olive-wood stick with pantomime gestures of welcome and jubilation.

He had changed a little since I had last seen him a year after the war. His face had filled out and he had grown a sweeping black moustache that seemed a slightly burlesque addition to his delicate and rather intellectual features. When he took off his army beret I was astonished to see that most of his hair had gone; his forehead now recedes smoothly three-quarters of the distance over his scalp, giving him, at a first glance, a deceptive air of middle age which a second glance quickly belies. It had all fallen out a few years before, during the space of three days. He has an alert, extremely personal sense of humour (which has served him well, as he has been the magnet for an undeserved sequence of troubles) and there must have been something odd about him from the start for Xan Fielding and me to have invented the code name of 'the Changeling' for him (which later became, for some reason, 'the Changebug'). His gift for play on words, for funny repartee, light verse, improvisation, unpredictable flights of imagination and his instinct for teasing the great, just on the right side of impertinence, earned him a universal licence as jester: but his charm and good manners coupled with his diminutive size and a strange lost look – he was always tired out from his innumerable lonely treks – made him a favourite among the mothers and daughters of a hundred mountain villages as well as among the rest of us.

★　★　★

I first met George one evening about the end of July in 1942, when I was lying up for a few days in the rocks above Vaphé in the Apokoronas, where the Vandoulakis family had long sheltered Xan Fielding earlier in the year. He was brought there by Perikles Vandoulakis and his sister Elpida – they came crawling through the bushes on all fours into my little hideout of boulders and thorn-trees and cistus, and George, who was in a muck-sweat from a long run over the mountains, handed over half a dozen letters from agents in Western Crete, all twisted into compact billets and carefully hidden in different parts of his clothing; they were produced with a comic kind of conjurer's flourish, after grotesquely furtive glances over the shoulder and fingers laid on lips in a caricature of clandestine security precautions that made us all laugh. He wore a black Cretan shirt, his clothing was in tatters and his patched boots – the semi-detached sole of one of which was secured to its upper with a thick strand of wire – were coming to bits on his feet. When he took off his fringed headkerchief to untwist one of his messages, his forehead was shaded by a raven black shock. A small, carefully tended moustache ran along his upper lip. He was small in stature and as fine-boned as an Indian, looking little older than sixteen, though he was actually twenty-one. He was lithe and agile and full of nervous energy. His eyes were large and dark, and his face, in repose, thoughtful and stamped by a rather melancholy expression which vanished at once in frequent fits of helpless and infectious laughter that almost anything seemed to provoke.

When my answers were written and safely stowed by George in their various caches, we lay about talking under the bushes till it grew dark, drinking from a small calabash of *raki* which Elpida had brought with her from the house, and cracking almonds with a stone. It was plain that George was enraptured with the excitement of our secret life, in spite of the appalling trudges that kept him for ever on the move in those merciless mountains. When the moon rose he got up and threw a last swig of *raki* down his throat with the words 'Another drop of petrol for the engine,' and loped towards the gap in the bushes with the furtiveness of a stage Mohican or Groucho Marx. He turned round when he was on all fours at the exit, rolled his eyes, raised a forefinger portentously, whispered '*The Intelligence Service!*' and scuttled through like a rabbit. A few minutes later we could see his small figure a mile away moving across the next moonlit fold of the foothills of the White Mountains, bound for another fifty-mile journey.

I had been smuggled into the island a month before by sea in John Campbell's[1] small ship. After hiding (mainly owing to my footgear having been torn to bits on the rocks) in Tom Dunbabin's cave on Mount Ida in Central Crete, I had made my way here to take over the western part from Xan Fielding. He was temporarily leaving the island under most peculiar and dangerous auspices (as the reader will see), with Colonel Andrea Papadakis, the self-styled leader of pan-Cretan resistance. Xan, who had arrived in January 1942, was an old hand and when he vanished to Egypt, not the least valuable of the many legacies I inherited from him was this strangely youthful-looking helper, George Psychoundakis. I immediately took him on as a guide and runner, and, until Xan's return a few months later, we made many long journeys together, sharing the rigours of cave life, dodging the Germans, waiting for parachute drops and trekking to the coast to meet secret vessels.

Two of the things I remember best were his telling me, through a day's march from dawn till long after sunset, the plot of a novel called *Kassiani*, about life in the Byzantine Empire. He reconstructed it in almost Macaulayesque detail. On another day in the crags above Asi Gonia, where we had gone to inspect a store of sabotage explosives, he recited an epic poem that he had written about the war. It covered the invasion of Poland, the Fall of France, the Albanian triumph and disaster, the German Invasion of Greece and Crete and Rommel's final advance. The recital lasted over two hours and finished on a note of triumphant optimism and presage of vengeance which he emphasized

1 Lieutenant (later Commander) John Campbell, DSO, RN.

by borrowing my pistol and firing it again and again into the sky with the remark that we would soon be eating the cuckolds alive. (The day after I had set sail from Mersa Matruh a few weeks before, it had been overrun by German tanks, and Campbell's boat had been forced to return to Alexandria, and, at the very moment of George's recital, the German guns were hammering the British line at Alamein. Formations of troop-carrying aircraft fifty and a hundred strong, laden with reinforcements for Rommel, roared almost hourly over our empty mountains, adding momentum to what might have seemed the inevitable overthrow of the Middle Eàst. German armies were advancing triumphantly into the heart of Russia. Our military fortunes were at their nadir.)

Like all Greeks from the mountains, George has an inexhaustible curiosity and a vast capacity for wonder. There was endless questioning about the outside world – about trains, political systems, how whisky is made, why the Scotch wear kilts;[1] what Churchill was like, how many sheep the average Englishman owns, religion, mileage, steam rollers and astronomy. He would listen gravely to the answers as the strange visions assembled in his mind. Not only had he never left Crete but he had only visited two of the three main towns of the island and these only half a dozen times: Canea, that is to say, the bomb-shattered capital on the other side of the mountains – smaller than Guildford, with broken minarets and a harbour that reflects Turkish cupolas like flawed rose-coloured pearls; and pretty Retimo under its massive Frankish keep. Unknown Herakleion – far away to the east, a great battered agglomeration heaped round the renaissance fountain of Morosini and girdled by an immense rampart from the time of

---

1 Battalions of the Black Watch and the Argyll and Sutherland Highlanders had fought in the battle of Crete.

the Venetian occupation – was almost too distant for speculation . . . Cairo, London, Paris and Berlin were as mysterious and as far beyond conjecture as life in the stars. The stony-hearted wonderland of America, from the sagas of old emigrants, sounded stranger still. Just as our daily contact with the Greeks was a source of stimulus and fascination, his sudden contact with strangers opened up great stretches of new territory: an imaginative expansion that ran parallel to the discovery of his own island that his duties as a runner involved.

The job of a war-time runner in the Resistance Movement was the most exhausting and one of the most consistently dangerous of all. It entailed immense journeys on foot at full speed over some of the most precipitous country in Europe, carrying messages between the towns and the large villages and the secret wireless stations in the mountains; humping batteries and driving camouflaged explosives and arms, and, occasionally, a British straggler in disguise, on the backs of mules through heavily garrisoned areas. He was in the game from the start to the very end. Three of the other early starters – of whom, in the early days, there were less than a dozen – were captured and shot, two of them after long imprisonment and appalling tortures in Ayia Jail. None of them were paid and there was no incentive but a sense of duty to their country and their allies.

They were all mountain boys. Most of them had pastured their families' flocks since they could walk. All were poor, and George's family was the poorest of all. Its only resources were a few sheep and goats, and even these were stolen by a neighbour while George was away on a mission at the other end of the island, leaving the Psychoundakis family with, literally, nothing at all.

His house stands in a lane in the lower part of the village, below the springs where the women are eternally thumping and rinsing and then spreading their laundry to dry on the boulders. The single room has a beaten earth floor and it is spanned by a smoke-blackened and cob-webbed archway which sweeps from one end to the other and supports the rough-hewn beams and the planks above on which a fresh layer of trodden earth forms the usual Cretan roof. This is pierced by half of a ribbed amphora embedded there as a chimney-pot for the neolithic hearth below. The furniture is a rickety table, a couple of rush-bottomed chairs and a great loom which occupies much of the floor. Strings of onions and dried tomatoes on the walls, a wooden mule-saddle and bridle and a couple of ikons with their little flickering oil dips are their only other possessions. At night the whole family sleeps end to end under blankets and homespun cloaks on a solid ledge running across the back of the room. Hens peck their way in and out.

George's father was an old man long past work. Now-adays, he sits beside the door all day long in a perpetual dream. His mother, Kyria Angeliké − cadaverously thin and dressed in a collection of patches sewn together − was always banging away at the loom, spinning by the fire and among the chickens with a distaff in one hand and a spindle in the other, or cooking whatever beans or herbs she had managed to scrape together for the family. She was as wrinkled as a walnut, and her lively, bright-eyed face spelt nothing but kindness and high spirits, except when her eager talk was interrupted by the half a dozen rapid signs of the cross and the accompanying deep sigh which are the ritual *leitmotif* of Greek feminine village life. She died three years ago and is bitterly missed by all who knew her. George's two pretty sisters, Rodianthe and Eléni, and his little brother Nicolas − wild and engaging creatures of about thirteen, eleven and nine at the begin-ning of the Resistance − were always bounding in and out, as nimble and as clear of worry as the mountain goats on the rocks overhead. It was on George's shoulders that all the family anxieties weighed, as they still do today.

He was born on the third of November, 1920. This is a minor local feast in honour of St George, celebrated at a spring where the cattle are watered just outside the village, so his parents had not far to look for a name. (St George, the patron and protector of Asi Gonia, is said to have appeared on a white horse at moments of danger and scattered the besieging Turks, and his name has special significance among the Goniots.) After two or three years at the village school, he lived as a shepherd until the events described at the beginning of his book.

Education in the Cretan mountains is brief, rudimentary and primitive. The old people are largely illiterate and many of the younger ones still find reading hard. The actual function of writing is a real grind, and the result is almost as uncouth as characters scratched on a cave wall with a bit of flint. This has nothing to do with the level of their intelligence, which is extremely high, or with their instinctive knack of quick, lucid and entertaining talk, which is almost universal.

In this literary wilderness, George would grub for whatever he could find among the scattered intelligentsia of the sierras – the schoolmasters, the doctor from the nearest town, the intelligent young priest from his own village, the sprinkling of retired army and gendarmerie officers. The material was sparse: a few translated novels, a theological work or two, some simplified mythology, some history books and descriptions of the Turkish rebellions and the Balkan wars, the inevitable *Erotócritos*. He devoured them all and when he had nothing to read, he would occupy the vast leisure of a shepherd by writing verses: homespun patriotic poems, theoretical verses about love or satires on local life. Occasionally he would avoid the traditional fifteen-syllable Cretan line, and attempt more difficult metres, tackling queer themes like his *Ode to an Inkspot on a Schoolmistress's Skirt*. But the one he had most enjoyed writing, he said, was an anti-feminist poem satirizing the women who, during the previous particularly bitter winter, had worn men's trousers to protect themselves from the cold when engaged on olive-picking in the fields. The whole village had been shocked by such wanton behaviour; and more shocked still to find next day, pinned to the door of the coffee-shop for all to read, a sheet of verses commemorating this shameful breach of modesty. George had been careful to sign them, not with his own name, but with that of the village cobbler . . .

★   ★   ★

The battle of Crete with which George's book opens, was one of the phenomena of warfare. The German parachute invasion, at dawn on the 20th of May 1941, touched off pandemonium. The savage ten days that followed, the uncertain sway of the battle, the courage displayed by everyone engaged, the final disaster and the miseries of the evacuation are well known. The important thing, for the purposes of this introduction, is the participation of the Cretan population.[1] The 5th Cretan Division – all the Cretans of military age, in fact – had been marooned in the mainland on their way back from the Albanian campaign. (How sorely their absence was rued!

---

1 The fact that there was no mention of this in the relevant volume of Sir Winston Churchill's *History of the War* has caused pain and disappointment. The Cretan share in the fighting is rightly stressed in the excellent official New Zealand history of the battle, *Crete* by D. M. Davin. For other details about German-occupied Crete, see Xan Fielding's *Hide and Seek*, and also, more recently, *Crete: The Battle and the Resistance*, by Anthony Beevor (John Murray).

The Cretans felt, and still feel, that if these extra numbers had been there, the battle might have gone the other way. Perhaps they are right.) All through those hot summer days the olive woods were a deafening chaos of automatic weapons and exploding grenades and mortar-bombs, of field and ack-ack guns and tank-cannons firing; the sky swarmed with alighting parachutists, machine-gunning divebombers, Junker 52s and troop-laden gliders either circling to shed their freight or falling in flames among the branches where they blazed and crackled all through the uneasy truce of each short night.

About six thousand were killed on both sides, and four thousand more badly wounded. It was a head-on crash of the world's latest homicide appliances and, from the first moment, both sides were astonished by the presence of old Cretans and boys and women, armed with rusty guns and sickles and sticks – soon to be replaced by captured enemy weapons – in the thick of the fighting. They fought with courage and cheerfulness throughout and suffered heavily. (I well remember a delegation of old men approaching our HQ outside Herakleion on the evening before we cleared out, begging for arms to continue the struggle until we could get back. Our brigadier,[1] deeply moved, handed over everything that still remained in the armoury.)

This had several results. A few of those who had played a leading part in the fighting took to the hills with small bands, so that there was the germ of an armed Resistance movement from the start. Another important outcome was that, immediately after the Fall of Crete, the German reprisals against the population were so fierce that all chance of conciliating the Cretans, had it ever existed, was gone. They were at loggerheads from the start.[2]

1 Brigadier B. H. Chappel, formerly of the Indian Army.
2 Captured documents prove that the Germans were hopelessly misinformed about the probable attitude of the Cretans in the event of invasion.

Fighting side by side is a great link, and these warm feelings were strengthened, in this case, by feelings of pity among the Cretans for the large numbers of allied soldiers who had been unable to escape from the west at the Sphakia evacuations. They wandered about the mountains in twos and threes, and their numbers were soon augmented by prisoners breaking out and taking to the mountains. The Cretans felt in duty bound to hide and feed them, and later on, when submarines began to call and take them off, the Cretans who acted as their helpers and guides and hosts at different points on the routes to the embarkation-points automatically became important strands in the network which was later to spring up. They were ardently pro-British and, with time, they became so firmly established that when much later on leftwing organizers began to appear, the political battle, from a Communist point of view, was already lost.

The Cretan Resistance movement was one of the most successful in Europe. It was never put to the final test – island-wide revolt in co-operation with an allied landing – for which the whole of Crete was longing. Unfortunately for the Balkans and Europe, the allied attack in the south of Europe was launched on Italy, and the Balkans were by-passed; but such an attack on Crete would have found the island united and organized to the last detail. Occupation is like an illness; but, however painful this illness was in Crete – and it was very painful indeed – it was spared the appalling internal complications by which other occupied countries were racked. The antagonism of Right and Left never reached the bitterness it attained elsewhere. Apart from a few trivial brushes, all passed off peacefully. The organization of resistance was, except for carefully thought-out attacks for reasons of wider strategy and morale, a defensive process of preparation and military intelligence and consolidation. Two of the most important tasks were the avoidance of isolated and unco-ordinated attacks on the enemy and the maintenance of political harmony.

Crete is famous, throughout Greece, for its revolutionary past, for its feuds and its lawlessness, and for the violence and the impetuosity of the islanders. But, to judge by results, a firm solidarity underlies all this, and it is an inestimable boon that Crete is, by tradition, united in one political allegiance, which happens to be the Republican Liberalism of their great fellow-islander Elevtherios Venizelos. One of the wisest heads in the island, however, and one of the best advisers in the formation of Resistance policy was Mr Emmanuel Papadoyannis, a life-long Royalist and opponent of Venizelism, former Governor-General of Crete, and, since the war, a minister in several important posts.

George's contact with the secret mission dates from the arrival of the first British officer, the late Commander Pool. Soon after, he worked with Jack Smith-Hughes – *Yanni* – who had escaped from the Germans, and who was later to run the Cretan section of SOE[1] in Cairo so well for the rest of the occupation. When British officers began to arrive, they were symbols of the free world in Cretan eyes: links with the distant dreamland of the African front, lonely swallows presaging summer. They at once became figures of importance, and, as time went on, they reaped, more and more, the benefit of the centripetal tendency of the Cretans. Their authority was immense, and – inevitably, under these extraordinary conditions – so was their freedom of action. They were chosen from all over the army, their qualifications being willingness and suitability for that peculiar kind of warfare, and some acquaintance with modern Greek or with the ancient variety – a far

[1] Special Operations Executive.

greater help for the modern than is generally supposed.

The ones that play the most parts in this book are Xan Fielding – *Aleko* – one of the earliest arrivals and author of *The Stronghold*, a description of life in the White Mountains, the area where he worked most of his time in Crete; Tom Dunbabin – *O Tom* – raggedest of guerrillas, a scholar gypsy, Fellow of All Souls in peace-time, distinguished classical scholar and author of *The Western Greeks* (about the early Greek colonies in Magna Græcia), who eventually became head of the mission; Ralph Stockbridge – *Siphi* – who is now Vice-Consul in Alexandria. These, with the present writer – *Michali* or *Philedem* – are the ones with whom George had most to do in the early days, and they were in fact, with the signallers Alec Tarves – *O mikros* (little) *Aleko* – and Matthew White – *Matthaios* – the only ones there. (One feels that, through long familiarity, George has a particularly soft spot for them.) There is a brief mention of Monty Woodhouse – *O Monti* – now in the Foreign Service, who was later to command the entire mission on the Greek mainland. Later arrivals were John Stanley – *Yanni* – Arthur Reade – *Levtheri* – now a lawyer in Cyprus, a writer and philhellene; Dick Barnes – *Pavlo* – a schoolmaster, with Harry Brooke – *Charis* – his signaller, an old hand; another *Levtheri* – Hugh Fraser, now in the wilds of Uganda; Denis Ciclitira – *Dionysios*; Bruce Mitford – *O Mitsos* – who has since returned to his Chair at Cambridge; Steve Verney – *O Stephanos* – now a priest in the North Country; Sandy Rendel – *Alexis* – who works on *The Times*, and has recently published an excellent account of his experiences in the eastern parts, *Appointment in Crete*. Most of these organizers were in their early or middle twenties. Tom Dunbabin and Arthur Reade were rather older, and the youngest was John Houseman – *Petros* – who arrived as a subaltern in the Bays at the age of twenty. He, like Jack

Smith-Hughes and John Stanley, is now happily married to a Cretan girl. It is impossible not to mention Sergeant-Major D. C. Perkins of the New Zealand Army – 'Kiwi' or *Vasili* – Xan Fielding's second-in-command, who after a series of almost legendary guerrilla attacks on the Germans, was killed in an ambush.

Of the Greeks who joined the mission in the Middle East, the most notable were the kind and tireless Niko Souris, an Alexandrian from a Cythera family, and Apostolos Evangélou – *Phtochos* – first Xan's then my signaller. He was a schoolmaster from the Dodecanese, a promising poet and a delightful man; he was captured and executed by the Germans after cruel tortures. Of visiting commandos on special missions the most notable are George, Earl Jellicoe, later an active politician, First Lord of the Admiralty and head of the Royal Geographical Society; David Sutherland, Ian Patterson and Bob Berry, the last two of whom, alas, were killed on two separate missions soon after; they all belonged to the Special Boat Service; and Bill Stanley Moss, who among his other works has published a lively account of the Kreipe operation, which has been turned into a very successful film.

None of them were regular soldiers except Harry Brooke, who had joined the Green Howards some years before the war, and served for a time in India, and Alec Tarves, who ran away from his home in the Cairngorms and managed, by concealing his age, to enlist in a highland regiment when he was fifteen. Both were now in the Royal Corps of Signals. The early infiltrations were run by Mike Cumberlege and John Campbell, who commanded tiny piratical craft – the *Hedgehog*, the *Porcupine* and the *Escampador* – operating from Bardia – or, when the Germans took Bardia, from Mersa Matruh or Alexandria – plying across appalling seas to the rocky southern coast. John Campbell is now back in his native Ireland. Mike

Cumberlege was captured late in 1942 in plain clothes on a sabotage mission in a little caique off the Greek mainland; after three years of prison, he and his companions were taken out, put against a wall and shot in Flossenburg prison four days before it was overrun by the allied armies in 1945. (Cumberlege's good looks, his humour, his general buccaneerish air and his single gold ear-ring made a profound impression on the Cretans. His and John Pendlebury's[1] death seem the most irreplaceable of the losses in British aid to the Resistance in Greece.) Nearly all these names are remembered with affection in Crete. Indeed, those who remained there longest are considered practically members of the Cretan family.

So the British Mission to Occupied Crete began: the secret infiltrations by caique or submarine and the forced marches by night across the German-infested plains. These were followed by long climbs up the most improbable peaks to establish a headquarters, each isolated officer with his wireless transmitter and signal-sergeant and little armed retinue of Cretan helpers and guides and runners. Sometimes they found an old hut or sheepfold, but they usually settled in one of the caves with which the hills abound.

The life was a troglodytic one. It was all right in summer, apart from the frequent German sweeps through the mountains, but full of hardships in winter, when it was often impossible to light a fire because of the give-away smoke, or sometimes even to venture outside, for fear of leaving footprints in the snow. At first, though this improved, food was scarce and poor. At other times, if the rocks or the ilex trees screened us from the plains, there

1 This one-eyed giant, who was shot by the Germans as he lay wounded, after leading a sally of the Cretan Guerrillas during the siege of Herakleion, has passed into Cretan folklore. A distinguished archaeologist before the war, a fine scholar and athlete, he had lived for many years in Crete and was much loved by all who knew him.

was something captivating about this cave-life. There is one refuge not far below the birthplace of Zeus on Mount Ida that I remember almost with homesickness, in spite of the snow and rain that blew into the cave's mouth, the stalactites that dripped on our heads, the smoke that reddened our damp eyes and the armies of vermin that manoeuvred in our torn and stinking clothes. We padded the wet rocks with brushwood and built a hearth. Here, waiting for runners from the towns with news of troop-movements or convoys for the Western desert, or marking time till the next wireless schedule to far-away Cairo, we would lie round the flames. The white-cloaked shepherds, who took turns as look-out, squatted with their guns across their knees. We would talk interminably, passing the *raki* round or a gourd full of wine, chopping up tobacco leaves on rifle butts to roll into cigarettes.

I could listen for hours to these indestructible old men and their tales, in Cretan Greek, of revolts against the Turks. They taught us innumerable couplets and long *Rizitiko* songs with Oriental modulations. They read our fortunes on the shoulder-blades of sheep, explained superstitions and incantations and expounded dreams, taught us how to curl up our moustaches, tie our fringed black turbans, mend our tall boots and arrange our mulberry-coloured silk sashes – the disguise in which we contrived to become indistinguishable, at least to German eyes, from the Cretans themselves.

They recounted comic incidents from the *Karaghiozi* shadow-play and exchanged the innumerable anecdotes of Nasr-ed-Din-Hodja, the legendary Turkish village priest. Strangest of all, as few of them could read or write, was the ability of some of these greybeards to recite by heart the whole of the *Erotócritos* (the most word perfect of all was George's own father, Uncle Nicolas). This is a fantastic Cretan myth in verse in a kind of Midsummer Night's

Dream setting, written in the seventeenth century. There are over ten thousand lines and it consists of rhyming couplets of decapente syllables modulated in a ritual, rather lilting monody. One would fall asleep for an hour or two, and wake up to find some gnarled shepherd still intoning . . .

But we were never in any of these lairs for long. Sometimes they were blown, their whereabouts becoming common knowledge. The villagers and shepherds were reliability itself – apart from occasional garrulity – but there was danger from *agents provocateurs* in Gestapo pay, and, all too often, we were put on the move again by enemy searches through the hills in force. Often they were armed with wireless detectors. We would hastily bury or hide our precious suitcase-wirelesses or, hoisting them and the batteries on our backs, take to our heels. On one occasion we spent a long oak-apple day in the branches of a tree while German raiding parties thrashed through the rocks and bushes below.

There were countless marches to the coast to meet secret craft. They brought in new agents or commando groups and evacuated stragglers or hunted Cretans for asylum or training in the Middle East. There were treks to remote plateaux for parachute drops of stores and arms – in vain, as often as not, owing to the moon or the weather – and to the towns or far-away villages for conferences: to Neapolis in the east to plan the defection and flight, at the time of Badoglio's armistice, of the Italian divisional commander and some of his staff; to Canea or Herakleion to make sabotage attempts, organize propaganda, inspect a clandestine printing press in a cellar, or reconnoitre the ground for some surprise operation. Meanwhile the guerrilla bands were growing, the information network covered the entire occupation machine, every formation and gun position and supply dump was pinpointed and signalled to Cairo and, as the years passed, it began to be clear – not that the Cretans ever doubted it – that we would win the war.

But the price of resistance was very heavy. Some of the best were caught and tortured and shot, and the concealment of a single British soldier, or an armed clash in the mountains, could mean the destruction of villages and the depopulation by massacre and execution of an entire valley. By the time the German garrison withdrew to a narrow fortified perimeter round Canea (contained there by the whole guerrilla strength of Crete till they surrendered at the war's end) the casualty list was disastrous.

★   ★   ★

When, three years ago, the homecoming celebrations in Asi Gonia were over, George and I set out on a round of visits to some of the villages that had helped us during the war, and during the following days I was able to catch up with his life since I had last seen him.

He had had a hard time of it. Owing to some bureaucratic confusion or the loss of the relevant documents in the Greek military archives dealing with his war service, and in spite of his British decoration,[1] he was arrested as a deserter and spent long months in the jails of Piraeus and Macedonia. His file was discovered in the end and the matter was more or less straightened out. This was a period of great misery – 'I was locked up in cells,' he told me, 'with brigands and communists and all the dregs of the mainland.' (It was during three days of this period of anger and misery that all his hair fell out.) In the end he had to do two more years' service in the Pindus mountains

1 He was awarded the BEM in 1945.

and Macedonia: a time of constant fighting in the fiercest period of the civil war against the communist insurgents of Markos and his successors. When he got back to Asi Gonia, he found his family in a state of dire poverty, and took a job as a navvy on the Argyroupolis-Asi Gonia road to try to provide for his household. It was a long, sad tale.

After a few days of trudging over the steep mountains, sometimes on foot, sometimes on mule-back, George told me that he had tried to write down, while he was being moved from prison to prison, all he could remember about the Occupation. He also told me, when we were staying with Father John Alevizakis, the brave old priest of Alones, that he had been forced to drop it during the civil war; but when he was working on the road, he had settled in a little cave on a nearby slope. Here, like a ragged St Jerome, he would write at night by the light of an oil-dip until he fell asleep and continue at daybreak until it was time to take up his pick again. I think he undertook this task as a kind of exorcism of the gloom of his circumstances. I asked him if I could be allowed to have a look at it, and without a word he dived into his knapsack, fished out five thick exercise books tied in a bundle, and handed them over.

From the first page, with its title *Pictures of our Life during the Occupation*, I was unable to stop. George squatted anxiously chain-smoking nearby, ready to explain any bits that were illegible or obscure. But it was hardly necessary. The memoir had plainly been written fast, but the writing was easily legible and full of character. The words were punctiliously equipped with breathings and accents and even, when he soared now and then into the 'literary' form, with iota-subscripts; there was hardly an erasure from beginning to end. Devouring these pages occupied all the recovery-pauses from the reunions that dotted our path. I finished them four days later in the Abbey of

Arkadi, and asked George at once to let me take them away with me.

It still seems to me that I was reading something unique in the literature of Resistance: a sort of primitive, Douanier-Rousseau war book. Dozens of accounts by officers who were dropped or infiltrated into enemy-occupied country have appeared, and are appearing still, but there has not been a single one, as far as I know, by any of the millions of men who formed the raw material of Resistance in occupied Europe. How odd and exciting it would have been if one of the Rualla bedouin, by a sudden miracle of literacy, had given us the Arab version of the Seven Pillars of Wisdom! This, *mutatis mutandis*, was precisely what George had done; and how fluently and easily and unhesitatingly! For the rôles were reversed, and the British officers and their signallers and NCOs, not the stage-mountaineers of most Resistance writing, were the foreign oddities; and it seemed to me that they were far better and more soberly appraised than their equivalents in English war books. Though here, as in his treatment of his fellow-Cretans, his preferences and prejudices are clear.

It is a completely truthful account of Resistance life. This is astonishing in a place like Crete, where the mytho-poetic enchantment is for ever spinning its bright web. When George sets down an event which he has learnt by hearsay from another part of the island, this magic has sometimes been at work on the details. It is just as one would expect, but the distinction between George's own first-hand experience and stories at second- or hundredth-hand, is always clear and always defined. There is no pretension to knowledge of the high-level background of the Resistance, of the decisions and negotiations, the structure and intrigue and the fluctuations of policy in the evolution of which he acted for years as the tireless messenger across those wild mountains. He merely records their outward symptoms. Nor does his book pretend to be a complete record of the occupation. The precipitous character of the country split the island up in separate hermetic worlds so that thunderous events taking place two mountain ranges away were reduced by distance to faint murmurs. On the whole, George was concerned with the affairs of Central and Western Crete, and many of the complicated events that took place in the eastern part of the island scarcely impinge on George's memoir. They were muffled doings, as it were a few rooms away, along dark corridors, scarcely audible. His journeys form a complex cat's-cradle between the eastern peaks of the White Mountains and the western ones of Mount Ida. Occasional strands branch away to Xan Fielding's Never-Never-Land of Selino in the far south-west; or north-west to Kissamo, or to the towns of Canea and Retimo, or across the Messara plain in the south-east to the rocky combes where our secret craft put in; once, right at the end, round the western cape of the island by caique, through the deserted islets – formerly the haunts of corsairs – off Cape Grambousa, and eastwards as far as Herakleion. But, over the wild ridges and valleys that link the two greatest mountain blocks of Crete, he must have covered many hundreds of miles. The same names occur again and again: his own village of Asi Gonia; Vaphé, Vilandredo, Alones, Yerakari; all the Amari Valley; Vizari, Phourphoura, Argyroupolis, Priné – known to us respectively by the code-names of Stubborn Corner, Warpaint, Bloodstone, Flails, Holystones or Hawking, Lotus-Land, Bosoms, Katzphur, Silverstone and Nepenthe – are landmarks that often recur.

★　★　★

As George was writing for his own benefit there was no need to describe either Crete or the Cretans, so it may be useful briefly to set the stage.[1]

Crete, the largest, the southernmost and the most solitary of the Greek islands, and the fifth largest of the Mediterranean, floats halfway to Africa. It is a hundred and sixty miles long and roughly thirty broad, though wasp waists and swelling salients vary this girth. It is such a steep maze of gorges and crags that distances as the crow flies have no meaning; the islanders themselves measure them by the time taken to smoke cigarettes, by hours gauged by the climb or decline of the sun, and days reckoned from daybreak to sunset; or, more often, during the Occupation, by the duration of nights. Thirty miles, in some parts, meant three days (or nights) of scrambles up rocks and breakneck, treacherous descents of landslides. Only in the rare plains is the reckoning normal, and even there the multiplicity of Germans made journeys a chain of detours that falsified all normal computation. All this expands Crete into many times its real size, and sometimes, in the central valleys, the sea seems as remote as from the heart of a continent. There are four main mountain blocks: the White Mountains in the west and Mount Ida in the centre, both well over 8,000 feet high; then, beyond the Herakleion lowlands the 7,000-foot agglomeration of the Lasithi Mountains – this is the easternmost limit of the territory covered in George's book – and, far away in the alien east – hardly considered by the martial and vainglorious west as part of Crete at all – the beautiful and pacific 5,000 feet of Seteia. Generally speaking, the south coast falls sheer and waterless into the immense soundings of the Libyan sea. Only goats and their wild shepherds inhabit these desolate regions. There are only

1 This can be skipped by anyone who knows the island.

a few hamlets where caiques can put in, the villages are little more than pastoral settlements, and the occasional monasteries are so thinly monked as to be practically hermitages. Save for half-a-dozen islets as barren as rusks, nothing lies between this and the far-away deserts of Libya.

The northern slopes are on the whole more gradual, subsiding to the coast under vineyards and olive groves where the ledges of the hills are misty with corn in spring-time. It is here that the only main road runs west to east, joining the three main towns – Canea (with the fine harbour of Suda Bay) and Retimo and Herakleion; these gather all the island's trade and civilization round their quays. Due south of the rolling vineyards of Herakleion, the hills flatten into the fertile expanse of the Messara plain. We had little to do with these opulent lowlands; there was no cover, enemy garrisons were thick on the ground, traitors were not unknown, and only the mountains held an uncertain offer of safety.

The Cretan landscape, then, is very diverse. The characteristic that is common to all its facets – Cretan songs call the island 'the crown of the Levant whose earth is pure gold and whose rocks are diamonds' – is an amazing, overwhelming beauty. All – the steep olive groves and vineyards, the massifs and canyons, the jagged mountainsides and the haggard planetary wastes above the woods and the flocks – are embedded in brilliant, shining, dazzling air. The high mountains where we lived had the austerity, the extravagance and sometimes the melancholy of the backgrounds of primitive religious paintings in Italy (though no Italian softness) or the vertigo of those insane and toppling crags – steel grey on purple, or ice blue on asbestos white – that surround the saints and martyrs on the ikons of Byzantium. This is the thorny landscape across which the reader must follow the small cloaked figure of George – stooping against snow and rain and wind in winter or racked in summer with parched longing for the next thin trickle of a spring – on those countless journeys from cave to cave.

The highland villages are built on ledges on the mountains' flanks (never, as in Italy, on hilltops to withstand a siege), so that the villagers, who are born irregular fighters, can retreat uphill and fire on the attackers from above. The church is usually on the outskirts and the real centre of the village is a clearing under a huge plane tree by a spring, under whose shade the villagers sit outside the *kapheneion* drinking interminable cups of Turkish coffee, gossiping, fingering their amber beads, and talking politics. The old men still wear the Cretan costume of dark-blue baggy trousers and jackboots, black shirts, purple sashes, embroidered blue waistcoats with arabesque patterns of black braid, and black headkerchiefs haphazardly tied, the whole reduced by wear and weather to a uniformly sombre whole. The young men are turbaned too, and clad in patched breeches and the inevitable boots (townspeople are scorned as *makrypantalonades*, long-trouser men). All wear moustaches, and the white beards of the old ones are topiared into a queer Minoan cut. The women are in perpetual mourning. Their faces are shaded by black coifs, their plaits are pinned across their brows in a crown or hang down their backs. They always appear to be carrying home pitchers of water from the spring, spinning or thumping away at the laundry-troughs.

Crete has always been a theatre for strange and splendid events. It was on the summit of Mt Ida that cloud-gathering Zeus, the son of Kronos and King of the Gods, was born. The reign of Minos, the arrival by sea of Europe on homing Zeus disguised as a bull, the odd practices of Pasiphaë abetted by Daedalus the labyrinth-maker and the slaying of the minotaur by Theseus in the labyrinth itself are some of the most remarkable things in ancient mythology.

King Idomeneus led a strong contingent from the hundred cities of Crete to the Troad and, as legend hardened into fact, the stupendous Minoan civilization emerged, and shot forth its rays over the waters of the Mediterranean.

The old Minoan island became part of the Byzantine empire. It was occupied by Saracen pirates, who were driven out after a century, and its reintegration to Byzantium came to an end during the Crusades, when the island fell under Venetian suzerainty, which again, after one of the longest sieges in history, was superseded three hundred years ago by a Turkish occupation which only ended a few years before the first world war. The savagely independent Cretans were in permanent sporadic revolt against these occupations and the history of the last few centuries is a long sequence of fierce, almost yearly insurrections and bloody reprisals. Sphakia, indeed, in the south-west, contrived to extort its independence by force of arms and discard the Turkish yoke. Its final liberation was mainly the work of one of the great figures of our century, Venizelos.

The warlike habit of these centuries had left a burning nationalism, a free spirit and the determination to resist foreign occupation at any sacrifice. It also bequeathed, in the wilder regions, certain lawless customs which, formerly aimed at the oppressor, now wreak havoc among the Cretans themselves. They are virtually weaned on powder and shot. Every shepherd goes armed; the worship of guns and a devastating skill in their use is a dominant characteristic of the Cretan highlands. The large-scale rustling of flocks, though it is on the wane, still continues. Marriages are often accomplished by the abduction of the bride by her suitor and a posse of armed bravos, and blood feuds, sometimes initiated by one of these two causes, can decimate opposing families over a space of decades and seal up neighbouring villages in hostile deadlock. The wild nature of the country puts these things beyond the nature of the law and fills the mountains with a scattered population of outlaws. So, in spite of the breathtaking surrounding beauty and the idyllic ritual of the year – the life of the sheepfolds, the dances at weddings and christenings, the great feasts of the Church, the treading of the grapes in autumn, the olive harvest in winter – no leaf-fringed legend haunts the shape of Cretan mountain life. It is invariably in the remotest, the rockiest and poorest parts of the island that these conditions prevail. Bitter feuds are ceaselessly weaving their baleful patterns, and even the Occupation, in which these mountaineers were so resolute and devoted, failed to suppress this minor universal warfare; private vengeance – especially in Sphakia and Selino – laid many villagers low. But a foreign traveller will only see the kind hospitality of these mountain people, their devotion to their friends, their humour and high spirits and a sweetness of character which is the invariable corollary of the hard conditions of their life.

★   ★   ★

Asi Gonia, George's home, is a large leafy village with rocks and boulders and cactuses jutting everywhere in its intricate warren of lanes. It stands half-way up one of the passes – only to be negotiated on foot – that pierce the barren range dividing the provinces of Canea and Retimo. Their flocks are jealously guarded from the Sphakians on the other side of the watershed; the Sphakians complain that the reciprocal balance is equal. All these villagers are immensely (and justly) proud of their warlike record; Asi Gonia has always been a hotbed of guerrillas, and the tradition finds expression in the bearing of the villagers: a patrician carelessness and dash, something dandified in the cut of their breeches and boots (however patched they may be), and a studied abandon in the tie of their heavily fringed headkerchiefs. They are dark-haired and swarthy and extremely handsome: piratical in appearance and dyed-in-the-wool Bohemians. Their eyes kindle and their grins widen at the suggestion of any rash scheme, especially if the scheme involves danger and a change. They may be taken as representative of the faults and virtues of the Cretan mountains. Irrepressibly energetic for all but drudgery and emulous in the extreme, they seek the bubble reputation; and, though the warlike arms-worshipping tradition of the island produces an inevitable fringe of braggarts and swashbucklers, the Goniots during the war proved as good as their most extravagant gestures, and all through the Occupation they were exemplars of pluck, steadfastness, generosity and resource. This was largely due to the good sense and the authority of Petrakas, George's uncle, a veteran of the Macedonian irregulars against Slav komitadjis before the Balkan wars, and the village's natural leader.

It was through just such mountain hamlets that George and I were travelling, and the news of returning friends moves fast; groups of booted and turbaned mountaineers, festooned with bandoliers and armed with rifles and pistols and silver-scabbarded daggers – 'bristling like lobsters', as they say in the island – advanced to meet us; welcoming rifles and tommy-guns blazed into the sky; black-clad girls, with plaits as thick as a wrist, emerged from each doorway along the steep lanes with glasses of *tsikoudia* or *raki* – the fiery spirit of Crete – and bowls of walnuts and olives 'to cover it'; and a round of banquets began. Chickens and lambs were slaughtered, the oldest wine was brought out, and only a robust constitution and the daily breakneck scrambles and mule journeys from range to range saved the long-lost friends from becoming, as time went on, stretcher-cases from over-eating and drinking. We had to get through seven or eight meals a day.

At night, during such reunions, the wine surges up to high tide, the floor-boards bang to the stamp of Cretan dances, the rate of the bow accelerates across the triple-stringed *lyra*. *Mantinades* – those instantaneously improvised couplets, each one capping its forerunner to a ritual tune – whizz through the air. Aquiline faces stream with sweat in the lamplight, and many of the turbaned heads are so weather-beaten and of so definite a cast that they might be hammered bronze; so compact of force and energy are some of them that one could almost expect to see smoke curling from their ears and flames from their nostrils. As though to oblige, every few minutes one of these booted figures, in spite of a token protest from the cylinder-hatted priest, pulls a pistol from his sash and empties it into the rafters. In an hour or two, the priest himself is shooting off *feu de joie*; and, by the time everyone reels away to bed, dawn is already slanting along the canyon.

There is a constant siege of questions about the fortunes and the whereabouts of stragglers who were housed, clothed and fed by these people in the bad times of 1941, 1942 and 1943, when the last of them were smuggled to Africa by submarine, caique and MTB: 'Where are Harry and Spike from Adelaide and Brisbane? Jack from Liverpool, and Walter from Ealing? Arthur the *Neozealandòs* with a Spandau bullet in his leg? Does he limp still?' The black-coiffed crones ask after them as though they were their own children, and cross themselves with heavy sighs, croaking a prayer that they got back safe to their mothers and fathers . . . It was in the rare intervals of such celebrations that I escaped into solitude with George's five exercise-books.

★ ★ ★

I have, with his permission, cut out a few short passages that seemed repetitive, and very few others which might possibly do harm or cause unnecessary pain; it must be remembered that it was written as a remedy for unhappiness, a private blowing-off of steam which was never meant to become public. There are only a few of these excisions and, where the back is robust enough to bear these blows, I have left the text alone. George's verdicts seem surprisingly just to me. The translation is literal, nothing has been inserted or touched up, and, within the limits imposed by translation, the style is unchanged.

The style is of interest. There are several influences at work. Firstly, there is the Cretan dialect, which deviates from Athenian Greek about as much as the speech of County Galway from the BBC. It is most attractive, but, as it incurs the teasing of the mainlanders on the score of insularity and rusticity, the Cretans' pride in their idiom is tempered by self-consciousness; which is why, on the whole, George tries to avoid it. Luckily it often creeps in. He himself talks with an unmistakable Cretan brogue and uses all the Cretan dialect words. But he tends, on the whole, to express himself in a more studied fashion than anything that is within the normal range of his fellow-mountaineers. He writes a serious Demotic with turns of phrase here and there absorbed from newspapers read aloud and from the Athenian wireless in the village *kapheneion*. Occasionally the Demotic – which is the lively, pungent popular speech of everyday Greek life – is sprinkled with expressions that are unconsciously remembered from the liturgy, and now and then the dead hand of the Pure (or Literary) style – that stillborn medium which tries to wrest the heritage of ancient Greek from the Demotic – lays its clammy touch on George's page. The idiosyncrasy of all these conflicting influences is full of fascination. It is inevitable that George's written language should be an amalgam. For a Cretan mountaineer who is able to write at all, the very act is a formal, Sunday-best affair; every available grace must be called in. This can sometimes overcast George's humour and ebullience with a kind of temperate sedateness; but, when he is really in his stride, it breaks through nevertheless, and as the pages follow each other, and the work grows easier and more confident with practice, the composite medium settles into a forceful and surprisingly adequate means of expression. He is at his best when Demotic and Cretan win the day. Sometimes when he is embarking on an exalted theme involving patriotism or the cruelties of the Germans or lamentation for the dead, he takes a deep breath and out wobbles a great magniloquent balloon of prose. However highflown these passages may seem, they are completely sincere. The reader may smile, but he must remember that a Cretan shepherd, even an illiterate one (which George is not), has a very much larger vocabulary than the average English shop-assistant can command, and an inborn feeling for self-expression and for rhetoric. A tongue-tied Greek is a very rare freak of nature.

After a peripatetic week, George and I parted company at the Abbey of Arkadi. He set off for Asi Gonia and I sailed back to Athens with the precious parcel containing his book. I translated it later on and went over the results with Xan Fielding. We divided the work of annotation, each, roughly speaking, covering the periods and the areas which we knew best. Occasionally, when a more personal elucidation seems necessary, initials are appended. Jack Smith-Hughes (whom I would like to thank) has been through the proofs and has added his first-hand knowledge to the footnotes.

George uses *Angloi* or *Englézoi*, irrespectively, through-out, for English, British, Scotch, Welsh, Irish, New Zealand or Australian, and I have kept to his usage in translation. Perhaps the use of the prefix 'Mr' – *Kyrios* in Greek – needs a word of explanation. The full military rank – '*Kyrie Lochage*' – 'Mr Captain' – or '*Kyrie Tagmatarcha*' – 'Mr Major' – was usually reserved for formal address. In everyday use the Christian name was usually used, preceded (George is most punctilious here) by 'Mr', when a friendly deference is felt to be more suitable than the coldness of army protocol. 'Uncle' is a term of affectionate respect to older men, and 'Auntie' to their wives.

$$\star \quad \star \quad \star$$

Returning to Crete yet again a few months ago, I found that George's family fortunes had gone from bad to worse; they are now complicated by troubles which, if they come to a head, are in danger of blazing into a large-scale blood-feud. There is no point in going into all the details here. It came about without any provocation on George's side, and, to lessen the possibilities of a fatal clash – a clash that might leave his family without any support at all – George keeps away from his village as much as possible nowadays, scraping together a miserable subsistence as a charcoal burner on the mountains of the Sphakian border.

Once more we kept each other company from village to village, and, though there was little in his spirited talk and his singing and in the rose stuck behind his ear – a symbol of the convivial mood all through Greece – to indicate all these worries, he was in a state of deep depression. Yet he had found time, between the incessant chopping and stoking that his grimy work involves, to go on writing. He read me long passages from a new book, which is a collection of the legends of his village and the neighbouring ranges, their proverbs and customs and religious observances. It was excellent, and, what is more, written in a pure fluid Cretan.

When we separated, he went straight back to his solitary pyres beyond Asi Gonia. One of the many pleasures that this work affords its translator is the thought of the moment when his brother or one of his sisters or his many cousins, breathless from a steep climb after the postman's visit, hands him the parcel containing the first copy of this book. There will be the ceremonious wiping of sooty hands; the cutting of the string, the excited unshelling of the cardboard and the brown paper, until at last, with a rich creak of binding and freshly printed paper, he opens his book.

$$\star \quad \star \quad \star$$

These notes were written in 1954 and with a couple of exceptions the careers of the participants – Greek, Allied, Italian and German – are not pursued later than this *terminus ad quem* for the sad reason that, during the interim the reaper has been very busy and such an ending might give this introduction the aspect of a long-drawn-out obituary.

Note to the Sketches

The six sketches on the following pages were drawn in Crete in the summer and autumn of 1942. They are the blurred and dog-eared remainder of several dozen which depicted many of the characters mentioned in this book, and they have only survived because they were smuggled out early on a timely submarine. I destroyed all the others in a moment of danger. They are inscribed with made-up names put there in case they were captured by the Germans, and the signature 'μ.φ.' stands for the equally false name of Michali Frangiadakis on my forged identity card.

PLF

George Psychoundakis. He is labelled Vlasios Bertodoulakis from his nick-name of 'Bertódoulos', the clown Bertoldo in the old Italian comedy which was formerly popular in Greek translation.

Πάτηρ Ἀθανάσιος Κεντριανός

Father Kyriakos Katsantónis of Ano Meros in the Amari. The false surname of Kedrianos on the sketch was taken from Mt Kedros, on the side of which his village stands. It was burnt down a year later.

Andreas Polentas, of Vrysses, Apokoronas, captured in Vaphé with Apostolos Evanghelou, with whom he was later shot by the Germans in Ayia Jail in the autumn of 1942. He is labelled 'Levkoritis' – 'White Mountain-man' – after our hideout in the White Mountains.

Kapetan Petrakoyeorgis of Margarikari. With Kapetan Satanás (Satan) and Kapetan Bandouvas, he was one of the three chief leaders of the Nome of Herakleion.

Kapetan Manoli Bandouvas, from Asites. One of the most important leaders from the Nome of Herakleion.

Aristides Paradeisianos, from the small village of Ay. Yanni, Amari, in the Nome of Retimo. He was named 'Ouranakis' because ouranos = sky = paradise, i.e. Paradeisianos.

PART 1

The Battle and After

The Battle of Crete

It was in May 1941 that, all of a sudden, high in the sky, we heard the drone of many aeroplanes growing steadily closer. In a short time they were scattering Death on all sides in a merciless bombardment of this southernmost edge of Europe. At first everybody thought it was just one of the usual bombings which took place every so often and which had been growing more frequent of late. But lo and behold! Out of the sky the winged devils of Hitler were falling everywhere.

The news soon spread to the farthest corner of the island. 'German parachutists are dropping!' the cry went round, and everyone – men and women, great and small – ran to the nearest scene of action to attack the enemy, armed as they were, with guns that anyone would have sworn were taken from some museum. And they would not have been far wrong, for the villagers had kept them hidden for many years in holes and caves and now, all eaten up with rust, they really were almost archaeological specimens.

They fought untiringly, day and night. But more and more Germans were continually being dropped. The first week passed and the second came and the Germans, who thought they would be able to capture this last remaining stronghold with ease, had got nowhere. Our brave allies kept up the counter-attack without a break and the enemy was foiled, too, by the upsurge of the soul of the Cretan race whose freedom they were bent on wresting away.

I was in my village of Asi Gonia at the time. It is a village far away from the main roads and it has always been distinguished for its spirit and its bravery. I was pasturing a few sheep on the mountainside when I heard that everybody was off to fight the Germans; so I too left my sheep and went down to Episkopi, which is about one kilometre from the borders of Canea and Retimo. (The road from one to the other passes through the middle of the village.) Every evening men took up positions on the seashore in case the Germans should attempt a landing during the night.

We listened to the BBC and to Athens in an agony of anxiety as to what they were saying about the battle of Crete. The fighting was getting fiercer every moment and we eagerly asked anyone coming from Canea or Retimo how it was going against the Germans. Our hearts leaped with joy when, each time, the same answer came back: 'We've eaten them up!'

The aeroplanes came and went like bees in a bee-garden, each time bringing more bombs and troops. It made us grind our teeth to see them hammering away at all the roads and, indeed, wherever they saw so much as a farm animal. 'Aaaa! You cuckolds!'[1] we cried. 'If only we had our aeroplanes and our troops here!' And our thoughts would fly to Albania, where our Division had been left behind.[2] 'If only the Division were here!' But, alas, we had nothing. Troops, arms, ammunition, aeroplanes – everything in fact was wanting, and our hearts[3] were the only things of which we were never short.

One day a low-flying aeroplane suddenly swooped

1 *Kerata*, cuckold, hornwearer. The commonest of all Greek vernacular insults.
2 Explained in Introduction.
3 Courage.

across the plain stretching from Dramia to Georgioupolis and settled on the seashore. 'Germans must be landing!' we cried, and ran towards it as fast we could. The machine had fallen by the sea and one wing was under water. A great gathering from all the surrounding villages ran shouting towards the aeroplane. 'Let's get at them!' was the universal cry. We were still two hundred yards away when a sudden burst of heavy machine-gun fire made us all duck. The German airmen, frightened at such a concourse, were firing into the air to stem the onrush and escape from the hands that would soon be on them. I am sure that they fired in the air, because we were so close that it would have been easy to kill a lot of us with the aircraft's cannon. But nobody was hit – not because the Germans were merciful, but because they knew they would soon be in our hands.

I had jumped into a ditch, and found five or six others lying flat beside me. Only one of them was armed, and, at that, with an old Martini in such a state of disrepair that after firing each shot he had to extract the cartridge-case with a ramrod before re-loading. (I remembered the old saying, 'Stand still, Turk, while I re-load.'[1]) About two minutes later, up drove an English tank from the out-post at Georgioupolis. We broke cover and ran towards it, while the Germans were surrendering to the Englishmen. Five airmen got out and climbed into the tank. We threw a last glance at the ones we wanted to throttle with our own hands, and, as they were being taken off to Georgioupolis, our anger exploded on the aeroplane. We cursed our friends the English for rescuing them, and the destruction of the plane began. Some broke off and took the machine guns, others the parachutes, the magazines, and the ammunition belts, until the plane looked like a

1 Referring to the old muzzle-loaders.

bit of bread thrown on to an ant-hill. Soon there would have been nothing left if some Englishmen had not turned up shouting 'No! No!' at the top of their voices. But we did not know what the word meant – to judge by the results, it might have been the order for its complete destruction. Then our own police interfered. 'Boys,' they said, 'the plane has scarcely anything wrong with it and they want to repair it and use it against the Germans. You mustn't destroy it!'

The policemen's words and the threats of the Englishmen, who by now had surrounded the plane with fixed bayonets, made us all listen to reason. We stopped, gazing now at the plane which stood dumb and motionless, now at the English sentries, and as we set off back, we explained to the villagers who were still arriving that there had been no fresh invasion, only a wounded aeroplane that had made a forced landing.

★　★　★

Back in the village, one day followed another and in Crete at large the unbounded will of the allies and the islanders began to give way before the overwhelming superiority of the enemy. Their blows fell with greater and greater fury. Seeing a handful of men putting up such an amazing resistance – a resistance that all the millions of the other races they had enslaved had not been able to offer – they went mad with anger. The destruction they wrought cannot be described and will not be set to rights for many a year.

Crete fell after a hard fight whose story is known to all the world. It would need a modern Homer, painting with the brightest colours, to sing the encomium of the Battle of Crete and tell the tale of the sacrifice of her people in the cause of freedom.

The barbarian footfalls of the Germans were soon heard

in the streets, and their still more barbarous voices. They reached to our very bowels and provoked a storm in the soul of the race like the hiss of a poisonous snake about to strike. They began to burn down villages and torture the inhabitants, loading them like beasts of burden, and killing them with appalling torments. The Germans proved themselves to be, in every way, utter barbarians. They were avenging, they said, their slain brothers-in-arms who now filled the whole island with graveyards.

But how could they justify this vengeance for their slain companions, who, along with them, had tried to drive us from our homes and dishonour and kill us, and settle in our stead? What did they expect us to do? Cross our hands and surrender? This our souls forbade us to do. Our history, too – an incorruptibly great and glorious one for many generations and thousands of years – had taught us a different lesson. No. Crete had to resist, and she resisted with all her might. And these strangers, strutting now in the guise of brave swashbucklers, should have been begging forgiveness for all the evil they had done to Crete; for their cruel attack upon the island and for all the barbarity that typified them; for their 'vengeance', as they called it. Now people beheld their brothers shot with their hands tied behind them, their houses burnt and their fortunes destroyed. Children were killed in their mothers' arms, and men and women, both young and old, fell together before the German bullets. Whole villages, with their churches and their schools and all that was sacred, were burnt and blown up; yet they talked of a New Order. What a monstrosity! But the daily mass-executions of hundreds and all the persecution and destruction the Germans then began, instead of terrifying the Cretans into loving them as they hoped, bred hate inside them and armed their spirits with the sharp weapons of future vengeance and liberation.

The Wandering English

As soon as the Germans were masters of the key-points in the island, the English troops began to withdraw. As they did not possess a single fighter or bomber plane, they were unable to resist the unparalleled blows of the German air force, and they were obliged, first to retreat, and then to evacuate Crete. But how could they all escape, with the Germans pressing them so hard? Apart from those taken prisoner, thousands of British stayed behind wandering hither and thither in the valleys and the mountains and in the towns and the villages too. The Cretans deemed it a sacred duty to look after these soldiers by whose side they had fought and whom fortune had brought from their far-off country to wage war and to shed their blood on our mountains. We gave them food and clothing so that they could discard their uniforms and move about more freely, and hid them in the most suitable places. Most of them were led away to remote mountain villages where the safety was greater both for them and their protectors, for woe betide the people and their villages if the Germans found them out.

I remember, as though it were yesterday, the first English who came our way asking to be hidden. We were sitting outside the coffee-shop when a villager came and told us some Germans were heading for the village. In those days, the wave of flight into the foothill-villages had begun to break up, and only a few people were there.

They had taken fright and were returning home. When our fellow-villager assured us that he had seen the Germans approaching with his own eyes, and only a little way off, we too, ignorant as we were of the Germans' purpose, jumped up like the other refugees, and fled in fear. Climbing the slope opposite the village to see what was afoot, we soon saw the supposed Germans coming towards us, led by several of our villagers. We ran farther off. 'Don't run away,' they shouted, 'they are not Germans.' Eaten up with curiosity, we asked who they were. Our joy cannot be described when they answered that they were English.

For most of us it was the first time we had set eyes on Englishmen. When we had joined them we tried to talk to them, but they could not understand a word. A fellow-villager who knew a few scraps of English which he had brought back from America started talking to them. They said the Germans would not be more than two months in the island so that we and they would soon be free again, and we all believed it. When they had rested a little while and eaten whatever we could prepare for them we led them away to a romantic – not to say frightening – valley half an hour away[1] where their sojourn could remain unknown for the time being. We reassured them and told them that they were completely safe here, and that they could come to the village during the daytime without fear. What did we not say, talking about these people! Soon more arrived, and they all formed a little company and talked away among themselves. They did not seem at all unhappy.

---

1 In Greek and Cretan mountains where the actual mileage is irrelevant, distances are always reckoned in time.

The First Germans in my Village

Not many days passed before four Germans arrived from Argyroupolis with an interpreter. They sat down at the coffee-shop, summoned the Mayor of the village, and at once began asking him questions. The first thing they asked was, had the villagers taken part in the battle against the parachutists? The Mayor answered that our village was so far away that we hardly knew that a battle had taken place. Then they asked if the village possessed any arms, but once more the Mayor said that the villages had given up all their arms to the country at the time of the Albanian war, and that only a fowling-piece or two still remained. The Germans said they must all be handed over, even fowling-pieces, and that for each gun that was withheld ten men would be shot and their houses burnt down.

'You must collect them all at the village police-station and the police will bring them to us at Argyroupolis,' they said 'and the wireless set must be handed over as well.' So the owner was called and told where and when it should be taken. Meanwhile some of the villagers had collected and were gazing at the Germans with curiosity. And the inquisitive ones were not a few, because many thought they were beholding some kind of strange animal.

The villagers thought it would be wise to hand over a few rotten and harmless guns – any old iron to deceive the Germans with – in case they had learnt that we possessed any arms. It would be best, they said, for the sporting-guns to be handed over as well lest the Germans should learn the owners' names from the list of licences in the records at Canea. So about a dozen sporting-guns were collected at the police-station, and about the same number of totally useless rifles. The good ones were hidden away as carefully as sacred relics – holy things to be used at the right time, when the signal of liberation should be given; and there were plenty, because, when the English retreated to Sphakia,[1] even small boys had gone down to the seashore and the valleys bringing rifles back with them.

The days followed each other and news came from all over Crete of the daily brutalities committed by the Germans. Every day we learnt of new burnings and shootings and fear grew inside us but also strengthened the hatred in our souls.

---

[1] The southern port from which they were evacuated.

Three Boys Burn an Aeroplane

June had ended, and in July – it must have been about two months since the fall of the island – three boys from a neighbouring village (Kastelos in Apokoronas), called Levtheri Daskalakis and George and Andrea Vernadakis, went down to the flat country near Asprouliano where the plane which had made the forced landing still lay. A German guard post had been set up close by to watch over it. But the boys went at midday when the men of the guard were inside eating, and, creeping up to the plane unobserved, they set fire to one of the petrol tanks. It went up in a flash, the whole plane catching in a moment and blazing like a firework. The Germans rushed out, but they did not see who had set fire to it, and (as we learnt later), fearing punishment by their superiors – for their only duty had been the guarding of this plane – they told the owners of the vegetable plots round about to say that they had seen nobody if the military authorities should question them: that the plane, in fact, had caught fire by itself. The gardeners said they would back them up in their report. Unfortunately a 'bad Greek'[1] called Evangelos Stagakis of Dramia went to the local German command-post at Episkopi and asked to be taken to the Kommandant. When the interpreter learnt that he wanted to reveal the truth about the burning of the plane, he turned him out.

1 i.e. a traitor.

But Stagakis started threatening the interpreter, and went on until he managed to appear before the Kommandant, to whom he betrayed the whole business. The men at the guard post were arrested at once and (we learnt) put in the lock-up where the Germans beat them up. To the devil with them. But what happened to the neighbourhood? A large German force immediately surrounded the villages of Dramia, Kastelos and Kourna and rounded up the male inhabitants. But the boys, forewarned, had left their villages. The Germans announced that unless the people who had burnt the aeroplane were given up, the villagers would all be shot. But how could the villagers have found them, even if they had wished to give them up? In the end, after all the denials of the villagers (who constantly repeated 'We don't know anything. How could *we* find them?'), it was decided that the blame rested only with the boys' fellow-villagers, the Kastelians; so the Germans began to threaten the Kastelians and especially the relations of the three boys. But they were determined to die rather than hand their children over to be killed. The matter was very serious. If they did as the Germans demanded, the killing of their children would weigh heavy on their hearts for the rest of their lives. They would never be able to still their consciences. So they decided to warn them not to come near the village, but to flee far away and take care never to be caught by the Germans, even if everybody else were killed. And then they waited, resigned to the firing squad. Meanwhile the boys (who had gone into hiding near our village), learning that all their own people would be killed for shielding them, began to be tormented in their minds as to what they ought to do. Finally they decided to give themselves up. They lingered in the neighbourhood to observe the actions of the Germans, in order that, the moment they saw the Germans about to execute their relations, they might surrender and take the road to Golgotha. But here, too, bad Greeks were in evidence. The then Mayor of their village, Stavros Romanias, learning that the boys were in hiding nearby, sent a man to verify the fact, and, when he had made quite certain, took a large number of Germans who set out in ones and twos for Asi Gonia. Fortunately we saw them before they reached the village, and had time to lead the English further off and then to escape ourselves. Unfortunately some villagers were mad enough not to escape, so the Germans arrested about a dozen of them and led them away to Archontiki. They gave them a certain time limit in which to betray the boys; otherwise they were to be shot.

The luckless boys, learning all this, and seeing that the Germans were in no joking mood, took the path of death with heavy hearts. Only Andrea, the youngest, was unwilling to give himself up, so he hid himself at the place called Koumara,[1] where some Psychoundakis cousins of mine, who pastured their flocks thereabouts, looked after him. As bad luck would have it, some fellow-villagers, relations of the people who were being held in Archontiki, losing patience and not knowing what the Germans were going to do with their kinsmen, set off one day to Andrea's hiding-place to persuade or compel him to give himself up. But the moment he saw them he took to his heels. They set off after him in pursuit, and he ran tirelessly for many hours. Some of the ones in front fired shots at him to make him stop, but it was all in vain. At last, when he had shaken them off, he fell into the hands of some others, who caught him, half-dead with exhaustion. They took him to Argyroupolis and handed him over to the Germans. He showed no signs of fear but laughed at them as though it were all a game of hide-and-seek.

1 The arbutus-berries.

The Germans took him to Canea along with the other two, where they were tried. Andrea, being under age, was only sentenced to six months' hard labour, but the other two, who were nearing twenty if they had not actually reached it, were condemned to death. So, after a few days, in a street in Archontiki and under the eyes of all the inhabitants, these two martyrs to freedom and death-deriders stood before the firing squad, – naked, hungry, barefoot and in chains. Their last moment was approaching. Their bonds were removed and their executioners, with rifles levelled at their bare breasts, were waiting for the word 'Fire!' The leader of the German party read out the sentence and asked if they had any last words to say. Daskalakis asked for a glass of water which they gave him, and the question was repeated to Verna-dakis, who said: 'A glass of wine and permission to sing a *mantinada*.'[1] Saying which, naked, barefoot and utterly exhausted as he was from thirst and hunger (for, during their confinement in Ayia jail they had been given neither food nor water), he mustered all the strength of his soul – and what greater strength is there? – and took to his heels. Straight away the firing squad began shooting after him as he ran. But neither the rifle bullets nor the bursts from the sub-machine-guns could touch him. He ran like lightning from lane to lane until he was out of the village. Then, as it was difficult to run further without being seen, he climbed up into an olive tree and stayed there until night fell. When it was quite dark he climbed gently down and, slipping through the sentries, fled far away. Later he escaped to the Middle East where he volunteered for the Air Force.

1 A Cretan fifteen-syllable rhyming couplet, usually with a sting in it. Sung in solo to one of half a dozen ritual tunes, the last half of each line being repeated, after the words 'Ela! Ela! Ela!', by the rest of the company. They are sung and improvised by all Cretans, especially in the mountains.

While they were chasing Vernadakis through the village, Daskalakis remained motionless in his place although he too had a chance of taking to his heels and escaping. 'Run for it!' several onlookers shouted, but he refused, saying the Germans would avenge themselves on his kinsmen. It would be better for him to die, he said. In a few moments the Germans were back again, and they opened fire on Daskalakis with fury. He fell at once, quite transformed and unrecognizable from the bursts of the German machine-guns.

Commander Pool[1]

A few days later, a wonderful piece of news reached the village: an English submarine had come to Preveli and landed a senior officer of the British Navy there. This was the first contact between the Allied GHQ in the Middle East and captured Crete. The submarine had approached the shore at Preveli in the Eparchy[2] of St Basil in the south of the Nome of Retimo, and, led by a guide, Commander Pool had landed and made contact with the Abbot Agathángelos[3] of the Holy Monastery of St John of Preveli. He undertook a short journey and made contact with other patriots, and, seeing that many British soldiers had not surrendered to the Germans but were wandering the island and being protected in the villages, he declared that the first work to be done was the evacuation of these men to Africa by submarine. The job of assembling them began. The news spread everywhere in secret, and the English were collected in little parties and led from village to village until they reached the shore at Preveli. All the soldiers who had been hiding in the Nome of Canea (except those in Sphakia) had to pass through our village.

The Germans got wind of the presence in the mountains

1 Commander F. G. Pool, DSO, DSC, died 1947 in Athens.
2 An eparchy (district, county) is a subdivision of a nome (province), which is under the jurisdiction of a Nomarch (Prefect).
3 The Most Rev. Fr. Agathángelos Lagouvardos, OBE, a wonderful white-haired old man, who died in Cairo in the summer of 1942.

of many British soldiers who had not surrendered, and
they understood still more clearly that many others, being
secretly apprised of the support of their wandering
countrymen by the people of Crete and of the flight to
Africa by submarine, had started breaking out of the prison
camp.¹ So they sent spies up into the villages to find out
in which ones they were hiding and from where they
escaped. Often the Germans dressed up as Englishmen
and pretended to be wandering soldiers; but the trick
seldom came off. Warning spread from mouth to mouth
and nobody was trusted unless he was recommended by
one of our people. Sometimes, however, the Germans
were able to take in unwary villagers whom they afterwards
arrested and shot. But Asi Gonia, like many other villages
of Crete, was a great hiding-place for these Englishmen.
More, it was the key to safety and to their passage through
the mountains, from the Nome of Canea to the Nome
of Retimo.²

For this reason the Germans sent their spies there one
day. Fortunately we saw through them and chased them
away with threats, shouting that unless they cleared out
of our village we would arrest them and hand them over
to the Germans. In some other villages, where they were
even more intelligent, they captured them and thrashed
them like donkeys (as they say), then, leading them off
bound, handed them over to the enemy! As the Germans
were unable to reveal their game, our village, and several
others, succeeded in creating an undeservedly good
impression.

So the flight of the English to Africa began. Every day
a new party reached the village and every day I was their

1 Because of the mass escapes, this camp, near Galata, was transferred to the
mainland in February 1942.
2 Thanks to its position on the Selli pass between the outcrop of the White
Mountains and Mount Drepanon. See map.

guide. I would lead them to the villages of Arolithi, Alones or Kali-Sykia and hand them over to others of our people to help them on their way. At Alones[1] I could put them into the hands of any villager I met because all of them were good and all eager to help; and, best of all, they knew how to keep their mouths shut. Their village priest, Father John Alevizakis was a golden-hearted man and a true patriot. All the village were enlightened and led in the right path by him, just as a good family is enlightened and led by its head. At Kali-Sykia I would guide them to the house of Stamati Stavroulakis, a fellow-villager of mine, and to several other houses. Up in the mountains above our village, at a place called Vourvouré, lived another fellow-villager of ours, the Infantry Lieutenant-Colonel Andrea Papadakis. He had a fine property there and a fine house where the English often lay in hiding.

1 A tiny village inhabited by two families (Alevizakis and Tsangarakis) and controlled by the magnificent old village priest, Father J. Alevizakis.

The March to Preveli Monastery

It must have been in the month of August that an English officer came to stay with Colonel Papadakis up at Vourvouré. He knew Greek well, and I think he had escaped from the prison camp at Galata. He was very young, stout, ruddy and fair-haired; his rank was second lieutenant, and his name was Smith-Hughes.[1] He had talked about the whole situation with Colonel Papadakis[2] and agreed to escape with him to Cairo, in order to get instructions there from Allied Headquarters in preparation for returning to the struggle in Crete and the organization of liberation.

Colonel Papadakis summoned his god-brother[3]

1 Major Jack Smith-Hughes, OBE, RASC, was twenty-one or twenty-two at the time but looked older. Oddly enough he had slightly thinning black hair. He escaped to the Middle East, returned again as one of the first Resistance organizers in occupied Crete, then returned to Cairo, where, till late in 1944, he most capably ran the Cretan Office of Special Operations Executive. He then continued his work in the island until the liberation, after which he was acting Consul in Canea. He married a Cretan girl. A barrister-at-law and author, he is serving in the army once more.

2 He must be distinguished from his second cousin, Colonel (later General) Nicolas Papadakis who was the first Military Governor of Crete after the liberation. He landed, accompanied by Jack Smith-Hughes, in October 1944.

3 'God-Brother' means somebody who has stood sponsor, as a godfather does, at a wedding or a baptism. In the Orthodox Faith, this binds him more strongly to the bride or groom, to the parents of the child baptized, and to the whole family, than blood-relationship. The Greek word is koumbáros from the Italian compadre; the Cretan dialect one of synteknos. This, however, only applies to the baptismal relationship. Some of us entered on many of these god-brotherhoods, a link which persists and which is maintained for life.

Petrakas[1] from the village and told him all this; he also told him to find fifteen well-armed men to escort them down to Preveli, from which point they were to escape. Uncle Petrakas was a widely respected figure in our village and as many would follow him as he wished. He summoned several of us (me among the rest) and we took our arms and followed him. We reached Phratì, a village about two hours away from Preveli, where we met Colonel Papadakis and Mr Smith-Hughes and some other English officers. We lay in hiding all that day and night and before the next day began to break we set off for Preveli. We went into hiding again twenty minutes away from the monastery and despatched a runner to ask for someone called Polio[2] who was to guide us that evening to a suitable embarkation point. After a while Polio came and talked with the officers, then left again. We were to remain there till evening fell, and, as soon as dusk began to thicken, set off for the monastery. We waited close by for a signal to go inside.

Soon someone shouted to us, and in we went. We sat down and ate what the monks brought us, and waited for orders. Our *Kapetanios*,[3] Mr Petrakas, was not slow to arrive; we were to prepare for the road. It seemed the

1 Kapetan Petrakas Papadopetrakis, MBE, was one of the most reliable and courageous helpers and guerrilla leaders in Crete. He had taken part in guerrilla campaigns as a boy in Macedonia, and had seen action in many theatres. Aged about fifty at the time with which we are concerned, he led a very efficient and well-disciplined irregular band and, in the troubles of 1948, was shot clean through the body between the lungs, but has suffered no visible ill-effects. Tall, baldish, blue-eyed and with heavy blond moustaches, his code name was Beowulf.
2 Cretan nickname for Paul.
3 *Kapetanios* or *Kapetan*, the Greek, and especially the Cretan, honorific name for a guerrilla leader; often usurped, especially in Cretan funny stories, in the region of Sphakia and elsewhere. Later, when this style was applied to some of us, it always produced a glow of pleasure, in spite of some of the spurious implications I have hinted at.

arrival of the submarine had been postponed and there was no work for us there. But, as we learnt later, this was really not true. It was some kind of pantomime (I don't know who was behind it) to prevent Colonel Papadakis from leaving the island. We left that evening, taking the road over Asomatos Marios,[1] and reached the Kouroupas Mountains. By the time we struck the Kanevos road day had already broken. We tried to find out if any Germans were there, as usually there was no lack of them. The motor-road from Retimo ended here, the German command-post of Spili was very close, and the Germans travelled hence by mule to the coastal guard-post at Plakia. Hearing that all was clear for the moment, we crossed the road two by two leaving Kanevos and heading for Kali-Sykia.[2] We sat down to rest by the village spring, and then pushed ahead through Alones and Myriokephala to Asi Gonia. Wherever we went, the villagers, seeing us carrying arms, almost exploded with joy. For those were very tragic days; fear and death reigned everywhere. So when they saw us fully armed, everyone thought something important was afoot and prepared to take up their guns and follow us. We calmed them down and told them they would be warned in time when the moment came.

★   ★   ★

The days followed each other swiftly. The news of submarines approaching Preveli had reached all ears, and wherever English were hidden, their protectors made haste to guide them that way.

Still more of the English took to breaking out of the prison camps, or from the gangs that were marched out on

1 *Asomatos Marios*, the name of a mountain.
2 'The Good Fig Tree': a village.

labour fatigues, and the Germans were growing anxious. More and more Englishmen kept arriving in our village daily. Whenever there was a mission[1] at Preveli, two hundred and more would assemble. A whole camp! Try as we might, it was no longer easy to keep all this a secret, and so in time it reached the ears of bad Cretans. A man in pain finds a little relief and comfort in talking about his pain to a friend, and thus it was with the woe-begone Cretan people when they heard the smallest thing that could give them a flicker of hope. When two men met, the news would follow the moment they had said '*Yassou*[2]... Have you heard anything?' And the word would fly from mouth to mouth, like a wireless. No other wirelesses existed! ... So the news about Preveli, finding its way into the orders of the day, at last reached German ears. And so, one evil morning, the monastery woke up surrounded by Germans. Fortunately, our people[3] had taken careful precautions, and nobody fell into the trap. But the Germans plundered and wrecked the monastery. They carried away the plentiful food supplies, the countless herds of goats and sheep and so on, and they banished the monks. Luckily the Abbot Agathángelos escaped and fled to Africa, so the monks were able to throw all the blame on him. The Germans then set up a strong outpost at the little harbour of Limni, where till then the submarines had drawn alongside, thus putting an end to all hopes of secret vessels approaching that stretch of the coast in future.

1 i.e. a submarine approaching for an evacuation.
2 '*Eis tín ygeià sou*', contracted to '*Yassou*' = 'To your health!' The most common and familiar Greek greeting.
3 'Ours', 'Our people' – i.e. anyone on the right (that is, the speaker's) side, or 'in the secret'. A very common Greek turn of phrase.

A Senior Officer Ill

However, another fitting place for this work was soon discovered.

Crete is surrounded by deserted shores, and the new point lay on the south coast of the Nome of Herakleion. The English soldiers hiding in the Nome of Retimo could only get there after a march of many days and still more for those hiding in Canea. But, as before, they were led from village to village, from eparchy to eparchy and from nome to nome until they reached their destination. Yerakari was their chief halting-place on this journey. 'Send them to Yerakari!' was the universal watchword. Yerakari, in the Eparchy of Amari and the Nome of Retimo, was one of the most beautiful villages in Crete. Though it is a very mountainous village, it is accessible by motor-road. But, most important of all, the inhabitants were all good patriots.

One day in the middle of October Kosta Grylos (from nearby Alikampo) came to our village. With him, in a wretched state of health, was an English major in the Medical Corps. Kosta brought him to the house of Petrakas on a donkey, accompanied by his soldier-servant. Uncle[1] Petraka called on me to accompany them to Yerakari,

---

[1] 'Uncle' is often a title of respect among peasants for older people. But George is also a blood relation of Petrakas.

and next day at the rising of the sun Kosta and I helped the sick man on to the donkey and we set out.

As we would be obliged to follow the main roads, we disguised him as an old woman. After we had dressed him up, he really looked like one, and if we were quizzed on the way, we decided to say we were taking our grandmother to a German doctor in Spili who, we had heard, was a kind man who might help her in her illness. Spili lay two hours this side of Yerakari. The soldier-servant was dressed as a Cretan and, if he kept his mouth shut, it was hard to tell him apart. It was a sunny morning, perfect for our patient's journey. We were unable, however, to reach Yerakari in a day; but we had been told the name of a friend in Lambini, in whose house we could sleep the night. We pressed forward and I asked various acquaintances in each village if there were any control-posts farther on, for this was the only danger. We were asked so many questions on the road that we lost our tempers, but took care not to show it. When we reached Koxaré, it was dusk. We went to a friendly house and got some milk for the sick man and then hastened on to Lambini. Night had overtaken us now and we were hurrying along the main road. I had never gone farther east than Koxaré and knew neither the way nor the distances, but we had learnt that it was one hour from Koxaré to Spili.[1]

We had gone some way when suddenly, at a turning in the road, we found ourselves at the entrance to a village. The moment he saw this, Kosta, who was in front with the donkey, turned to me and said, 'Spili! We must go back!' in a frightened voice, and hurriedly wheeled the donkey round. I followed him out the way we had come without a word, and when we had gone about two

[1] The local German headquarters.

hundred yards I stopped him and asked him where we were heading for.

'I don't know,' was his answer.

'Wait,' I said, 'I'll go and find out where we are. It can't be Spili, as we haven't walked more than an hour and they told us Spili was two.'

'Let's get off the road,' he said.

'Let's,' I said, and we climbed up among the olive groves, and, unloading the sick man from the donkey, spread a blanket on the ground and laid him there to rest. Then I went off to the village, and, halting outside a house, put my ear to the window. I realized there were no Germans there and knocked on the door. Someone said 'Come in,' so in I went.

'Good evening, gentlemen,' I said, and they answered, 'Good evening.'

'Please, what is the name of this village?'

'Myxórouma.'

'How far is it to Lambini?'

'About a quarter of an hour,' they answered.

The famine was just beginning and everyone those days was heading east to the Messara Plain to buy wheat. The road was crowded with such travellers, so I pretended I was one of a party of three, and, as none of us had been in those parts before, we didn't know how late people were allowed to stay out at night.[1]

'Don't worry,' they said. 'This isn't Spili, and there are no Germans here. But, if that's your destination, you will be late and the Germans will open fire on you.'

'We've got some friends in Lambini, but we don't know the way there either.'

'It isn't hard,' they said. 'We'll guide you,' and one of them followed me out to help us on our way. Asking him

1 Because of the curfew.

to wait a couple of minutes while I called the others, I ran off to them like lightning. We helped the sick man on to the donkey and rejoined our new friend. The darkness was on our side and our lie went undetected. He led us on a bit and put us on a different road. 'This way,' he said, 'you'll be in Lambini in ten minutes.' We said goodnight and thank-you to this good man and set off. By the time we reached Lambini it had started to drizzle. But luck helped us a little, for someone in the middle of the village, whom we asked about our man there, said, 'I know the family, but not that Christian name. Let's go and find out.' He took us to the house of the family. The name I had been given really did exist, but the owner of it had been in America for over forty years. What were we to do? We knew nobody else in those parts.

Our new guide asked us where we came from. We said that we were Apokoroniots,[1] and that we knew nobody else there. 'Apokoroniots!' he said. 'Don't worry. Come with me. I'm from Apokoronas myself – from Megala Chorafia[2] – but I married into this village. My name is Kelaïdis.' We followed him and, when he asked us which village in Apokoronas we were from, we told him the truth, both as to our villages and our names. And, as there was nothing else for it, we also entrusted him with our secret. This made him still more eager to help. Meanwhile we quickened our step as the rain was growing heavier. He said he would take us to the house of a kinsman, who would look after us. He summoned the woman of the house and took her outside to tell her the secret. But his kinsfolk were scared to take us in when they learnt we had Englishmen with us.

1 Inhabitants of the Eparchy of Apokoronas, near Canea.
2 'Great Fields'.

Then, in a towering fury, he took us to his own house, wet through with the rain by now. 'There's not much room here, boys,' he said, 'and we must shift as best we can.' His little house was newly built; indeed, not quite finished. Both he and his wife were full of enthusiasm and delight at the honour of giving hospitality to our party.

We ate and drank our fill, and managed to find some milk for the sick man, for he could swallow nothing else; then they made up a good bed for all of us in the guest-room,[1] with plenty of blankets to keep out the cold. When day began to break we got up, made ready, and set out. Our noble-spirited host came with us a fair distance, about an hour, leading us to the hilltop above the village and overlooking Karines, in order to avoid Spili. Putting us in the right direction to strike the Spili-Yerakari road, he bade us farewell and left. We thanked him warmly for his help, which had been great indeed, and pursued our journey.

I will never forget the poor doctor in the bitter winds of those mountain tops. He was terribly cold on his donkey, shuddering all over and one word – '*cold*'[2] – was always in his mouth. In vain we did our best to comfort him and keep him warm. But, 'I'm cold,' he kept repeating. We crossed a great plateau with many streams on top of the mountain range, called the Plateau of Yious. Then we took the downhill slope towards Yerakari, and halted outside the village.

I went in alone to find the man to whom I was to entrust the doctor – Mr Alexander Kokonas.[3] I soon found him. His house lay at the edge of the village and he showed me which way to lead the others there without attracting

---

1 The *mosaphir-oda* is usually by itself on a storey above the big living-room.
2 In English in the text.
3 Reserve Captain Kokonas, OBE, schoolmaster of Yerakari, a saintly figure and one of our best helpers.

attention. This lay along a stream-bed and the donkey refused to budge. It was very steep, so we abandoned the donkey, and Kosta carried the sick man on his back as far as Mr Kokonas's house. Here he found every care at once as well as medical attention. We left next day, relieved and happy because we had fulfilled our mission.

★ ★ ★

Alas, when I got back to my village a great disaster awaited me. During the night, unknown people had come and stolen all the sheep my father possessed, about sixty of them. I ran from one village to another trying to find them, but all in vain. The sheep had vanished for ever. I was miserable, for sixty sheep meant salvation to a family, especially in those years. What was I to do now? Should I, too, take to stealing, as the custom is in those villages?[1] No. It didn't even pass through my head. Kill the people who had stolen them? Nor that, either. Take them to court? That too was impossible, as our State no longer existed and the courts had come to a complete standstill. Only the shadow of them was still kept up, for form's sake. So I left God to punish them, which He did after His fashion and in His own time. I resumed my peaceful way of life as before.

---

1 i.e. on the slopes of the White Mountains and the borders of Sphakia, the most notorious region for cattle-rustling.

PART 2
English Espionage

The Coming of Mr Jack Smith-Hughes

It must have been about the twentieth of October 1941 that Uncle Petrakas told me to accompany him up to the house of Colonel Papadakis at Vourvouré. There we found the officer we had guided to Preveli in August, when he left Crete by submarine – Mr Jack Smith-Hughes. With him was an English signal-sergeant, Mr Stockbridge.[1] They had come from Africa and landed on the southern coast of the Nome of Herakleion, somewhere near Treis Ekklesies,[2] and made their way to Colonel Papadakis through the Amari. That day was the beginning of an organized espionage service against the Germans. Colonel Papadakis told me that I was to be their regular runner. Taking all due precautions, they set about planning and organizing a whole network of observation and information. Mr Smith-Hughes was named Yanni, and that is what everybody called him. He wore Cretan costume (baggy trousers, high boots, a black shirt and a black-fringed turban), but anyone could pick him out as an Englishman at a mile away, especially when he was dressed in those clothes! So we persuaded him to wear long trousers. Mr Stockbridge we called Michalaki.[3] He never

1 Later Captain Ralph Stockbridge, MC and bar.
2 'Three Churches'.
3 His name was later altered to *Siphi* in order to avoid confusion with the translator's, also Michali, of which *Michalaki* is a diminutive, both being used indiscriminately for the same person.

went anywhere, for his duty lay with the wireless transmitting set which was disguised as a suitcase. My first journey as runner was to Priné with a letter for the Infantry Colonel Christos Tsiphakis,[1] whom they told me to ask for at the house of Mr George Robola. I fulfilled my mission as I had been instructed, and then I set out almost every day, bringing back letters and information to Vourvouré from all over the place. I am small in size and my general appearance and bearing failed to arouse the faintest suspicion. So I could go wherever I wanted without fear . . .

November had come round when one day they gave me a couple of letters to take to the Amari; so I made for Alones, where I slept the night. Next morning I took the path leading to Karines, in order to meet a friend of ours there, Stavro Zourbakis; reaching Elenes in the evening. A god-brother of Colonel Papadakis lived here, but he was not at home, so I pressed on to Yerakari, which I knew from the last time I had passed that way with the sick doctor.

'What a shame it was,' the schoolmaster said. 'After all that trouble, the poor man died in Ayia Paraskevi.' There, in spite of the danger from the Germans, (and, indeed woe betide them if the Germans had found him there, even dead!) they buried him in the village cemetery with great honours. That night I first met the Koutellidakis family – a fine, patriotic one – and George Koutellidakis, an officer of the Engineers. I left as soon as day broke, heading east through Kardaki, where I met Sotiri Monachoyiòs, and Ano Meros, where I met Father Kyriakos Katsandónis, and Ay Yanni, where I met Mr Emmanuel Papadoyannis.[2] I met them each in haste as I was in a

---

1 Later the leader of the National Organization of Crete (EOK) for the Nome of Retimo, and a post-war governor of Crete.
2 Former Governor-General of Crete, a Royalist, therefore anti-Venizelist, deputy, and, since the war, a Cabinet Minister in two governments.

hurry to reach my destination, which was Platanos.

I got there early. I found our friend Bibakis's house and gave him the Colonel's letter. We met Niko Souri[1] on the way to the coffee-shop and he introduced us. Niko was a Greek from Alexandria, working in the English service for rounding up soldiers from all over the island and organizing their escape to Africa. We talked for a time and agreed to set off at dawn next day. I was tired to my bones.

And next morning we left Platanos with the rising of the sun. Then a strange thing happened to me − a trick of the eyesight. I looked at Niko and could find no resemblance between him and the man I had met the night before. I gazed and gazed at him all the way but utterly failed to recognize him, to find even the faintest similarity. I could have sworn a thousand oaths, and was only comforted by the thought that he could be nobody else. I understood then that my great weariness the night before must have made me see him otherwise, and today, when I had recovered a little, I saw him as he really was.

We set off westwards on the southern flank of Mount Kedros and, reaching Koxaré at long last, sat down in the village to rest. But we found walking afterwards all the harder. How tired we were! It is hard to describe our weariness and the aching of our feet. We turned our fatigue into a joke. Finding two bits of wood we broke them, and used them as walking sticks to hobble along on like a pair of cripples. Our sitting down, instead of refreshing us, had made us both wrecks. With all this we reached Kali-Sykia by evening and went to the house of Stamati Stavroulakis, where we lay all night. In the morning, an hour's march brought us to Alones, where we stayed till

1 One of the best organizers and hardest workers in the Service.

the afternoon. Vourvouré was not more than two and a half hours from Alones, and we set off in time to get there by evening. This was my first long march, and it was a more exhausting one than any other I had made. It was not really so long compared with others I undertook afterwards (some of which were no cups of coffee), but I had not got used to it yet. Niko stayed with us a day or two, and then left again for his base in the Herakleian regions.

★ ★ ★

Each time there was a vessel from Africa, I had to go and meet it with the reports of the Service for GHQ, and bring back the mail for the Englishmen, coming from Cairo and elsewhere. I remember twenty-eight journeys in succession, after which I lost count, for they became innumerable.

At the beginning of December they sent me off to Margarikari. My tactics on the march were to know few people, in order that few should know me, even if they were 'ours' and good patriots. I kept my mouth shut with everybody, even to the point of idiocy, and these two things kept me safe to the end. It took me two days' walking to reach Margarikari, where I asked the way to Mr Petrakoyeorgis's[1] house. It was in the upper part of the village, a large newly built house, still only half finished. Mr Petrakoyeorgis's family were there as well as a few stragglers. In the evening about sixty Englishmen arrived, waiting to be led to the coast so that they might escape. They were lined up and given food for the journey.

---

1 Petrakoyeorgis, a tall splendidly bearded man, owns considerable property in the south of the Nome of Herakleion. He was, with Bandouvas and 'Satan', one of the three important guerrilla leaders of central and eastern Crete.

The house that evening was like an armed camp. Mr Smith-Hughes had given me a letter for Mr Petrakoyeorgis's brother, the doctor. I found him and handed it over. The letter asked him to give me a pair of ammunition boots. He gave me a fine, solid pair, so I seized them and put them on with joy, throwing away the old rubber shoes I had been wearing.[1] Now I really could walk! I bade farewell next day and left for Vourvouré.

Up at the Colonel's hideout we had no food and could find none to buy. The Colonel had sent off some cloth (which he had been keeping for a suit) to try and exchange it for wheat, money no longer being of any use. But his messenger brought it back, as nobody would give him enough for it. So we were up against it; though we kept going with a little bread and herbs[2] cooked by Mrs Papadakis, and sometimes managed to buy a sheep from my village. Another vessel was supposed to be arriving at the end of December, over in Herakleion Nome; so off I set for the Abadia villages taking a mule with me belonging to the Colonel. He told me to get some of the supplies arriving with the ship. But the animal was a dreadfully slow one – I only just managed to reach Myxorouma by evening, where I spent the night at the *khan*[3] of Uncle Yanniko, as everyone called him. The *khan* was bursting with people from all the villages and eparchies of the west, all heading for the Messara Plain to buy corn. I pretended (which nobody could doubt) to be about the same business.

Uncle Yanniko was a good little old man. He lived in the *khan* with his old woman, and never took any money from the strangers that slept the night. All you had to do

---

1 i.e. shoes soled with old motor-car tyres.

2 *Khorta*, a name which embraces not only the edible white grasses but also the leaves of certain plants.

3 *Khan*: Turkish word for inn with stabling.

was to buy a cigarette off his stall or a bit of bread or some hay for your beast. There were only two or three beds where his friends invariably slept, the rest of the world curling up on the floor or in chairs. It had been raining a little and I huddled up close to the hearth, where I dozed off a little while, though the cold kept me from sleeping long. As soon as day broke, and Uncle Yanniko was stirring, I drank a few *tsikoudias*[1] to warm me up, and left. I passed by Uncle Yanniko's often, and our people were always kindly received and looked after. He never asked me who I was or whither bound – and perhaps that is something you would find with few people in Crete.

My goal was Sata, a little farmstead in the Abadia near to the village of Klima on the frontiers of Retimo and Herakleion. I arrived early and went to the house of the Paradeisianòs family. There I found Kosta, a reserve artillery lieutenant, a fine man and a good patriot. I gave him the document I was carrying and he set off at once for the coast where the ship was to come. My duty was to wait till they got back from the mission. I waited some time, about fifteen days because the bad weather had held the operation up. I was still there at Christmas. Meanwhile, snow had fallen – a rare thing thereabouts, because it is low and faces south. Kosta's brother, Yanni, was employed at Timbaki,[2] and he often came to the hamlet. He would entertain us by playing the *bouzouki*.[3] I was very worried about this long delay, but I had to wait. At last Kosta came. I took the things he had brought from the ship and set off. They were little enough: a tinned ham weighing

1 Cretan name for *raki*.
2 Timbaki was the site of a large new aerodrome the Germans were building with forced labour from all over central Crete.
3 The *bouzouki* is a long-necked mandoline, used exclusively to accompany *rembétika* songs, those of the wide-boys, that is, the apaches and hashish-smokers of the large towns and ports.

five kilos, two tins of condensed milk and a few *okas*[1] of sugar. I got to Karines by evening and spent the night there at Zourbostavros's house. (His wife, Kyria Heleni, was a woman of pure gold, and so was his daughter, Popi. They were always overjoyed to see us, and if we went that way without calling at their house, there were always complaints.) I got back to Vourvouré and Mr Smith-Hughes left for Egypt, where his mission was to organize the Service in Cairo.

★   ★   ★

Soon another officer reached our headquarters. It was Captain Xan Fielding, whom we always called Aleko. He was put ashore at Soutsouro beach on the south coast near the Lasithi-Herakleion border. He was of medium height and did not look at all like the usual fair-haired kind of Englishman. In Cretan costume he passed as a Cretan a hundred per cent, but, though he spoke Greek very well, his accent, at that time, was a give-away. Another officer came with him, a captain whose speciality was sabotage. For this purpose he carted many and strange explosives about with him. This gear reached my village on the backs of various boys in the Service, who grew more numerous as the days passed (one of them was Kosta Koutellidakis from Yerakari, a very good and courageous boy). We hid these things in an historic cave above my village called the Khainospilio, the Cave, that is to say, of the Khainides,[2] as the Turks called them. The Liberation Committee of Crete had taken refuge there in the old days, and from there they used to send out their orders to the rebels.

1 An *oka* is the old Turkish measure of weight, roughly three pounds.
2 Members of a resistance movement formed in the early part of the Turkish occupation and based on the forts of Grambousa, Souda and Spinalonga which was still in Venetian hands.

Another committee which had come from Athens also hid there, and one day they encountered a Turkish army on the hill above the cave. One was captured, another leapt over the cliff (called the Turkish Gallows to this day), the third climbed into an ilex tree, where he promised his silver dagger to St George, the patron of our village; and, though all the Turks passed underneath it, nobody saw him and he was saved. The Turks cut off the head of the one that was captured and used it as a shooting target. They built a *koulé*[1] on top of this hill and it bears this name. So the region has played its part in modern days just as it did in the time of the Turks.

We hid the explosives in the Khainospilio and set one of my fellow-villagers on guard – Stelio Barbounis – lest other villagers should find and tamper with them; also to prevent their whereabouts becoming common knowledge – a highly dangerous thing. There must have been six loads of various types of very high-powered explosives, magnetic ones with time fuses and delays, etc., also two rubber boats. Meanwhile as days passed and things began to get more dangerous from every point of view, Uncle Petro[2] (for that is what we all called him) had already organized a good intelligence network of the whole district in case the Germans got wind of us and launched an attack. Two sentries were posted to observe the Argyroupolis-Kallikrati road leading past our village and through Vourvouré. Others watched the road from Myrioképhala, others the one from Marouloi. The same applied to the Kallikrati path, though this was thought to be less dangerous. The men on watch had to do their duty without letting anybody know what they were up to. They were to keep us posted of the slightest German activity.

1 Turkish tower.
2 Petro, Petrakas and Papadopetrakis are all the same person.

Mr Aleko left Vourvouré after a while and went to Vaphé, a village in Apokoronas. There he remained in the care of the Vandoulakis[1] family. He hid in the vineyard of Uncle Antoni, above the village by a farm called Araviti. Almost every day I had to take him messages there from the wireless set and bring back his answering signals. The distance was six hours and more on foot, depending on your pace and the obstacles encountered.

The Sabotage Officer stayed on some time in Vourvouré. He was a most peculiar man. He went about in military uniform and refused to wear Cretan clothes. He also had pyjamas, a wash basin, and a thousand and two mysterious objects. He wore a row of medals on his breast, and had a rucksack full of physio-geological books which he studied all day long. He uprooted specimens of every kind of plant he encountered, and laid them – still with the earth clinging to the roots – on the table. Then he would open his books and study them from their leaves to their roots. But he was not only in love with different kinds of weeds, but with stones as well. Every coloured stone, or stone slightly different from all other stones, he would pick up and analyse carefully, again searching through his books. Then he would put it away in another rucksack, which his guide carried. It was soon full, and his guide, a young Cretan boy (I can only remember that his name was Grigori) told us, that he would hide every now and then in order to throw some of them away as he was unable to carry on walking under the weight. The other Englishmen, who teased him because of all this, told us he was a very brave man and that he had been wounded in the head in some battle, and, it seemed, never quite

---

1 Two branches of this family lived in Vaphé. The house of Nicholas Vandoulas (Uncle Niko) came to be known locally as the 'British Consulate' as so many stragglers had received food and shelter there. His brother, Uncle Antoni, lived next door.

got over it. Indeed, G H Q recalled him after three months and he returned to Cairo. Fortunately he only remained a little while in Vourvouré.

We had come to an end of our supplies and could find no more. Mr Aleko at Vaphé decided that the only solution was for an aeroplane to bring us some from Cairo. They conferred among themselves, the decision was taken, and a signal was sent to Cairo giving the dropping area and the signals. They awaited the reply. Meanwhile, it seemed there was some misunderstanding between the English and Colonel Papadakis, and Mr Michalaki the wireless operator left the Colonel and joined Mr Aleko. I was away when this happened, so when I got back, only Colonel Papadakis was there, and he told me nothing. But something else happened in those days. It seems that the Germans had smelt something, for they had ordered the Greek police – the gendarmerie sub-garrison at Argyroupolis – to arrest Colonel Papadakis at Vourvouré and bring him before them for interrogation. The second-in-command of the gendarmerie at Argyroupolis was Second-Lieutenant George Phasomitakis. But he was a fellow-worker of ours – he knew all about our Service up at Vourvouré, and he wrote to Colonel Papadakis warning him which day he would come, so that nobody should be there. Perhaps this is why Mr Michalaki left; but I understood there had been some kind of quarrel. I stayed with him for three or four days of wind and rain and snow.

We had nothing, absolutely nothing to eat, so we remained fasting for all three days. On the third day I found something in an old basket – some vetch, which they used as fodder for the cattle. I knew that it was edible, and I told Colonel Papadakis, but he said it was poisonous. He was right, but if you boil it seven times the poison vanishes, so I put it all in a saucepan and started cooking.

We had a strong fire and plenty of wood, and we let it boil for a while, then poured away the water and put in fresh; and of water, praise be to God, there was no lack, because the spring was only ten yards from our kitchen; so we brought it to the boil again. Our cooking took several hours. I only wanted to boil them four times, but as I had already told him it needed seven, he sat down in the kitchen to make sure I did not boil it less. Evening had fallen when our food was ready and we sat down to eat. We poured away the water, put on salt and oil and fell to work. I ate with a ravenous appetite. But Colonel Papadakis paused at each spoonful, and who knows what was passing through his mind, for, in spite of his hunger, he only ate one helping. I can't remember how many I ate. I only remember I thought the taste delicious, and ate enormously. As we finished our meal, Colonel Papadakis said:

'Well, we have eaten and God send we live till the morning.'

'Don't worry,' I told him, 'nothing will happen.'

We slept well and when we woke up I asked him how it had been.

'All right,' he said, 'but the thought of what might happen kept me from sleeping much; otherwise everything seems all right. But don't you feel you are carrying a great weight in your stomach?'

My stomach, however, had not grown heavier, but much lighter; it always feels heavy *before* I eat.

The weather had greatly improved. There was bright sunshine, so we parted, for the day the police were due was not far off. He told me to go down to the village, because he meant to hide somewhere, then after the police had searched Vourvouré in vain, we could all go back. I went down to Asi Gonia and in two days' time saw the gendarmerie climbing the mountain. They went through the house and, finding nothing, reported to the Germans that it was impossible for anyone to live up there during the winter.

The author, George Psychoundakis, during the war

Wireless station officers and others in the White Mountains. 'Manoli' (Geoffrey Barkham) on the far left and Pavlos Vernadakis next to him

The White Mountains above Koustoyérako

'Aleko' (Xan Fielding) without his shirt and Cretan 'andartes' in the White
Mountains

'Yanni' or 'O Tom' (Tom Dunbabin) second from left and others in Central Crete

Left to right: 'Michali' (Patrick Leigh Fermor), George Psychoundakis and Vangeli Vandoulakis in the Kyriakosellia Hills

Yanni Tzangarakis

'Levtheri' (Arthur Reade) outside the beehive hut

'Manoli' (Geoffrey Barkham) on the right with Pavlos Vernadakis and two Cretan girls

'Michali' (Patrick Leigh Fermor) and party outside the hideout and wireless station on Mount Kedros wearing bandoliers especially for this photograph.

'Matthaios' (Matthew White) who was in charge of the 'set' in cloth cap on the far left, George Tyrakis with binoculars, 'Michali' (Patrick Leigh Fermor) wearing bandolier and black shirt in the centre, Bill Ledgerwood, an Australian who was smuggled out later in 1943 at the back on the far right, Niko Souris, standing in front of him, Yanni Tzangarakis sitting in the front on the right and next to him sitting on the left, Aristides Paradeisianós. George Psychoundakis is away carrying messages

The hideout on Mount Kedros

'Michali' (Patrick Leigh Fermor)
outside the hideout

Two guerrilla shepherds – good examples of the 'andartes' (guerrilla fighters).
They formed part of Kapotan Yanni Bourdzalis's unit and helped on the
approach march – but not in the capture – of the Kreipe Operation

Asi Gonia

The Aeroplane with the Stores

Soon the long-awaited telegram, saying that the aeroplane with the stores would be arriving in a few days, came through from Cairo. I don't remember where I had been sent, but I was not present at the drop. But when I got back, I learnt the whole queer story.

Colonel Papadakis had summoned a number of people to the dropping area to collect and guard the stores; these were people who had nothing whatever to do with the Service, so he would not be obliged to give them anything except his thanks. Petrakas was the only member of the Service that he called for, but he told him to bring nobody with him. They assembled in the evening at the place where the aeroplane was expected, at Koutou, that is, high on the mountain close to Manika.[1] The place was flat and perfect for our purpose. They prepared branches of dried shrubs for the signal fires, of which five were to be lit in the shape of the English letter V, the sign of victory. By the time the hum of an aeroplane was heard in the distance all was ready. The moon, shining in the starless winter night, began to grow steadily dimmer, and then to fade away. The aeroplane drew close and the fires were quickly kindled. As the plane flew overhead, the moon was completely gone, for there was a total eclipse

1 Near Kallikrati in the Sphakian Mountains, where some of the worst rogues in Crete lived on the run.

of the moon that night in February 1942. The plane began to circle above the fires and the men below were waiting for the things to drop. I do not know what passed through their minds at this moment, but they got the idea that they were hearing two planes, one following or chasing the other; and one idea starts another. 'They are German planes!' they cried. 'We have fallen into a trap!' Colonel Papadakis said that they were dropping parachutists to catch them, and that everyone must disperse at once. Mr Petrakas, however, found this hard to believe, and refused to run away. Then came the sound of parachutes whistling through the air. 'Can't you hear them?' Colonel Papadakis said to Petrakas once more. 'They are dropping parachutists. We must be off as fast as we can.' Again Petrakas said he didn't agree and he would make sure with his own eyes. He went over by himself. But coincidence followed coincidence that night, for quite by chance some cattle thieves happened to be passing that way, driving stolen sheep. Seeing the fires and hearing the planes, and thinking that Germans were abroad, they had hidden behind some rocks beside the pathway. Uncle Petros approaching unawares the very place where the robbers were hiding gave them a fright – they thought the Germans would see and capture them. They leapt from their hiding-place and dashed off from stone to stone as fast as their legs could carry them. Uncle Petros, hearing their footsteps and peering in the same direction, saw them crouching like shadows behind a rock. He had no further doubt that Germans were there, and hurried back by the quickest way. As he turned, he saw a parachute stretched out in front of him, and became still more perturbed. How was he to know that, a few yards farther off, at the end of the parachute cords, lay a great barrel? The gloom of the moon's eclipse was no help . . . As soon as he had joined the others, he said, 'Let's be off as fast as we can.' The ones who had believed it from the first waited to hear no more, and they all cut the mud[1] together. They stopped some way off and asked Petrakas exactly what he had seen. 'I heard their footfalls,' he said, 'and saw two or three taking up positions behind the rocks and, on the way back, I saw their parachutes.' They crossed over to the opposite mountain beyond Kallikrati in order to be well out of the ambush and in a position to see what was happening. Hiding at the place called Chavidi in a cheesemaker's hut, they awaited developments. Fortunately they then had a mind to approach and see what was going on. So Colonel Papadakis sent forward his little nephew whom he always had with him, Levtheri Kalitsounakis of Kato Vasamónero in Retimo. Levtheri was still a young boy. He planned to walk innocently across the dropping area, pretending to be on the way to Skaloti. He would then see if there were any Germans there and what they were up to, and if they didn't see him, double back; if they did he was to push on to Skaloti. Levtheri started off and a fully armed fellow-villager of mine – Spyros Katsanavakis, who worked for Colonel Papadakis up at Vourvouré – followed at a distance. And what did Levtheri see the moment he reached the little plateau? – rocks covered with parachutes harnessed to huge barrels and containers! There were no Germans anywhere and he realized they had all been taken in. He climbed to a high point and signalled to the man following him, who joined him. One of them sat and guarded the things, the other ran shouting for the rest. They all returned as quickly as they could, bringing mules with them from Kallikrati to transport the stuff . . . A number of parachutes had dropped some way off, but they found and collected them all except two or three with little barrels of sugar

1 Slang for 'be off in a hurry'.

and flour which had struck rocks and broken open, spilling their contents.

When I got back, I went to Kallikrati to find out where they had gone, because they must have left Manika after the drop. Uncle Petros saw me as I crossed the village and told me the whole tale. He was furious that Colonel Papadakis had called in outsiders to fetch in the stuff, and when he, Petrakas, said that he should give some of it to the men in the Service, the Colonel had flatly refused. He asked him at least to give a couple of leather soles to Stelio Pervanakis who guarded the explosives in the Khainospilio, so he could get a pair of shoes made, as he was almost barefoot. But even that was refused. Then Uncle Petros said, 'God-brother, if everyone thinks of his own interests, we will never get on together. From now on, god-brother, we go our own ways.' Colonel Papadakis answered something. They parted, and after that Uncle Petros never consented to work with him again.

Colonel Papadakis had hidden everything from the English, only producing a few items, saying that everything was lost or destroyed. Out of the whole of that drop, nobody in the Service got even a pair of socks. In fact, the Germans got it all in the raid on the Colonel's private hiding-place.

Soon Mr Michalaki arrived from Embrósnero and set up his wireless in a cave called Pyrovolos, high in a peak between Kallikrati and Manika. The cave was perfect for our work. It was very large and there were deep places where we could work the battery-charging engine. We collected our drinking and washing-water from stalactites, Mrs Papadakis cooked for us in Kallikrati, Levtheri, Colonel Papadakis's nephew, brought it up to us, and we arranged luxurious couches for ourselves inside the cave from the branches of various shrubs that were better than the softest mattress.

It was March now, the weather was fine and the sun on the mountain top was very hot. The Service, from now on, worked excellently. From Uncle Antoni Vandoulakis's vineyard at the Araviti farmstead above Vaphé Mr Aleko could easily collect all the information Headquarters demanded, and send it on to the wireless set by Uncle Antoni's children, when I was not at hand. Very often he would send Perikles.[1]

It was very seldom I could sit down and rest for a day. There was no time for it in this kind of work.

[1] One of Xan Fielding's first guides, who subsequently became Mayor of Vaphé. Compromised by his Resistance activities, he was later arrested by the Germans and on his release was evacuated for his own safety to the Middle East, where he volunteered for further activity in the Greek mainland.

The Second Drop

Our food ran out again and we impatiently awaited another aeroplane. I remember one day sitting down with Mr Michalaki to eat some grass cooked with snails. The saddles of the snails had all got broken and they covered the grass with little fragments so that it looked uneatable. But there was nothing else and we had collected the wild herbs ourselves from round about. If only we had some bread! But there was none. (When we were hungry, we used to set about the food with our bare hands, forks would have been too slow.) We took the grass blade by blade, picked off the broken snail-shells and ate it with much laughter.

Everybody suffered from hunger during the Occupation, but 1942 was the worst, especially the winter, when we nearly starved. It was then that the snail kingdom suffered the fiercest inroads. Every night, armed with oil dips and torches, the villagers would set out in hundreds in search of the priceless treasure which was the most luxurious fare to be found in house or inn. On one such night of general snail-gathering, our second aeroplane with stores passed overhead, bound first for a bombing sortie over Canea. Seeing lights by the hundred, the pilot said to himself, 'That's where they must be waiting'; for he flew lower and circled above the flickering oil dips. Terrified, they all dowsed their lights. The machine flew still lower and, thinking it must be German, everyone ran for shelter. The pilot dropped his load and flew away. When the parachutes opened and started whistling through the air and thumping the ground, the snailers (for that is what they were called) ran away as fast as their legs would carry them, one shouting that bombs were dropping, another parachutists. A parachute-load of flour burst on a rock near a woman. Suddenly covered in flour, she almost died of fright, shouting, 'Woe to us ill-fated ones! They are dropping bombs with gas inside and I am done for!'

Someone else there, a shepherd from Asi Gonia called Meladakis, suddenly came upon a container. He opened it, and, lo and behold! It was full of boot soles! He hoisted it on his back and ran to his companions who were down below at the sheepfold. The news soon spread, and everyone ran to join the search. Yet others learnt the news in the villages close by, a whole campaign was soon on foot, and everything – mostly hides and boot soles and flour – had been gathered before day broke. God, they declared, had come to their help.

So our luck was out with our second drop as well!

At the Cave of the Winds

We must have been about twenty days in our new cave when we heard that the Germans had got wind of us; so we had to change our hideout at once. We got our gear together and went to the other side of Kallikrati, between there and Asphendou. It was a low hill with a little cave at the top called the Anemospilia, or Cave of the Winds. Clumps of vegetation covered the crest of the hill, and the cave was invisible. A wonderful refuge. We had water from a *sterna*[1] on a little plain nearby called Lambonas, and food from Kallikrati. We stayed there the whole of April and nearly all May, and our work went forward splendidly.

One evening in the coffee-shop I learnt that Father Andrea, the priest of Kourna, had heard the Germans were coming to surround our village at 2.30 a.m. that very night. Some believed it, others not, but everyone except a few old grey-beards left the village. We took to the steep mountainsides that almost encircle our village, and scattered and hid.

There were two or three others in my hiding-place, so we lay down and slept. After two or three hours we started softly rousing each other. 'Wake up, poor wretch,' the word went, 'the Germans are coming down over the pass.' Although they did not talk at all, we could hear

[1] A deep rain-water cistern.

their footsteps clattering louder than a regiment of cavalry. We clambered up the mountain-side to keep out of the trap and see what they were doing when it grew light. When dawn began to break we nailed our eyes on the village, and were able to make out the Germans. There were a great many and they had invested the village on all sides. They were rounding up the women and children and driving them into the church. Once we heard them firing a machine-gun inside the village, and the sound of heavy shooting went on for five to six minutes. We feared that, having found a hidden gun or something, they had started executing people. At about midday they let everybody loose, and the women and children returned to their houses. Then the Germans left their positions round the village and mustered at the school and elsewhere. The women, feigning indifference, came out to tell us that no evil had befallen. They had all been driven into the church, their papers[1] had been inspected, and the Germans had asked the Mayor where we had hidden the Englishmen and Colonel Papadakis. They searched all the houses for arms. Fortunately none were found anywhere, for when the warning came, we had hidden all the arms the men were not actually wearing, and lots of the women had bullets and pistols hidden on them. If they had searched them, they would have found any number. The shots had been the Germans firing after someone escaping, luckily without mishap. (It was a fellow-villager, Andrea Markakis.) Others in the village had eaten much wood[2] in the Germans' effort to find out if the fugitive was Colonel Papadakis or one of the Englishmen. But they answered that it must have been somebody who had run off because his papers were not

1 Identity cards issued by order of the German Commander.
2 Been beaten up.

in order. Then everyone was assembled at the school and the Germans asked for eggs and food. They left in the afternoon and we returned to the village. They had taken off Stelio Barbounis (the one who had watched over the explosives in the Khainospilio), as he was wanted by the Greek police as a sheep-thief.

I headed for our hideout to tell them what had been happening in the village. When I had heard the Germans coming down the pass during the night I had destroyed some letters I was carrying just in case; so I had to go back anyway, to get new ones. 'Quite right,' Mr Michalaki said when I told him. He prepared new ones and sent me off.

I set out for the Amari. A new officer had arrived there, Mr Monty,[1] and I found him at Sata in the Abadia with Kosta Paradeisianos. I gave him the correspondence and sat down to wait. While he was reading he asked me an odd question.

'When you go through Patsos, do you give our letters to a Greek sergeant in the British Army from Cyprus, married to a girl in the village?'

Mr Monty's question astonished me.

'I would be incapable of doing such a thing, Mr Monty,' I said. 'Mr Aleko will be able to bear me out, for he knows the sort of work I do. Besides I have never been to Patsos in my life.'

'I don't know who it can be,' Mr Monty went on, 'but one of our runners has done exactly that.'

Mr Monty was right, as I did not fail to find out.

When Mr Monty had prepared what he had for me and told me I could go, I took the road home, and resumed my regular work at our headquarters.

1 A mistake of George's; Monty (Capt., later Col., the Hon. C. M. Woodhouse, DSO, OBE) had then been in Crete several months, but George had never met him before.

About the fifteenth of May 1942 another new English officer came to our hideout. He was called Mr Tom Dunbabin[1] and he had arrived a fortnight before from Cairo with an operator and a fresh transmitting set. He was to stay in the Amari, as the espionage network was growing steadily thicker.

One day Mr Michalaki told me that he was preparing to leave for Cairo and he asked me if I would like to go with him. I said it was as he thought fit, and he promised to take me. My delight knew no bounds! At last I would see Egypt, about which I had heard so much. But later Mr Michalaki summoned me and said he had thought about it and decided to leave me behind to help a new wireless operator who was coming, and I could go later. I did not let him see it, but I was very upset, as the joy of the journey had already got hold of me. But Mr Michalaki guessed my sorrow, and said that, as he had promised, he would take me if I insisted, but if I was willing, he would much prefer me to stay on for the present.

'I'm not unhappy,' I said, 'not at all, really. I am quite willing to stay – I am not really as eager to go as all that.' So I stayed. I confess that I told him a lie because I didn't want to upset him. As soon as dawn broke next day, Mr Michalaki, Mr Tom and Mr Tom's guide, Kosta Paradeisianos, left us and struck the path.

We set about hiding the wireless, the batteries, the charging engine and all our stuff until the new operator should turn up. Then we abandoned our hideout. Colonel Papadakis took his wife and three little children, and went to Alones, where they were hidden and protected by all the good villagers, for the Germans by now had outlawed the Colonel, his wife and his children one by one, also

---

1 Captain (later Lieut-Colonel) T. J. Dunbabin, DSO, MA, Fellow of All Souls.

his maid Anna Mantadaki from Myriokephala. Mr Aleko took me with him to the Apokoronas.

Here Perikles told me a funny thing that had happened to Mr Aleko. One day when he was in their vineyard by the farmstead of Araviti, he saw two Germans just over the wall. He had been writing in his diary and still had it in his hand. He got up and walked slowly to the other side of the vineyard, and then took to his heels. The Germans did not see him but went into the vineyard, to see what they could steal. They found nothing, but coming to the little hut, they saw Mr Aleko's empty plate lying there with some bread. Woe betide if they had suspected! But they didn't, and they left. As for Mr Aleko – he carried on until he reached the cheese hut of Patsouros (George Patsouros was a friend of his) and, telling them what had happened, sat down to go on with his diary. But they shouted for him to come over and eat some yoghurt with them. As this was his favourite food in Crete, he got up and went inside, leaving his diary on top of a little rock. He told us they were sitting in a ring, all eating out of the same saucepan. A loud sucking noise came out of their mouths with every spoonful, and they were smothered with yoghurt, from their toes to the tips of their beards and whiskers. You could have eaten anywhere, he declared – inside the saucepan or out, on the ground, or off their boots – there was yoghurt everywhere.

'Join us,' they said, 'and partake.'

'No thanks,' he said quickly, and went out of the hut. But another disaster was waiting for him outside. Some pigs that were rootling there had found his diary on the little rock and, by the time he had got there, they had eaten it all up. He began shouting, 'All Holy Virgin! They've eaten my diary!'

Patsouros asked why the devil he had left it there.

'I didn't know pigs ate diaries,' he said, and, turning

away very sadly, he went back to Vaphé, where he learnt that the two Germans had wandered through his lair. When I arrived he had come down from the vineyard and I found him in the house of old Uncle Nikoli Vandoulakis, Antoni's brother. It was separate from all the others and was highest in that steep village. He was a wonderful man, and so were his wife and his daughter Elpida, the kindest, bravest and best of girls. They had turned their house into a general rest-house for wandering English soldiers after the fall of the island, and they befriended and housed the officers of the Service with the utmost willingness, likewise anyone who had a hand in the work of Liberation. In the vineyard they had an Australian lieutenant, one of the prisoners of war who had escaped from the Germans. They called him Johnny. Mr Aleko told me to guide him to the Amari so that he could get away to Egypt with Mr Michalaki. We left at once, and slept that night in my village. We got no farther that day as he could only walk very slowly, his broken shoes having badly mangled his feet. But we had to hasten, in case we should be too late for the boat.

We left my village very early and reached Angouselliana by midday. We sat down in a vineyard to eat the eggs and bread we had brought with us, but he couldn't eat for the pain in his feet. He only took some very cold water offered us by a kind man, and when we had had a good rest, we took the road again. But the farther we went the harder it became for him to walk. When we reached the point where we had to cross the main road near the Retimo-Spili-Ay-Yanni fork, our path was blocked by a party of Germans. They must have been marching to Spili or Koxaré. We waited in the ditch until they had all passed, and nobody saw us; and when they were some way on, we continued our journey. It is not more than an hour and a half from there to Karines, and we still had five hours of daylight. But, in spite of all my efforts to help him on and cheer him up, we didn't get there. He fell down half an hour from the village and said: '*Okhi allo, Yorghi. Poly arrostos. Edo ypno!*' ('No more, George. Very ill. Here sleep.')

I was very sorry for him and felt his pain deeply. I found a good place among the bushes, cut some branches and made the beds so that we could lie down at once. He was fast asleep almost before he lay down. But I could not go to sleep at once for many reasons. It was not yet dark and I had to keep watch unless anyone should spot us. He had taken his boots off the moment we sat down, and his feet were in such a pitiable state that I confess that, had it been me, I wouldn't have been able to walk at all. When we woke up in the morning, he couldn't put on his boots at first; but bit by bit, after long efforts he managed to get them on. As he hadn't eaten anything the day before, I produced a couple of eggs that I still had and implored him to eat something, lest he should grow even weaker. He tried to eat but it wouldn't go down and he had to spit it out. We just managed to get to Stavro Zourbakis's house in Karines and Kyria Eleni found him some milk, of which he managed to drink a glass. Seeing a deep mountain stream above Patso he asked me if he could bathe in it as it might make him feel better. And he really did get a bit better after his bathe, so we pushed on. There was a great sadness in his face and I often tried to make him laugh. 'Never mind, Johnny,' I told him, 'everything will be all right when you get to Egypt,' and laughed, telling him various amusing tales. But all in vain. All he did was to say: '*Panayia mou! Kako paidi! Ego pethaino kai esy gelas.*' ('All Holy Virgin! Bad boy! I die and you laugh.')

Next day we got to Sata. George Tyrakis[1] took him

---

1 George Tyrakis, aged about twenty-four at the time, was one of the best helpers of the mission. He played a prominent part in the Kreipe operation.

over and set off to catch the others up who had set off for the coast. I made for Mr Tom's hideout, which was a little higher than the foothills of Mount Ida[1] and immediately above Apodoulou in the Nithavri area. Our operator Mr Michalaki was there, getting ready to leave for the coast. Kapetan Satan,[2] one of the very first of the Kapetans to take arms in the mountains, was leaving as well. He was armed with a gun that looked like a Turkish Mauser, heavily adorned with silver. He raised it to his lips, kissed it, then gave it to George Voskakis, saying '*tesilimi*'[3] and begged him not to shame it. After that, nearly all of them left for the coast and I went to the hamlet of Sata to await their return from the mission, as Mr Aleko had told me to bring our new wireless operator back with me.

They returned in three days. I asked what had happened to poor Johnny and was downcast when I heard that he had missed the boat on account of his slowness. It had sailed away two hours before he reached the beach! But he wouldn't have to wait long as there was another secret vessel in a few days, and he had not gone far afield. So he managed to get away at last.

1 Usually called *Psiloriti* in Greek.
2 Antonios Gregorakis, one of the best guerrilla leaders of occupied Crete, and a friend of Pendlebury's; he died later on in Cairo.
3 From the Turkish word *teslim*, meaning consignment or bestowal.

Manoli and Vangeli

When Mr Tom came, he handed over to me two young gentlemen, both Greeks, that I was to take with me. We found a beast on which to load their gear and moved off.

'Under what name shall I introduce you?' I asked them. One said 'Manoli', the other 'Vangeli'. When I said we were bound for Apokoronas to find Captain Aleko, one of them asked which village. I said: 'Vaphé.'

'Which house?' Vangeli then asked.

'The house of the Vandoulakis family,' I answered. I saw he was smiling. Then he asked, 'Right up at the end of the village? The last house?'

'Yes. You seem to know those parts.'

'I know them a bit,' he said, still smiling.

'How? Have you ever been there?'

'Have I ever been there? Do you know old Nikoli Vandoulakis?'

'Very well. I've often been to his house, and Mr Aleko is a guest there now. Indeed, it is his house we are heading for.'

'Well, the old man is my father.'

'Your father!'

'Yes,' he answered, so I told him what village I was from, and many tales about his village and his family and so on. He had been serving with the Greek Army in the Middle East as a second-lieutenant, and come to Crete seconded to the Allied Headquarters with instructions to put himself at the orders of the English officers there.

The other young gentleman, who was from the island of Patmos in the Dodecanese, was called Apostolos Evangelou, but I only learnt his real name after the Liberation. He was a wireless operator, and we called him Manoli at the time. He was very intelligent and cultured and one of the best men I ever met, looked at from every angle. Such goodness of character is not found in many men.

With our laden animal, we looked like blackmarketeers and little we cared, for wherever we went, this appearance allayed worse suspicions.

Three Germans were commandeering animals outside Kaÿméni Ay-Yanni.[1] God was watching us, for, had we gone on, Manoli and Vangeli with their fine new clothes and smart air would have aroused their suspicions, so rare did such things then seem in our parts. When they unloaded our stuff, it would have at once seemed suspicious, and would have set them searching. We all three had pistols and could easily have killed them[2] in case of need, but this would not have helped much, because all the blame would have fallen on the inhabitants. But there would have been nothing else for it, had they found the wireless stores, the codes, the new crystals, the orders and so on. Warned by a stranger, we took another path and arrived in Alones that evening. There we found Colonel Papadakis with his family, whose hideout was now in the forest opposite the village. The operator remained with him, and I pushed on with Vangeli next day to find Mr Aleko.

When we reached Vaphé, I went to Uncle Nikoli's house. Vangeli, lest any fellow-villager should see him, was to come on later when I whistled to show no strangers

1 Burnt St John.
2 'Cleaned them up' is the Greek phrase.

were in his house. But there was no one there except his own family, so I greeted them and sat down. Their happiness was also mine, and I could not keep it off my face.

'What are you looking so happy about, Georgie?' they asked.

'Because I've got good news,' I said.

'What news?' they asked.

'Aha! At this moment none in the world could be better!'

'Well, tell us then, and put us out of our agony!'

'I'll tell you at once – with a whistle.'

They followed me inquisitively to the door where I gave a whistle, and, with one leap from the garden, there was Vangeli in the courtyard, and in the arms of his father and mother, who loaded him with kisses.

As they could neither have expected nor even imagined such a surprise they were almost flying with their delight!

His sister Elpida's joy was also beyond describing. They brought out bottles at once for us to drink his health and welcome. Then all his cousins arrived – Antoni Vandoulakis's children – and one of them went to fetch Mr Aleko from the vineyard. When he arrived, they were introduced and Uncle Nikoli placed his best wine on a table richly spread, for among the other good things of his household, Uncle Nikoli had wonderful wine and *retsina*[1] and *raki*. We drank plenty of everything and told each other lots of stories. Later we left Vangeli alone with Mr Aleko to talk about the private matters of the Service. That day was the twenty-eighth of March 1942.

Meanwhile, my clothes and boots were falling to bits with all my long marches, in which there was never a

---

1 *Retsina*, wine reinforced with resin, is the usual drink of the Greek mainland, but very uncommon in Crete.

break. I saw that I would never get anything from the parachute drops under Colonel Papadakis's well-known handling. 'They've stolen the lot,' he declared every time. One day I went to Vaphé and told Mr Aleko that I could no longer move about, as I was practically naked and barefoot.

'Don't worry, George,' he said. 'Some time we'll strike lucky with these drops, and then we'll all be fixed up.'

'Mr Aleko,' I said, 'I fear that will never be if Colonel Papadakis has charge of them. The things get stolen every time, and what remains is hardly enough even for him. We are always done in.' And I told him exactly how the stores 'went astray'.

Mr Aleko realized I was right and at once wrote a signal, and a letter to the Colonel telling him all this. He said I must hand in the signal with all speed as he wanted an answer, for which I was to wait for three days.

It was night when I got to the mountain ledge. I handed over the letters and the signal and sat down to rest.

I had not settled down long before Colonel Papadakis called me over. I knew what he was going to say and went over at once. He started the discussion in front of the others, I think expecting me to deny everything I had said to Mr Aleko. But I can only love, honour and feel shame with people that show love and affection to me.

So he began. 'Now, George, how long have you been with us?' Feigning indifference, I said, 'I don't know, Mr Papadakis, I don't remember. You know better than me.'

'I'm asking you how long you have been with us,' he repeated angrily.

I gave the same answer with still greater semblance of apathy.

'What's all this you've been telling Mr Aleko, you wretch?'

'What have I been telling Mr Aleko, Mr Papadakis?'

'That I hide the stores dropped by parachute and steal them and give nothing to anybody – and I don't know what else besides!'

'I told him nothing but the truth. I could have told him a lot more, but it's not my business. But those stores are meant for just these needs of ours and I'm not going to run about barefoot and naked and remain silent for eternity while you hide them all and let them get stolen!'

'Listen,' he cried, 'just listen to the pig, daring to talk to me like that!'

'Do you want me to say I *didn't* tell Mr Aleko all this? What should I have answered when he said all I had to do was to wait for an aeroplane to be clothed and shod?'

He grew angrier still, and started shouting at me: 'Get out of here! Your service with the English has come to an end!'

'If the English depended on you,' I said, 'it would have come to an end long ago.'

'I'm the leader of the Resistance in Crete and from now on never set foot here again. Heaven knows what you have been and said! I'll report you to Mr Aleko and find out the whole thing – and then, woe betide you, you wretch!'

'And mind you *do*!' I shouted. 'If you don't I'll tell him myself.'

All this took place in front of the operator and Myron Samaritis. Then he jumped up and struck me over the head with his hand, telling me to get out of his sight.

'I've got orders,' I said, 'to wait here, and you can't turn me out. You can hit me as much as you like. I won't raise a hand against you out of respect for your age; but I'm not leaving here just because you want me to. I have others to answer to.'

'If you don't leave within a minute, I'll kill you. I give you a minute.'

'I refuse. I've got other orders, so do what you like.'
Then Samaritis and the operator came up begging me to
leave, as I had made him so angry. Manoli took me aside
and tried to persuade me, saying he would fix everything
up about the answering signal. As he was one of the few
good men in the world (as I said before) and as he insisted,
I did not wish to go against his prayers. So I left, telling
Mr Papadakis that I was going straight to Mr Aleko to see
what he had to say and if I really had no place with the
English and had to leave the Service, as he said.

'Don't you dare say anything to him,' he said, 'or woe
betide you, you swine!'

He thought he could frighten me with his threats. I
went to my village, and set off to find Mr Aleko early
next morning.

As soon as he saw me, he thought I had the answer to
his signal. 'Welcome back, George,' he said. 'Anything
for me?'

'Absolutely nothing, Mr Aleko.'

'Then why did you come back so soon?'

'I didn't leave. I was thrown out.'

'Who by?'

'By the leader of the Resistance in Crete . . .' And I
explained the whole tale.

He stood up at once, took his haversack[1] and his stick,
and said, 'Off we go, George. We'll go there straight away
and I'll tell him he can quarrel with you every day, but
he can't sack you unless I give the order. I saw right from
the start, George, that we couldn't work together, that's
why I left for other quarters. He was always telling me he

---

[1] The Cretan *sakouli*, or haversack, is an elaborate affair, woven of bright
colours, with red predominating. As the patterns vary from village to village,
it is possible for an expert to spot at once where the owner comes from. The
most splendid come from Anoyeia.

was the boss of the whole thing. He even tried to give orders to me.'

The moment we reached the hideout, Mr Aleko called for Colonel Papadakis. They went a little way off by themselves, sat down, and argued for at least two hours. When he came back, Mr Aleko called me, and repeated what he had said when we had first set out: 'You are to stay. He can't turn you out.' From that day Colonel Papadakis not only left off talking to me, but looking at me as well. When we were all sitting in the hideout, he would turn his back on me, and if ever by chance his glance crossed mine, it was always furious and charged with hate.

I confess I regretted all this and some of the things I had said. But he had provoked it all. It was June 1942 when all this happened.

Once, when I got back from the Amari news had come through about a German comb-out of the area, so we had to change our hideout again. In some low mountains between Alones, Rodakino and Kali-Sykia we found a perfect place in an endless wilderness of little peaks. Colonel Papadakis took his family about with him everywhere, as the Germans were after them too. I didn't want to talk to Colonel Papadakis, but he addressed me first; so I had to answer. But only when forced to by the needs of the Service. Evilly and coldly, that is to say.

Rumours

Returning a little later from a mission in the Messara plain, I found the whole area in the throes of a German drive. The entire district was panic-stricken and on the way back I had to dodge from village to village with great caution. I was even arrested (and then released again), because my inter-nome pass was not in order.

Reaching Margarikari, I found the whole village deserted. I only saw one old woman – the mother of Petrakoyeorgis – but she was very old. Perhaps she hadn't been able to get away. She recognized me and, the moment she saw me, began crying, 'Fly, my child!' I saw something serious had happened and, without waiting for further explanation, cut the mud. It was a pity I hadn't asked the way, so I got on as best I could. There was not a soul in the streets of Grigoria, the next village. Twenty yards from the last house I saw some freshly dug earth with several stones on top. Someone had obviously been killed there. Indeed, as I learnt later, the faithful gendarmes of the Gendarme Commander in Herakleion, Polioudakis,[1] had caught one of Petrakoyeorgis's messengers in Grigoria, told him to run, then fired at his back, killing him and burying him on the spot.

1 Polioudakis was one of the most notorious of the few traitors and collaborators in Crete. He was convicted by a war-crimes tribunal after the war and shot.

I carried on along the road, but, seeing the twigs of a fire smoking, hid. After a little while I left, and, where the road crossed the little brook where I had seen the fire, I saw some blood on the road and realized someone else must have been killed. It was another of Petrakoyeorgis's boys. The same gendarmes had shot at him, then, finding him lying wounded in the brook, despatched him.

I got away as quickly as I could and reached the Amari, where I told all I had seen and learnt their news.

Reaching the village of Yerakari, I went to Captain Koutellidakis's house, and found him very frightened indeed. He kept shaking his head and biting his lips, saying: 'Poor George!'

'What's the matter, Mr Koutellidakis?' I said.

'What?' he said. 'Haven't you heard? Haven't you sniffed something?'

'Absolutely nothing. What's happening?'

'Listen, George,' he said after a pause, 'I want to ask you something, and, if you know the answer, don't keep it back from me.'

I grew anxious to know what this uneasiness was all about. 'Tell me,' I said, 'and if I know the answer, I'll tell you.'

'They told us that Mr Tom and Mr Aleko, after the disasters in Libya, had decided to surrender themselves, their wirelesses and all their gear to the Germans. That is why they have fixed a meeting here in our village to discuss how and where to go and give themselves up. What do you think? Have you gathered anything of the kind?'

These words left me absolutely staggered; I asked him where he had learnt all this.

'What! Don't you believe it? We were told it on the best authority.'

'Yes? What is the name of the trustworthy fellow who told you these astonishing things?'

He refused to tell me his name, but went on asking me if I had got wind of nothing.

'I'd only believe such a thing,' I said, 'when the sky turned into seawater. But I insist on you telling me who this intelligent person is?'

'It's — from —, Mr Tom's guide. He told Mr Kokonas the schoolmaster, so we informed our people in Retimo, and we have all determined not to let them surrender. We would kill them rather. As a matter of fact, I told Mr Aleko as much in the last letter you took him, when you passed this way. I said, "Mr Aleko, before taking such serious decisions, it would be best to consult us, for perhaps nothing would happen to you – but what would happen to us? Where should we go?"'

'Mr Koutellidakis,' I said, 'the moment I get there, I'll ask Mr Aleko to show me the letter so that I can explain it, because I am certain he didn't understand what you were getting at. I'm certain, too, that his anger against the person who told you all this will know no bounds.'

I bade him farewell, rose, and left in order to arrive the quicker at our hideout as I had been held up so long – ten days at least – and they must have been very anxious about me.

Mr Koutellidakis and Mr Kokonas were understandably perturbed, for their informant had been the best known of Mr Tom's runners for some time. The Germans at that time were advancing on all fronts. In Russia they had reached Stalingrad and in Africa they had captured the whole of Libya from the English and were stretching out their hands towards Egypt. It was the most crucial moment of the entire war and the whole world was in great despair lest the Germans should triumph. And, as the saying goes, 'Even iron bends in the fire.'

When I reached our lair they all asked me what had happened to hold me up so long. So I told them the whole story, then went and sat on one side with Mr Aleko. I asked him if he had still got Mr Koutellidakis's letter. He said he had, so I asked him if he had understood its contents.

'George,' he answered, 'I simply can't make out what he is getting at!'

'Show it to me, and I will explain it word for word.'

He produced the letter and picked out the phrase which said 'they had no right to take such serious decisions without consulting the others', etc.

'I will explain it, Mr Aleko, as I'm certain you haven't understood. If you go to Yerakari, you are in danger of being caught and bound and even killed.'

'What do you mean, George? Speak up!'

'News has spread among our people over there that you and Mr Tom are about to give yourselves up to the Germans, and that you have appointed a rendezvous in Yerakari for the purpose of discussing it.'

The moment I had said this he leapt to his feet with his whole face ablaze with astonishment and anger.

'Who has been spreading all this, George?'

'— Mr Tom's guide,' I answered.

Mr Aleko's anger was beyond all describing. 'I'll shoot him dead with my pistol the moment I set eyes on him,' he said.

'Don't worry, Mr Aleko,' I said. 'I denied it all categorically and calmed them down.' We talked for a long time and then joined the rest of the company under a tree.

Shifting the Wireless Station

I stayed there a couple of days, then left for Yerakari. A new wireless set which we had ordered from Cairo had arrived there for us.

I took the road with Siphi Alevizakis[1] from Alones, a short chap, but absolutely tireless on the trail. We took Colonel Papadakis's beast to carry the wireless set.

We got to Yerakari very early next morning and loaded the set on to one side of the beast and twenty *okas* of wheat on the other. Crossing the plateau of Yious our beast was so slow as to be beyond bearing. We meant to cross the heights of Karines to avoid the villages and all dangerous points. But I thought we would never arrive that way, and decided to go through Spili. When we had almost reached the village I pointed out a pathway to Siphi, telling him to avoid the village altogether and meet me at Dariviana. So we separated. 'Take care,' I said, 'and don't worry if I'm a bit late, because, as you see, our beast is a ruin.' As soon as I got into the village, two Germans approached me from behind and gazed enquiringly at the beast, which, large though it was, ambled so slowly. '*Poly xylo avto!*'[2] ('Much stick that') one of the Germans said.

1 Son of the village priest, later arrested by the Germans and executed.
2 Pidgin Greek.

'*Poly xylo*,' I said, '*ochi mantzaria gaidaros kaputti*.' ('Plenty stick, no food, donkey done for.')

'*Ochi ochi kaputt*' ('Not, not done for'), the other said, '*Poly xylo*,' and started laying about the beast. Get thee behind me, Satan, I muttered to myself. I don't want your company. I wondered what would have happened if they found out that one of the sacks held a transmitting set for espionage purposes. Then I had another thought: perhaps they'll think me a black marketeer and try to take my wares. (This often happened, especially in that village, but more often among the gendarmerie.) Then I plucked up courage and thought, after all, why should it happen to me?

The two Huns were still following me, thumping the beast, and swearing at it to make it get a move on. Fortunately, at the door of a house with a vine trellis shading the courtyard, several girls were standing and smiling, because my Germans were beating the donkey or for some other reason. My friends stopped and tried to flirt with them, asking if the grapes on the vine were ripe, and so on. I got rid of these pain-mongers joyfully, and turned up a narrow lane in case they followed. I avoided the Greek Police Station and passed in front of the German Kommandatur. I reached Siphi in half an hour; he was sitting down just outside Dariviana. We had left Yerakari very early, but it was deep night when we reached Koxaré – normally only a five hours' journey. Our beast fell in the middle of Koxaré and refused to get up. A few villagers helped us, and managed to get it on its feet with a thousand difficulties. But, a hundred yards out of the village, it fell again. We unloaded the stuff and managed after a while to get him up. We saw it was hopeless to go on, yet we wanted to be clear of the village. I took the set on my back, Siphi shouldered the wheat, and stooping beneath our burden we got the unloaded beast moving. It couldn't go on much, however, and soon fell again, even without its load. We gave it some wheat, then took up the set and the wheat again and the saddle too and dragged on for about five hundred yards off the road and among the olive trees. Here we found some bushes among which we hid and slept. When we awoke in the morning we went to the place we had left the donkey, which had not only not got up, but had not moved an inch. I told Siphi I would push on with the set, while he should follow with the beast and the wheat in a week's time.

That was that. I humped the set – it must have weighed twenty *okas* – and by nine o'clock I had reached our hideout. Siphi went straight to Alones that evening.

Colonel Papadakis and Mr Aleko
[Xan Fielding]

It was at the end of July that we started getting our gear together. The Greek submarine, the *Papanikolis*, was to put in at Rhodakino and take off Colonel Papadakis and his family, and Mr Aleko as well. Vangeli Vandoulakis was to go as far as the beach and we were to leave for Vaphé with Manoli our operator and all our stuff to await his return. I set off with Manoli on the first of August while the others headed for the south coast. We spent the night in my village and moved to Vaphé next day. There we found a young English officer that I had never seen before. It was Mr Patrick Leigh Fermor. We called him Michali. He had a rough-and-ready hideout two hundred yards higher uphill from Vangeli's house in a little hill covered with rocks and wild shrubs. He talked to Manoli in French and in English, both of which Manoli knew a little. He also asked me in Greek if I spoke any English. I had learnt one phrase which I pronounced so well, that when I said I spoke no English, nobody believed it. He made me say the same phrase over and over again – '*I steal grapes every day*' – and laughed a lot.

Vangeli arrived on the fifth of August. The mission had only been completed the night before. He recounted all the strange circumstances of the operation. They had waited from the first of August, but no submarine was to be seen. Colonel Papadakis thought he was being made a fool of in some way, and wanted to kill Mr Aleko. He told Vangeli that he would get him raised to the rank of lieutenant if he killed him but Vangeli refused, repudiating the very idea. At one moment the Colonel said, 'I order you to kill him!' Vangeli could no longer hold himself in, and declared that he took orders from nobody, as he had been sent to the island to give orders, not to take them. When Colonel Papadakis saw that there was nothing doing he tried to persuade Manoli Yana from Rhodakino to kill Mr Aleko if the submarine failed to arrive in the end. Manoli Yana is a logical man and a brave *pallikari*,[1] and would never have done such a deed.

As dawn ended the last night, it appears that a fishing boat was captured by the submarine which had been waiting there all night without seeing them, or being seen. When the crew of the submarine saw that the boat held no Germans, they sent her in quest of the men who should be waiting on the shore. The little boat hunted along the shore until it found the waiting party, but they trusted neither the fishermen nor the submarine in case she were German.

So they sent the boat back to tell the submarine they would not believe them unless there was an English officer of a certain name on board. Off went the boat to the submarine with the message. The submarine-commander gave the name 'Hughes', but also asked for a name among the people waiting on the shore.[2] As soon as the fishermen got back with the well-known name of Smith-Hughes, they believed at last that it really was their submarine, and sent the boat back with the names of Mr Aleko and

1 A warrior, particularly a guerrilla fighter.
2 Jack Smith-Hughes was on board, having landed the night before in a vain search for the party. The *Papanikolis* was commanded by that famous Greek naval figure, Commander (now Rear-Admiral) Spanidi, who was later head of the Greek Delegation at SHAPE.

Colonel Papadakis. The submarine approached the shore, and the little boat ferried everybody on board.

Later we were told that the flight of Colonel Papadakis and his family had reached German ears even before he had left, and that the Germans knew just when and where he was to leave. But, if this is so, we don't know why they did nothing about it.

In White Mountains and the Arrival of Mr 'Michali' [Patrick Leigh Fermor]

As soon as Vangeli returned we started shifting our station to the peak of Simalókorphi, high in the White Mountains above the village of Askiphou. All Vangeli's cousins were set in motion to help us. With us, too, came the lawyer Andrea Polentas,[1] who lived in Vrysses, a very energetic man and a good patriot. It was his intention to take the place of Colonel Papadakis. Everything was new in our new hideout. The operator had only recently arrived and it was the baptism of the new set we had brought from Yerakari. We had a new leader and a new English officer. Mr Michali was a tall man, full of life, with a beautiful moustache and curly brown hair. He wore Cretan breeches and boots, a black shirt and a fringed turban, and he had dyed his whiskers and hair in such a way that he seemed the image of a true Cretan.

All this was the pasturing region of the Karkanis family, and Manousso Karkanis was always there to help us. It was very high in the mountains with the sun, blazing fiercely, almost burning us up. But we found two huge rocks, and between them we built a beautiful hut of cypress branches and other shrubs and bushes. The climate is very strange in those parts. You shiver in the shade and burn in the sunlight, which means you have to

1 Secretary of Papadakis's Resistance Committee.

sit a little while in the sun, then a little in the shade.

It was a wild, steep place and the distances were enormous, for which reason things did not work very well; but we were only to remain there a month and then leave, for winter starts very early in those high mountains. My job as runner here was very exhausting and I hardly ever had a day's rest.

The transport of supplies was a problem, but the Karkanis family of Askiphou and the Vandoulakis family of Vaphé were a great help. It was decided to ask for another aeroplane to come and drop the things we needed. The answer came back in a few days and a dropping-place was found at Niato, a little plateau below our hideout. It must have been on the seventh of September, when I was taking a letter from Mr Michali to Manoli Vlepakis at Kephala. I stayed there the night and watched the English aeroplanes bombing the harbour of Suda Bay. Our aeroplane too had come with the bomber formation and dropped the stuff on Niato during the bombardment. There was a fight between English and German planes, and one German plane was hit. It flew off in the direction of Retimo in bad trouble, burst into flames and fell blazing to earth at Prassès. A bit of it struck the mountains above Asi Gonia among a flock of goats, killing several. When I returned to our lair next day, they had collected the things, but unfortunately the aeroplane had loosed off the stuff from a great height and the wind had scattered it far and wide, right out of sight, so that men from the mountain village of Kalo Lakko found it. Only heavy things dropped in the right place, explosives and limpets[1] and so on. Some time later the Karkanis family found a large bundle of English cavalry breeches, which the Service had sent us

---

1 High-explosive charges designed to be fixed on the hulls of ships by means of magnets and detonated by delayed action fuses.

from Cairo, as they are almost the same as Cretan breeches.

One day Mr Polentas asked me if I had a monthly wage arranged with the English. I told him that I was not working for a monthly wage, but for our country, and received money from nowhere.

'Yes,' he said, 'but it would be a little help for your family.'

'Well, that is as may be, but I don't expect it, Mr Polentas.' And he said it was all arranged and would be gone into – now that Colonel Papadakis was absent . . . (and would not be coming back either).

At Photeinou. Mr Tom Dunbabin's Lair on Mount Ida

Towards the end of September, the weather began to get worse. We had to be off before the first rains came. I had the feeling that things were not going well between Mr Michali and Mr Polentas,[1] I don't know what the disagreement was about; anyway, Mr Michali was eager to change his lair for several reasons.

One day he called for me and told me to take the set and leave by myself without breathing a word to a soul.

'Only tell me where I must go, Mr Michali.'

'To Photeinou.'

'In that case Yanni Tsangarakis[2] ought to come as well, to go on in advance as it's his village, unless you need him.'

'I'll let Yanni go with you,' he said, and, calling him, he told us both to leave together. I put the suitcase wireless into a *sakouli* so that none should see what it was, and slung it on my back.

We got to Photeinou in two days, and hid the wireless till Mr Michali arrived with Vangeli and Manoli the operator. We set up the station at the valley of Scholari,

1 George is wrong about tension between Andrea Polentas and me. We got on very well. [PLF]
2 One of the best, bravest, most trustworthy and hard-working of the runners and guides, he was accidentally shot dead next year in tragic circumstances.

a quarter of an hour east of Photeinou, where many of the villagers have their fruit and vegetable gardens. Chief among these was Stavro Peros.

Uncle Stavro, a wonderful, kind-hearted old man with snow-white hair, whiskers and beard, was always laughing. Three of his sons, Siphi, Andrea and Antoni, and a daughter married to Kanaki, Yanni Tsangarakis's brother, lived in the village. All Uncle Stavro's eighteen children were brave patriots. The village was very small and the villagers all lived together like one family; so, with care, we would be able to work well there.

The village of Armenoi, the biggest German supply dump in the whole Nome of Retimo, was only three-quarters of an hour away. Many Germans were billeted nearby in Koxaré, and the main Retimo–St Basil road ran a quarter of an hour from the new station. Our lair was perched among the rocks above Uncle Stavro's garden on the western side of the little canyon. It was a very small cave indeed, and the set was put in a hole which could just hold one man, under a rock a little way off. Ten minutes south-east of the cave was the place called 'the Meadow Gate', where the Germans had dug many trenches, as it dominated the whole basin of the Eparchy of St Basil. There was not a single tree, and I didn't think much of it. There was nowhere for the battery-charging engine, so we had to smuggle our batteries into Retimo, where Vangeli Papalexakis recharged them. His brother Manoli lived at the little farm of St George.

This farmstead took its name from the little chapel which was part of the building. Old Petro Papalexakis's children – Manoli and George and the rest – had always been at Colonel Tsiphakis's disposal from the start, and so were at ours too. We hid the batteries there, loaded them up again at daybreak and went *via* Mikri Gonia,

Kastelo, Ay Georgi and Armenoi to Photeinou. I often walked this route with Mr Michali, when on his way to Priné, and bit by bit he learnt the path and used to go there alone, in spite of the fact that we ought not to have let him go by himself, in case his accent in Greek betrayed him. Nevertheless, one day he set off alone from Priné, heading for Photeinou. He told us he had met an old crone outside Kastelo, and before he could wish her good-morning she said:

'Where are you going to, my child?'

'To Angouselliana, auntie,' he answered.

'And where are you coming from?'

'From Phre.'

Then she asked him his name and a thousand and two other things. He told her that he had '*mia oulia*' at his destination (Cretan dialect for '*doulia*' – work, a job), that he was sorry she was so old, and so on; a pack of lies. 'Go towards the good,' he shouted as he left, and 'God and the Blessed Virgin look after you,' and all sorts of other wishes. He had got the knack of Cretan turns of speech, they amused him immensely and he was always imitating any odd expression he had heard. He turned the old crone's question into a sort of a proverb, and always croaked to any of us, when setting out: 'Where are you off to, my child?'

Once, as I was returning to Photeinou, I heard the sound of much shooting in the direction of our lair, and ran through the village to see what was afoot. I could see two stooping figures creeping from the direction of the height where our lair was. A bit farther off a little girl was running in the same direction. When I asked her what was up, she told me the Germans were after her Uncle Nikoli. This was one of the boys that came to our hideout, so I thought the Germans must have discovered it – in which case, woe betide us all! I didn't know what to make of it. The firing continued, so I thought it best not to approach till I knew what was going on. 'If they've found anything,' I thought, 'I'll see them setting fire to the village soon enough . . .' Two hours passed and all was quiet.

Back in the hideout, they told me the whole story.

About a hundred and fifty Germans had arrived on the opposite slope a little distance from the cave, and had started a battle practice. Nikoli Alevizakis, not knowing it was merely an exercise, thought they must be chasing our people.[1] He took to his heels at once, but the Germans saw him running and dropped their exercise to pursue him. If he hadn't managed to hide, he would certainly have been shot. When Mr Michali and Yanni Tsangarakis saw them from our cave, manoeuvring about five hundred yards away, they managed to make a stealthy getaway to the other slope of the high ground and hide. The operator, meanwhile, was in wireless contact with Cairo, and seeing the Germans manoeuvring and firing, concluded that they were aiming at him. But when he saw the bullets were not falling round about, he plucked up courage, took off the earphones and waited motionless; for in the place where he was hiding, the slightest movement would have given him away. Fortunately, the incident with Alevizakis on the other side drew the Germans farther off, to our great good fortune.[2]

When all was over, we teased poor Manoli because, when he thought the Germans were shooting at him, he

1 i.e. of the hideout.

2 The Germans actually were closer, and Manoli the operator, bent over the wireless with the earphones on, failed to see them, but kept on tapping morse while three Germans passed between him and our cave, a hundred yards away. Miraculously without being seen or heard, Yanni Tsangarakis and I, meanwhile, lay down with our rifles cocked, in case they should spot the set. Yanni, who knew his village was in danger of being burnt down, kept crossing himself and repeating 'O, my poor village . . .' [PLF]

didn't use his pistol. And he, joking too, said, 'As soon as I took the earphones off, I took my automatic and aimed – straight down the muzzle of their machine-gun, of course, to block it up . . .' When the danger was past, there were plenty of these jokes, but we thought of more serious things when night fell. We collected all our gear and moved to another cave, a deep hole only three minutes from the village. It was at the top of a hill above the village, and you couldn't see it unless you were actually on the spot. A great improvement! We got the charging machine going, for there was no danger of being heard.

The aeroplane was due to come again and drop us food and stores, and Yanni persuaded Mr Michali to let them do the drop in the area just beyond our hill. It was the end of October[1] and we awaited the plane three nights running, but it was raining and blowing so hard that nothing came. We broke up, as the signal had told us to wait only three nights. I was at my village the next night, which was fine, and the plane came searching for us. But, not seeing the flares, it flew off to Mount Ida where Mr Tom had his hideout, and as he too was due for a drop that night, both planes dropped their stores in his area.

A few days later an English airman came to our lair. His plane had been shot down over Herakleion. Three of the crew were burnt to death in the plane, three baled out by parachute, one of whom was captured, the other two falling into the hands of Cretans, who hid them. Mr Tom took on one of them in his hideout, sending the other to Yerakari, where I went to fetch him from Captain Koutellidakis. He and Mr Michali used to sing together every night and they would talk and laugh for hours. He

1 1942.

had been the wireless operator on the plane, and perhaps he might come in handy.[1]

★   ★   ★

With the growing frequency of these German manoeuvres, we developed the evil suspicion that the Germans might have got wind of our presence, and decided to shift at once.

Before I had time to settle down, Mr Michali shouted for me, and said we must set off for Alones. We reached it after a three hours' march, where we found Father John Alevizakis, whom we asked if we could set up our wireless station there. Father John at once assembled the chief villagers and they were all delighted to look after us. Mr Michali thanked them for their love and their eagerness to help and we left as night was falling, for there was no time to lose. We did nearly the whole of our journey in the dark, and as soon as we got to our cave, we collected our stuff and left again before daybreak.

We settled in a low stone hut in a goat-fold belonging to the Tsangarakis family. Now that we had two wireless sets and, purely by luck, two operators, Mr Michali determined to get two stations going. One he left here with the airman as operator, sending Manoli off to Vaphé with orders to set up his transmitter in our rock hideout above Vangeli's hideout. Vangeli was to stay with him as officer on duty (to transmit information) while Mr Michali would base himself with us at Alones, going to Vaphé from time

1 Flight-Sergeant Jo Bradley, DFM, MM, from Blaenau Ffestiniog, Merioneth. A charming man, who sang beautifully in Welsh, to the delight of the Cretans. When my operator Manoli was captured, and later executed, he became my operator till he was evacuated by MTB next year. After he and his comrade had baled out SE of Herakleion, they were hidden and led to safety by Grigori Khnarakis of Thrapsano. [PLF]

to time. Soon after, we learnt that our parachute stores had been dropped on Mount Ida, where Mr Tom, having collected them, was awaiting us.

I left at once with Mr Michali, heading for Mr Tom's hideout among the peaks half-way up Mount Ida above the village of Phourphoura. It was a steep climb.

Mr Tom at once took us to the cave where the things were hidden. This cave lies on the very edge of a sheer precipice, among the last wooded peaks of the mountain; – below, from Phourphoura, it looked like the utmost limit of the horizon. It is a very peculiar cave, hard of access even for shepherds: you have to approach from above, and tread with care in order to avoid going headlong over those sheer and enormous precipices; you advance to the right behind a needle of rock, like a mountain goat, climbing first up and many times down, before finding the cave. From there all the villages of the Amari are spread out below you in a panorama. The cave has a large opening but does not go very deep, but in spite of this, it is invisible from all sides, owing to the narrowness of the precipice. We lit a fire as soon as we had climbed inside and made some tea. Opening several tins, we dug out some biscuits and busied ourselves with eating and drinking. Bully beef, ham, bacon, sausages, biscuits, chocolates, rum, tea – all this came like a boon on top of our weariness. And there were sweet-smelling aromatic cigarettes and tins of tobacco and beautiful pipes.

We stayed there several hours while Mr Tom and Mr Michali shared out the stores in piles. Ours I put on one side while we sang hosannas unceasingly. We wrote everything down on a bit of paper; and among the other things were twelve long-barrelled Smith & Wesson ·32 revolvers. Six of them were for us and I was the first to receive one. This was the granting of my fondest wish. We divided up all the bullets equally except for mine, for

I got at least a hundred more bullets than those allotted to any other pistol. When we had finished, we scrambled down again to Mr Tom's lair, which was half an hour from the cave, and spent the night there. We descended to the Amari valley next day where we drank plenty of their excellent wine with friends in well-known villages, then set off for our own lair at Alones.

Next day I returned with Father John's son, Siphi Alevizakis and a beast to take some of our share of the drop. It was then I learnt the full story of how it happened. When Mr Tom learnt the date of the drop, he summoned some people to help collect the containers. Among these were Kapetan Petrakoyeorgis and Kapetan Bandouvas[1] with their *pallikaria*. After the parachutes had fallen a discussion started about the distribution, the stores consisting, as I have said, of two plane loads. When Kapetan Bandouvas learnt that they were to be stored by Mr Tom and distributed later, he claimed that the whole lot was destined for his band, and that he would handle the distribution. But Mr Tom firmly stated that this was his responsibility, for only he knew how they were to be divided up and to whom they were to go. When Kapetan Bandouvas saw that he could get no further with Mr Tom, he declared he would seize the lot by force. He turned to his men with the words:

'Stand to your arms, men!'

Whereupon, Mr Tom sat down on top of the stores and addressed Bandouvas and his men with the words,

1 Manoli Bandouvas, from Asites near Herakleion, was the most important and powerful of the Cretan guerrilla leaders. Of peasant stock, he was almost illiterate, and all his correspondence was conducted through a scribe. Massive and heavily whiskered, he had a very forceful personality and wielded immense influence on the simpler mountaineers. He was quite fearless, but also headstrong and domineering, and, as in this case, prone to rash acts. Since the war he has become a figure of some political and commercial importance in the Nome of Herakleion.

'Go ahead then, gentlemen, and shoot an unarmed man.'

Kapetan Bandouvas retreated before Mr Tom's determination and, calling his men together, he left forthwith. I learnt all this from Mr Tom's party and could hardly believe it at first. But later on I knew it was true, because I often heard the phrase 'Stand to your arms, men!' from the English officers themselves when they wanted to tease us. I also gathered that there was not much love lost between them and Bandouvas, while they had a strong respect for Petrakoyeorgis.

Losing no time, we loaded our beast and left next day and reached Alones by the night after without encountering any trouble. We went straight to our lair and after we had unloaded, Siphi left for his house, and I, being tired out, lay down to sleep. As soon as sleep had hold of me Siphi,[1] the operator, woke me up by shaking me, shouting the phrase: 'Blessed Virgin! *Perhaps now all kaputti.*'[2] They told me that one of the boys, cleaning his pistol, had pulled the trigger by mistake, and, as it had been pointing in my direction, they thought the bullet might have killed me. I rolled over and fell asleep again saying I hoped they would be more careful. These boys from Alones used to congregate in the hideout to keep us company, and also in the hopes of learning what was going on, as we could get any station we wanted on the wireless set.

1 Jo Bradley, the Welshman, was called by this Cretan diminutive of Joseph. He learnt fluent Greek during his Cretan sojourn.
2 The pidgin-Greek-German word *kaputti* had caught on everywhere.

The Capture of our Wireless Operator

Time passed slowly. One day followed another and we had been at work now for thirteen months without any serious mishap with the Germans. They had been on our heels from the start, but by keeping on the move and hiding all over the place, they could never lay hands on us. But, as time passed, the Germans sent out more spies, and their knowledge of us and our hideouts increased. They would never have managed to accomplish anything without the garrulity and carelessness of certain people.

About the twentieth of November we learnt that, at nightfall on the eighteenth, the Germans had surrounded the villages of Embrósnero, Vaphé and Vrysses, arresting thirty-seven people, and, among others, Mr Andrea Polentas, our man in Vrysses, and poor Manoli, our operator in Vaphé, and Perikles Vandoulakis.

Vangeli Vandoulakis was in the courtyard of his house in Vaphé, when suddenly he saw the Germans. He jumped over the wall into the garden. The Germans opened fire on him at once, but, in spite of the short range, he dodged the bullets and got away. Manoli, meanwhile, was encoding some messages inside the house. Hearing the command 'Halt!' and the firing just outside the door, he leapt to his feet. All he managed to do before the Germans burst in was to hide the papers and cyphers in his pocket. As soon as they saw him, the Germans cried: 'Ah! You are the operator!' Several of them at once stood guard round him while the others searched the house. It was completely surrounded.

Vangeli's sister Elpida happened to be indoors and, though she heard them shooting at her brother and saw them arrest Manoli, she kept her head. She saw Manoli slip the secret papers into his pocket, and, without losing a moment, she took a jacket of her brother's into the room where Manoli was under arrest. She told him to put on this coat, and helped him remove his own and put on the other. Then she went into the kitchen where she emptied the pockets and hid the papers down the front of her dress.

After searching the whole house and finding nobody else, the Germans took Manoli away with the thirty-seven other villagers they had arrested, and flung them into the terrible Jail of Ayia where Charon[1] had set up his dark kingdom.

The moment the Germans left Vaphé with our operator, Elpida quickly took the wireless and the other incriminating things a little way off, and hid them; conducting herself, although she was a woman, with all the sense and coolness of a brave man. After dark she carried the wireless, the heavy charging-engine and the batteries to a cave outside the village, and, taking a rifle, hid within sight of the cave for over two days till her brother and her cousin, Andrea Vandoulakis of Nippos, found her and took charge. The day after the arrests the Germans returned and searched the house of Uncle Nikoli, taking up the floor to the very foundations, in search (it seems) of the wireless transmitter. Finding nothing, they broke everything in the house to bits and left.

All these doings were the work of the traitor Komninas.

---

1 i.e. Death. Charon, in modern Greek folklore, is Death himself, not just the ferryman of the Styx.

He lived in Vrysses and it seems he was one of the spies taken on by the Germans from before the war. He was with the Germans in Vrysses every day, and Mr Polentas had made friends with him. He had 'taken him in hand', as he put it, to get information from him about the movements of the Germans and so on. Mr Polentas's great mistake was meeting him at all and, meeting him, not seeing through him. He used to take him to listen to Allied stations on a receiving set which he had kept hidden from the start. Probably, as time passed, he had talked to him about our transmitter at Vaphé, and our operator. The Germans knew just what Manoli looked like – that is why they said 'Ah! You're the operator!' the moment they set eyes on him. So Komninas, wearing a German officer's uniform, was able to arrange the simultaneous arrest of Mr Andrea Polentas and his god-brother and lead the way to the hiding-place of the receiving set. They went straight to the Vandoulakis's house without even a glance at any other.

In a few days' time the Germans let everybody go except Manoli the operator, Mr Polentas and his god-brother; and on the twentieth of December they were all three led before the firing squad under the black tree in Ayia Jail, and shot.

They kept Perikles a few more days, but thanks to his skill in answering them, he was released after countless interrogations.

The Return of Mr Aleko

At the end of November 1942, or the beginning of December, a messenger came to Mr Michali with the news that the former operator of the wireless set, Mr Aleko, had landed again, so he set off to meet him.

Mr Aleko arrived with another officer and a wireless operator, and they all took up quarters at a place called Gournes in the White Mountains, in the region of Karé and Kyriakosellia.

I set off at once from Alones with Mr Michali and went to Gournes. At the bottom of the gorge there stood a little church dedicated to St Paul and several *mytata* or cheese-huts. The newcomers had settled in the last *mytato* to the left of St Paul's. Vangeli Vandoulakis took Manoli's set there, and work began again. The *mytata* are conically shaped like limekilns or beehives, and they are all roofed with those great flat slabs of stone that lie about the mountainside. The entrances are so small that you have to crawl in on all fours, and we all huddled together inside on soft branches close to the fire because, outside, snow was already thick on the mountain, and it was very cold. They told us the tale of their landing.

The Greek submarine *Papanikolis* brought them to the south-west coast of Selino, near Souyia, without forewarning anyone by wireless to wait on the beach to give the landing signal. The submarine stopped over half a mile from the shore, they got into a boat with all their gear, and the submarine sailed away. They tried to land but the sea was very stormy, and they struggled with the waves in the dark for several hours.

When they were close to land at last, a wave dashed the boat against the rocks. Most of their stuff went to the bottom and they had to swim for it. They were very cold when they reached land, so they tried to light a small fire among the rocks to get warm. Some villagers from nearby Koustoyerako, who happened to be close by, saw the fire and thought they must be Germans. They were all armed, so, creeping through the rocks, they stealthily surrounded the strangers round the fire, and took aim. One of them suggested that they should get closer and find out more, just in case they were not Germans. So they crept up, and decided that they must be English, not German, as they could hear them speaking Greek now and again in their English accent. Then they approached them openly and everybody introduced himself. These villagers from Koustoyerako all belonged to the Paterakis family.[1]

So then they took the strangers and looked after them, and sheltered them for the night, returning to the shore with them next morning to help fish up most of what they had lost the night before by diving.

When they had rested there a bit, Mr Aleko took Manoli Paterakis with him and came to Gournes where we all met.

Mr Aleko, Mr Michali, the new officer Mr Levtheri and the wireless operator talked among themselves for hours, then Mr Aleko called me up and said, 'George, I didn't forget what you asked me to bring you when I left – a good pistol and a good watch. I hear you got a pistol at the Mount Ida drop, so here is the watch.'

[1] A magnificent shepherd family of several brothers, all of whom participated in the Resistance.

He gave me a most beautiful Swiss wrist-watch. I took it with joy and thanked Mr Aleko for his gift. We stayed there about three days, then I set out for Alones with Mr Michali and Mr Aleko. We left the wireless operator and the new officer under the care of the Kourakis family (and especially of Levtheri Kouris), all of them villagers of Kyriakosellia.

From Alones I accompanied Mr Aleko to Priné, to a meeting with Colonel Tsiphakis.[1] We went *via* Velonado, heading for the Mudros gorge. But it had been raining hard and the river was in flood. So we pulled off our high boots and our breeches, and waded across. Mr Aleko said he wanted to go by the Monastery of Rustika to greet a monk there who was a friend of his. When Rustika came in sight, he sat down to smoke a cigarette and as he smoked, an old woman came in sight, probably going from Rustika to Mudros. While she was still some distance away, Mr Aleko wished her good-day. The old woman at once started making the sign of the cross again and again, imploring God and all the Saints to watch over him and bring him safe home to his country, his home and his mamma, and so on.

All this surprised Mr Aleko very much, and, when she continued on her way, still murmuring and crossing herself, he asked me if the old woman were simple or what? 'Far from it, Mr Aleko,' I said, 'she's very intelligent.'

'Then why does she carry on so daftly?'

'Surely it's not daft to pray to God to bring you and the other English safe home?'

'But I don't look English, dressed like this, and it's not written on my forehead . . . how did she know?'

---

1 Major, later Colonel, Tsiphakis, a regular officer from Priné, near Retimo. He was head of the EOK for that nome, and he played a leading part in the successful defence of Retimo against parachutists. A man of education and good sense, he filled his difficult rôle with great credit.

'Even if you had it written on your forehead she would be none the wiser, as I'm sure she can't read or write. She knew it because, sitting down, we ought not to have wished her good-day before she did.' So I told him all our ritual about greeting, and he said, 'Well, I've learnt something new today, but, Holy Virgin! it doesn't matter a bit which of us greets first in England!'

'Yes, but here in Crete it means at once that you are English. It doesn't matter who speaks first if you are both walking, but otherwise, the one who is on the move must greet first.'

We went to the monastery and found his friend the monk.

This was during the fast of Advent, for Christmas was drawing near. The good monk, after greeting us, drew up chairs, produced some wonderful wine and a *mézé*[1] of veal that he had put by against Christmas. We ate and drank our fill, thanked him, said farewell, and left, and then pushed on to Priné, where we remained two days, Mr Aleko conferring with Colonel Tsiphakis and Mr George Robola[2] and his sons and all our friends there.

Returning to Alones, we found our hideout had been shifted to another place, almost five minutes out of the village. Once more the whole village was at our disposal for whatever help we needed, and the villagers took it in turn to cook meals for us, bringing out their wine, and offering us all they possessed.

On Christmas Eve Mr Aleko and Mr Michali gave me

1 The Greeks never drink without eating, and the *mézé* may be olives, cheese, fried potatoes, roast liver, chopped apples or pears – or almost anything.
2 Uncle George Robola, a prosperous elder of Priné, was among the staunchest and kindest helpers of the mission. His code name was 'Priam' and he had been very much affected by the accidental death of one of his many fine sons. Tall, dignified and quite fearless, it was his delight to entertain us under the noses of the Germans, and, puffing away thoughtfully at his *narghilé*, to discuss the politics of the last half-century for hours on end.

leave to spend Christmas in the village with my family, telling me to stay about ten days and rest, for, as they themselves declared, fatigue had almost turned me into a shadow. I set off at once for my village, where I stayed till the fourth of January. On the fourth, before dawn broke, I took the path to Alones and when I got there, the sun had only just risen. It must have been while I was still half an hour off when I heard two rifle shots; but I took no notice of it, because there was gunfire going off all the time, every single villager having a rifle. At all events, as I had been away a few days and didn't know what had been going on, I left the usual Alones–Roubado path, and took to the side of the mountain. When I reached the top of the last peak, from which you can see the whole village, I heard more firing, and started to smell a rat. I crept up behind a rock, and looking down, saw that the village was full of Germans. Just below me, about ten were climbing up the slope towards my vantage-point. If I hadn't heard the second shots, I should have walked straight into them. I hid like lightning. They reached the peak, looked all round, and started off down. It looked like an advance-guard or a patrol. Climbing higher still, I sat and watched every movement in the village. About midday, I saw them gathering from all the hills and woods round the village, and then moving off down the road to Argyroupolis. They had many civilians with them. All I could think of was: What has happened to our people there? The place where our hideout lay was full of Germans.

I had learnt that our headquarters had been shifted yet again during my absence because there had been a lot of German movement about Christmas time. I was certain they must have known something positive about the English to have gone in such large numbers. I could not go down to the village, even when I saw the Germans marching off, because some might have remained behind. I didn't know what to do. In the end I decided to return to my own village till I learnt what happened by the 'Cretan Wireless', as the English called it – that is, the mouths of men. Anything that happens is blown at once through all Crete from mouth to mouth on the very same day. I went to Uncle Petraka's, and found our two wireless operators, Siphi and the new one who had come with Mr Aleko; they had stayed on in Alones after Christmas. The new one was called Aleko[1] too, and to distinguish him from his officer, we called them the Big and the Little Aleko. Little Aleko had stayed in our village before Christmas, so he knew the way more or less. The lair had been shifted two days before to a point half an hour above Alones in a little stone hut they built for them on the spot. There was a hole nearby which they used for the battery-charging machine. The moment they heard the firing and the Germans in the village they all climbed into this hole, and when night fell and the Germans had gone they climbed out again and 'cut the mud' in the direction of our village. How they crossed the mountains in the dark and found our village is a marvel, for only one of them knew anything about the region. God must have guided them. Soon we learnt all that had happened in Alones. The Germans found a wireless battery hidden in Father John's garden. They caught Siphi, one of the priest's sons, and, when they searched him, found a letter from Mr Michali to his father in his pocket, sent some time ago. The letter contained something incriminating, and it could easily be seen that it was written by an Englishman.

[1] Sergeant Alec Tarves, MM, Royal Corps of Signals, a Scotsman from the Cairngorms, who had run away from home at fifteen and joined the Seaforth Highlanders. He served all through the occupation in Crete as an operator. He was much loved by everybody and was known as Little Aleko or 'the Tinker'.

They didn't arrest the priest then, but came back for him next day. Fancy thinking they would still find him there . . . ! They ransacked the entire village and searched the woods but found nothing. All their attention was fixed on the woods below the village where the set had been working two days before – they didn't bother to search above the village, except a little distance, and so didn't find the English with the transmitting set after which they kept asking. It seems that they had been well informed. They arrested everyone in the village who didn't belong there and many of the villagers, but some managed to slip away among the heather and arbutus bushes on the way to Vilandredo.

The Aloniots, when they saw the Germans had gone (and without the English), rushed to the hideout, took all the gear and hid it in the same deep cave as the charging-engine. They were not anxious about the English, as they knew they must have found refuge somewhere. They informed us where they had hidden the stuff, and advised us to get it without delay. We had to do it by night as the Germans were still going and coming in Alones. Uncle Petraka told me to get some other chaps to help us. So I got some cousins – Marko Psychoundakis, Ioannes Psychoundakis, Petro Kokkinakis and Andrea Leladakis. We left with Mr Michali and Yanni Tsangarakis just before nightfall. We were about eighteen altogether. Unluckily, I had put my ankle out the day before while fooling about, and could scarcely walk. Thus I could only go halfway and had to turn back, as I understood that soon I wouldn't be able to walk at all. The rest went to the hiding-place, hoisted all the stuff on to their backs and brought them for miles over the rocks to our village, in the rain and the dark.

The Germans are After Me

Returning home, a slow steady rainfall overtook me on the way. I thought of all the others heavily laden and slipping about the rocks all night in the downpour and the darkness. That night I didn't leave the village to sleep in some cave as I usually did. I followed to the letter the proverb which says: 'Watch your clothes and you will only lose half of them.' By now my foot was in pain, and it was raining hard, so I thought I would risk it.

I bathed my foot in hot water to bring down the swelling, and then fell asleep. I didn't wake up very early, as I had had little sleep these last few nights. Suddenly my mamma was shaking me to wake me up. 'What's the matter?' I asked. 'Germans, my child,' she said. I said, 'Never mind, mother, don't you be afraid. You mustn't *look* frightened.' I got up, put on a shoe but couldn't get the other on, as my foot was still more swollen. While I was trying, three Germans came into the house,[1] whistling and shouting. '*Oli apano, parti!*' ('All get up, *parti!*')[2] My brother and sisters were asleep still, so I woke them up, as 'our friends' were shouting furiously. '*Tempo! Tempo!*' When we were all ready, I said, '*Where parti?*'

1 George's house has only one room.
2 '*Parti*', perhaps from '*partez*' learnt by the German troops in the invasion of France, invariably came into any Cretan imitation of Germans talking pidgin-Greek. '*Tempo*' ('look sharp about it') is even harder to trace.

'*Klissia, Klissia,*[1] tempo!'

We went out quickly. I was in front, and I whispered to my parents and brother and sisters, 'Fall into line, and the ones at the back, dawdle.' So they made a line and our three friends followed.

By the time we had gone a short distance I was at least forty yards in front of the Germans. At that point there is a little brook beside the path. I looked back at the Germans, and, as they seemed to be looking the other way, jumped into the brook. Signalling to my family to quicken their pace, I turned my one foot into four to cover the thirty odd yards that would carry me out of sight. And, indeed, I got away without being seen, or without them noticing until they had got to the end of that narrow lane. At the end of the little river bed I climbed out at the chapel of St George and tried to creep past, but on the other side were two German sentries. What next? I thought of hiding in the chapel, but remembered that Germans always searched churches. I thought, too, of climbing into one of the half-dug graves in the churchyard of St George, but the Germans made regular hunts through graves after hidden arms. Standing there wondering, I saw the two Germans go into a garden in search of something. I took advantage of this by sneaking away and ran along a dried-up river bed under some plane trees in the direction of the cave. Some other Germans saw me there and ran to catch me, but I managed to dodge them among some bushes on the bank, and climbed up the side of the mountain called Koutoulóprinos.

I headed for home when they left the village at last, but was waylaid by an aunt of mine before I got there. 'Run, run!' she said. 'Don't go home or they'll get you!'

I learnt that they had asked for everybody's identity

[1] *Ecclesia* – church. Pidgin-German.

papers. In the end, failing to find the name they were after, one of them asked if there was anybody called Psychoundakis present. 'Which Psychoundakis?' a cousin of mine asked, 'there are lots of them.' He had half pronounced the name George when someone gagged him with his hand. They took several Psychoundakises off with them, threw them into Ayia Jail and interrogated them for three days in Canea. They asked what relation I was to them, where I was, and what work I did. They answered nothing that could harm me or even interest the Germans, and were allowed free.

Two days later a party of twenty from the Gestapo came to find me, asking for me everywhere in the village. Three Gestapites took up a position outside the village with the informer who had betrayed me, in order to point me out and identify me when caught. The others arrived at the village at the double and asked the first villager they saw to point out George Psychoundakis's house.

'Which George?' he said. 'There are several of the same name.'

'The son of Nikolas,' said the Germans.

'Ah! I don't know that one,' he was about to answer, but a rain of blows fell on him. 'I'll take you there,' he said at last, and led them to my house. My mamma was standing outside. 'That's his mother,' he said, 'and that's his house,' then he made off before catching any more.

Some of them questioned my mother, others surrounded the house and searched it.

'Are you the mother of George Psychoundakis?' they asked.

'Which one?' she said, 'there are several.'

'Of George, the son of Nikolas Psychoundakis.'

'Yes, I am.'

'Where is your son?'

She said she had had no news of me for at least three

months. I had left, she continued, to try to get a job with the Germans in Canea, as I had heard there was plenty of work going. They said I was wanted in Retimo for interrogation, and if I didn't go there before the seventeenth of January, they would set fire to the whole village.

When they had made a thorough search without finding me, they asked for my mother again, who had gone to my uncle's house next door. A German went in and asked her – my mother herself – where my mother was. She answered that she had gone out to pick cooking-herbs on the mountainside. So they left.

Nobody had been able to make out who the traitor was, as he remained outside the village with the Germans, muffled in a raincoat and with his face covered.

This time I had been away from the village since dawn, as, when our people had brought all the things from Alones, we had hidden them near the village and taken the wireless operators off to Gournes in the White Mountains, where their colleague was. Mr Aleko sent me with a letter to Mr Tom, telling me to ask for him at Mr Papadoyannis's house, as Mr Tom had shifted again and only Mr Papadoyannis knew where he had gone.

Reaching the Amari, I took the downhill slope from Ano Meros to the river, which I crossed by the old Turkish bridge – Manoura's Arch as they call it – then followed the river bank to where the path re-ascends to the village of St John. Suddenly I saw Mr Papadoyannis and his nephew Aristides Paradeisianos on the opposite bank, hiding behind the trunk of a large olive tree. Their eyes were glued to the path leading from Ay-Yanni, and although they were exactly opposite and only a little way off, they hadn't seen me yet. I realized they were on the lookout for Germans coming down from their village. As I had come in search of exactly these people, I retraced my steps to the bridge to cross over to the same bank.

Looking back at them, I saw them suddenly jump up and run for cover into a dense olive grove. It needed no clairvoyance to grasp the fact that they had spotted some Germans. Although I had seen none, I started running to get over the bridge the quicker, and ran to hide in the same thick olive grove. The moment I was over the bridge, I saw half a dozen Germans at exactly the point where I had turned back – not a hundred yards off, that is to say. They saw me running and levelled their rifles to fire. There is a watermill a few yards from the bridge, and at that very moment several men, who had come there with sacks to get their corn ground, rushed out and asked me why I was running. The Germans saw them half a moment after they saw me. The Germans must have taken fright, thinking they had fallen into an ambush of guerrillas, for they remained motionless, I don't know how many minutes, with their fingers on the triggers. All I said to the men at the mill was 'Germans!' Within a couple of minutes I was out of sight. When the Germans realized there was no danger, they unfroze, and went to the mill. They arrested everybody there and asked who it was that had been running. Not one of the poor wretches had any idea who I was.

★   ★   ★

I had been searching over two days without finding Mr Tom. They were to the north and a little to west of Phourphoura, high above the village in the foothills of Mount Ida. Manoli Paterakis of Koustoyerako was also there, and east of the hideout and a bit higher up the mountain was a tiny cave – a hole rather – which just had room, but only just, for the operator and his set. It was always dripping with water, rain or no rain, and everything there was permanently soaking – we called the place

'Matthew's Hermitage', for Matthew[1] was the name of the operator, a splendid chap – a man of pure gold, as you might say. His life in the hole was a true martyrdom, for when it wasn't raining, he sat outside his hermitage and got busy killing some of the lice, which seemed to have fallen in love with him. He must have loved them in return, for he only hunted down the big ones, which he put in a Player's cigarette tin. He condemned them to death by starvation and when he had filled the tin (which would not take long) he swore he was going to take it back to England with him as a souvenir of Crete. At night he covered himself up with a groundsheet so that the drops could fall on it from the stalagmites. The noise of their falling made a kind of lullaby. He took it all as a joke with never a word of complaint, and he always made us laugh when we saw him, because his clothes were invariably in tatters and he never washed, not even his face. But one couldn't help being sorry for his woe-begone state.

1 Corporal (later Captain) Matthew White.

The Raid at the Beehive Hut

Next day I left for our hideout in the White Mountains. Reaching my village I found Mr Michali and Mr Aleko there. They were both anxious about my absence, for I had been away some time. I told them all my adventures, and next day, with Yanni Tsangarakis as well, we all left together for the Beehive hut at Gournes. In Vaphé we waited for it to get dark in order to move under cover of night. As we left, dusk was falling. But Mr Aleko had a nail in one boot, his foot was in agony and he could walk no farther. He stayed in a little hut not far beyond Vaphé on a bit of land belonging to Antoni Vandoulakis. Perikles remained with him and the rest of us pushed on. Night had fallen by the time we passed through Tzitziphé, Phré and Pemonia.

Reaching Kyriakosellia, we woke up Levtheri Kouris and had something to drink, and then prepared to climb the mountain. He wanted us to sleep the night in his house, and start the climb just before daybreak. None of us agreed, although he said there was no danger. 'Levtheri,' I said, 'I said that too, one night, and stayed in my village and next morning I was a German prisoner, though luckily I got away.' He insisted no more, so off we set. By day it would have taken rather more than two hours to climb up to the Beehive. But, tired out and half asleep as we were, we took at least double the time. Every now and then we sat down to smoke a cigarette and only the cold kept us all from falling asleep where we sat. The hideout had been moved high, high in the mountains, on the right slope of the Gournes canyon. In spite of our hunger after this long march, we forgot all about food and lay down to sleep. But before sleep could carry us away, Vangeli Vandoulakis went out of the hut for a minute, and, coming in again, said, 'There's a terrible noise of rifle and machine-gun fire down in the villages. I bet they are Germans.'

All of us – Mr Michali, Mr Levtheri,[1] Yanni, Sergeant Alec Tarves the signaller and Levtheris Kouris – got up at once to listen. Dawn was beginning, and we moved a bit farther up to see what was going on. All idea of sleep had vanished. It really was the Germans making a raid on the foothill villages, for soon we could see them plainly in the villages of Karès, Rhamni, Melidoni, and Kyriako-sellia. We watched through binoculars and saw them far below us in the plain on the flat roofs of the houses, in the streets and all over the place. They seemed to be there in large numbers. One of us remained as a lookout, the rest went to boil some tea. Before we could drink it, however, the scout ran to tell us the Germans had taken the path up our mountain; they must have had some information, for they were coming straight up.

We went out and watched them, and they were soon exactly opposite on the other side of the hollow, heading direct for our first Beehive lair at Gournes.[2] There were about sixty of them with three or four civilian guides. A few minutes later we heard a great noise down in the gorge. One of us went forward to see what was happening,

1 Captain, later Major, Arthur Reade (of whom more later) accompanied Xan Fielding on his return to the island. Ever since his arrival, he had been living in and operating from the Beehive, in co-operation with the inhabitants of the local foothill villages.
2 We had abandoned it shortly before.

and what should he see! Still more Germans, at least twice the amount of the first party. We let them all advance deeper along the gorge and made our plans at high speed. 'The Germans are obviously after us,' we said. 'Everyone must scatter and hide where he can, and after the danger is past we will meet again in accordance with the situation.' We then dispersed in all directions. Vangeli Vandoulakis was to remain with Mr Levtheri, the newly arrived officer, as he couldn't move fast, to hide somewhere nearby. Mr Michali and Yanni Tsangarakis would find a refuge higher up the mountain, and I was to climb with Little Aleko to the other side of the watershed and find somewhere to hide there. We thought that if the Germans were heading for Gournes, they would see that we were there two days ago and begin a search. The snow higher up was already deep, so they would be sure to come in our direction, as it was clothed by a cypress forest.

There was not a second to lose. We had no time to hide the things, so we left them piled up in the hut. If (but we didn't think they would) they returned by that path, they would find everything. For this reason we had to hide as widely scattered as possible.

I took Little Aleko and we ran. We circled the northern side, hoping to avoid the snow as our footprints might give us away. We heard rifle-fire below, and looking down, saw more Germans coming up the mountain from many points. I told Little Aleko we ought to cross to the opposite peak to get out of the German cordon. He didn't want to and hid himself under a precipice, while I pushed on to the opposite peak which a thick mist was beginning to cover up. When I reached it so much mist had fallen that I couldn't see where I was. At that moment I heard a noise of firing and explosion in the direction of our hideout, as if all Hell had been released. I thought at once that they had met some of our party and that they were shooting at each other. But what could we do – six men against at least two hundred Germans? The firing went on for five minutes, then stopped. I remained in the same place a long time, filled with anxiety about the fate of the others. The thick mist hid everything and I did not dare to move for fear of falling on top of the Germans, or over a precipice. I decided to go down and head for Kyriakosellia and find out what had happened. I took the downward slope in the mist, and almost reached the foothills. But there were Germans there too. Luckily I heard and saw them in time.

I climbed up again, and descended towards the village of Kampos, but on the way down I heard rifle-fire in the village and saw that the Germans were there as well.

I wondered what to do. Had those cuckolds captured everybody? I'll find somewhere to hide, I thought, and went up the mountain again. Meanwhile, dusk had begun to fall. I had had no sleep the previous night and nothing to eat for twenty-four hours. But what worried me was: what had happened to the others[1] and how could I escape?

I headed downhill yet again, making a wide circuit. Night had fallen when I reached a foothill village between Drakona and Kampos. When I was a hundred yards from the first houses, I heard running footsteps coming my way, and, at the same second, the whole village was lit up with electric torches. I realized Germans were there also, and the footsteps were those of villagers escaping to hide. So I ran uphill again in the dark saying to myself that, to be on the safe side, I must expect everyone to be a German. I must be seen by nobody. I climbed a height half an hour above the village and went round the farther

---

1 Arthur Reade, Yanni and I hid in a thick cypress tree, and over a hundred Germans passed underneath. Later when the mist and snow started we went farther uphill, lay up in a hole, and next day headed for Kampos. [PLF]

flank of the hill. Suddenly I saw the mountainside opposite ablaze with lights. I didn't know what it was at first and was very frightened, but when I reached the top of the hill I saw they were searchlights.

I climbed halfway down an overhanging precipice without realizing it and almost fell down the rest. I wore myself out all night trying to get away from that accursed precipice. Climbing down, utterly exhausted, I flung myself full length at the bottom to sleep a little, betide what may. I slept a little while and was woken by rain falling on my face, so I pulled the hood of my cape farther down over my head and pressed closer into the side of the rock. Waking up again a little later, I felt a weight on top of me, but thought it was an illusion caused by my exhaustion. I opened my eyes. Day had broken, and what did I see? The whole world was white with snow, which had also completely buried me. I got up and beat it off and then headed downwards.

The snow line was now right down on the plain. I found a vineyard with a hut, so I went inside, fell down flat and slept till the afternoon. Waking up, I made a plan. I would go down into Canea[1] and catch a bus. Having an identity card with a false name I had nothing to fear if they questioned me. I found a suitable place, free of snow, on the steep slope, and hid my binoculars and sub-machine-gun there taking good note of the place, in order to find it again easily. Then I took the Drakona pathway, and, meeting a shepherd outside the village, got into conversation. I told him I was from Alikampo in Apokoronas and that I had had some sheep stolen the night before which I was trying to find. Unfortunately the snow had started, putting a stop to my quest. I told him a thousand and two lies, asked him the news and

[1] The capital of Crete, and the nearest big town to this range of mountains.

what the Germans had been after in the village over there last night (meaning the last village I had tried to enter the night before, at dusk). He told me they had made a great search, and that he had heard they had found some guns; the same had happened at Kampos and the Germans had arrested all the men they found in the village. The shepherd had some good wine, which he gave me to drink, and he also gave me a few olives and lupin-seeds. It was the second day without food, and my appetite was ravenous. I greeted him and left. Not having time enough to go even a third of the way to Canea, I crawled into a cave, hid myself well and slept till dawn. The moment day broke I went down to the main Suda-Canea road. What do I want to go to Canea for now? I asked myself. Let's save time and see what happened to the others. In Suda I sat for a while in a coffee-shop and had just enough money with me to buy half an *oka* of oranges. Then I continued my way, reaching Tsitsiphé in the afternoon. I headed for the place called Pateloures, where we had left Mr Aleko.[1] I found him there and told him all our troubles, and he told me the rest were all safe. The Germans had gone to our first hideout at Gournes, but the civilian guides they had taken by force were from Karès. These men who, it seems, knew the secret, must have thought we were still there, for they took the Germans to the first cheese hut near the chapel of St Paul. The path to the hut we were *really* in had been beaten flat through the snow with our footprints, but the Germans didn't put two and two together. They waded up to their ears to our first hut, and surrounded it on all sides. Then, firing a few mortar-bombs, they opened up with rifles and tommy-guns and charged. All they got was a pile of stones. This was the noise I heard when I thought they had clashed

1 Xan Fielding.

with our people. Then the mist enveloped them too and their commanders at the Khan of Babali fired signal flares, ordering them to leave the mountains.

We owed the safety of our gear, perhaps our lives, to the mist, as otherwise they would have found our station.

When the Germans had abandoned the mountain and our people – Mr Michali and the rest – had realized what had happened, they returned to the lair and then settled in a cave between Kyriakosellia and Kampos, where a few days later Mr Aleko and I joined them.

Here Mr Michali, Mr Aleko, Vangeli Vandoulakis and I took a beautiful photograph. Mr Aleko was hunting down lice in his lowered breeches, and refused to change position. So I had one of him with his trousers down. We also took one of Captain Reade, 'Levtheri' that is. I don't want to let slip this opportunity of putting down some anecdotes about Mr Levtheri.

He was a very tall, red-haired man. He had let his beard and whiskers grow to look like a Cretan, and each hair of his beard and whiskers grew separate from the others, which gave him the appearance of a porcupine. You could tell he was an Englishman from a mile away, especially as he found the greatest difficulty in getting about over rocky country. He could drink more than anyone I have ever seen in the whole of my life; but without getting drunk. He liked to have a drink when he woke up during the night and, if possible, with company. At such times he would flash his torch round the hut or the cave to see if anyone was awake, and signal to them to get up and come and join him. But he never wanted to disturb anyone. He had better manners and feelings than anyone I have ever met in spite of the short time I stayed with him and the few times I saw him, for I was usually away on the roads. On one occasion the Cretans told him they could not drink without a *mézé*. He asked what *mézé* was needed, and nearly every day after that he provided a sheep. But he did not know how to roast *kebabs*, and he would take a great bit of meat and hold it out to the flames, thus cooking one side which he would then eat, holding the rest to the fire again to roast. This made us all laugh, and we showed him how to cook meat on a spit. I was an expert at *kebabs*, and when I was there, I would be his cook.

Something happened while I was away, about which I heard from the other boys, and which is worth recording.

He had ordered a sheep to be sent up from Karès. They sent it up by a boy, saying that his father wanted it to be a present. But our people in the hut said they wanted to pay for it, and gave the boy about 80,000 drachmas. One moment when they were all out of the hut, the boy remained alone inside. He saw Mr Levtheri's leather belt there, and took ten gold sovereigns out of it. When they saw, later on, that the sovereigns were missing and that the boy had gone, they realized he had stolen them. Early next morning one of them got ready, without saying a word to Mr Levtheri, to go down to Karès to get the sovereigns back, because everybody was ashamed about this theft. But before he left, who should arrive but the boy's father. He had the ten sovereigns in his hand and he addressed Mr Levtheri, who knew Greek well, saying: 'Mr Levtheri, I sent you the sheep as a gift. I can't accept all this money you gave my boy in payment. Please take them back.' And he gave Mr Levtheri the money. But Mr Levtheri said: 'I gave them to him as a gift so please accept them as we accepted yours.'

He kept the money after some demur and thanked Mr Levtheri. His son had hidden the 80,000 drachmas, but given his father the sovereigns, not knowing what kind of money they were. Our people asked Mr Levtheri, as soon as the old man had left, why he hadn't told him that his son had stolen the sovereigns. 'It wouldn't have been right,' he said, 'to insult that good old man by saying that his son was a thief.' This old man from Karès often came up to our refuge after that, bringing honey and walnuts and *tzikoudia* and wine and sheep and other things in order to pay back the great gift he had received.

Mr Levtheri still had with him the hollow rubber lifebelts they had used for the landing near Koustoyerako, which he now used as containers for wine and *raki*. He never wanted them to be empty although he constantly spent his time emptying them.

All these things happened to Mr Levtheri while he was hiding high up in the White Mountains, in the snow and bitter cold.

As the other English officers told us, Mr Reade was one of the most distinguished barristers of London. He had been a personal friend of Elevtherios Venizelos and he loved him deeply. He had particularly wanted to visit Crete to become acquainted with his actual fatherland; and he had adopted the cover name of Levtheri for Venizelos's sake. Later he asked to be taken to the summit of the White Mountains, which has been named after Venizelos, and, in general, he was passionately eager to learn all he could of the personal life of Venizelos and collect anecdotes of his struggles up in the mountains. But alas, Headquarters in Cairo did not leave him long in Crete, and more was the pity.[1]

[PLF]

---

1 Arthur Reade's departure from Crete was a very great loss to us all.

Escape

A fugitive from justice was also hiding in our new cave. He was called Stelios Koyiannis, of Kampoi, and we used him sometimes as a lookout, and sometimes for bringing supplies. Later he was used for transporting arms and the like.

January was almost out when Mr Aleko took me with him to Priné, to see Colonal Tsiphakis. We spent two days at my village on the way back, because Mr Aleko wanted to examine the explosives stored in the Khainóspilio. While we were together in the cave I made the suggestion that I should go to Cairo for a little while, as my running had really exhausted me through and through. After all, lots of others went there on much flimsier pretexts than mine, so why not me, I thought.

'But, George, what will you do in Cairo?' Mr Aleko asked.

'I don't know, Mr Aleko. What does everybody else do who goes there?'

'But don't you know that they'll probably grab you for the Greek army?'

'But I *am* a Greek, Mr Aleko.'

'Yes, but it's a pity, after you've been with us in the Service such a long time, suddenly to change over to the army.'

'Well . . . I don't know,' I said. 'You fix it up as you think best.'

'All right, George, I'll think it over and let you know.'

We left the Khaïnides' cave and went to Uncle Petraka's house. In the afternoon Mr Aleko called me, and we went outside for a moment.

'George,' he said, 'I've thought about it, and I'll send you down.[1] You are quite right. You must rest for a bit, you've had a very tough time.'

I thanked him, we went indoors, and next day we left for our hide-out. It had moved yet again, to a little hole close to Kampoi, that was very hard to find. It opened into a real subterranean room inside the rock. Stelios Koyiannis had known of it and taken Mr Michali and Mr Levtheri there. It was now the beginning of February 1943. Next day Mr Aleko sent me to the Bridge of Babali to bring back a stranger to our cave who would be arriving from Canea by motor-car. Perhaps, he said, he might turn up with one of our people, perhaps alone, for which reason I was to be sitting on the trunk of a fallen olive tree, so that he could pick me out. He was to approach me and say: 'Shall we go?'

He also told me, laughing, that I was to bear in mind that he was a communist. 'Don't worry,' I said, and set off. I went and waited for him, and he arrived with (I think) Perikles Vandoulakis. I took him over and we left at once, taking the path through Pemonia. It was only when we were near Kyriakosellia that he opened his mouth: 'Are we going far?' he asked. 'Almost two hours on foot,' I said. Then he asked me what sort of a person Mr Aleko was. I said he was an Englishman, and began to describe his height, features, complexion, age, and so on. He asked me nothing else. We reached the lair and I helped him down the hole, which was rather difficult, as the entrance was so narrow. Inside it was all stalactites and water.

1 To Africa, that is.

'Greeting, Mr Niko,' Mr Aleko said as soon as he saw him. And then, with a laugh, 'Behold our house!' I went out and left them to talk. It was night and I soon fell asleep. As soon as day broke, I got up and went to the place above Drakona where I had hidden my binoculars and tommy-gun a few days before, and brought them back to the lair. The communist had left. I stayed a day there and the next was Saturday night. We had a *glendi*[1] in the cave, and what a *glendi!* We drank lots of *tsikoudia* and red wine and sang '*Pote tha kamei xesteria?*'[2] – 'When will the sky be clear?' – they had all learnt it and liked singing it whenever they could. The dawn of the sixth of February 1943 broke. I greeted them all and left. The secret vessel, which would take me back to Africa with it, was due in a few days. Mr Michali gave me a whole bundle of maps to take to Colonel Tsiphakis at Priné, and I was to wait for him at Yerakari, as he would be arriving there a bit later. I went through my village to see my family, because I didn't know when I would get back. I told nobody I was leaving. I left Mr Aleko to let them know later. I set out for Priné. A German sentry at the guard post stopped me at the Kouphi turning of the Argyroupolis-Archontiki road. He whistled and shouted '*Komm!*' '*Kalimera*,[3] *kamerad!*' I said. '*Kalimera,*' he said. '*Gut Papier?*' '*Ja kamerad, gut papier,*' I said, showing him my card. He said '*Gut,*' almost without looking at it and gave it back. It was the first time I'd ever been asked for my papers. I had all the maps hidden inside my tall Cretan boots, but didn't feel anxious.

I got to Priné and gave them to Colonel Tsiphakis straight away. He said he had heard I'd been captured and

1 A party.
2 An old revolutionary song against the Turks, dating from early in the last century.
3 Good-day.

killed when the Germans made the Beehive raid. So I told him the tale briefly. He said that Mr Aleko had remarked of me, laughing: 'They'll get the lot of us, but not that cuckold.'[1] Colonel Tsiphakis gave me several packets of papers for Mr Michali. I think they were reports for the Greek Government in Cairo.

I reached Yerakari next day, and waited for Mr Michali, who arrived next morning. He had Vangeli and Perikles Vandoulakis with him, also Doctor Paizis from Canea, Father John Alevizakis of Alones, and Siphi the RAF signaller, whose plane had been shot down over Herakleion some months before. All of them, except Mr Michali, were leaving for Cairo, but he was to accompany us to the shore. We all left next day for Apodoulou. Here there was a general muster of everybody who was leaving for Africa. Petrakoyeorgis was there with his guerrillas, his daughters,[2] his fifteen-year-old son Herakles and his brother the doctor. From Herakleion had come Apostolos Katechakis, the son of General Katechakis, and Mr Aristides Kastrinoyannis. We all set off in the direction of the coast. By day, we could move through the mountains as far as the village of Platanos. But beyond that we could only march by night, lest anyone should see us crossing the Messara plain. We had to approach and cross the plain and hide on the coastal mountains the other side, all in one night. So, as soon as night fell, we left Platanos, passed through Grigoria and Margarikari, and hid in a cave there somewhere between Kysos and Galia. At suitable points

1 In this case, a term of endearment.
2 One of these girls, Tassoula, was the heroine of the great abduction case five years ago. She was kidnapped and carried away to the top of Mount Ida and married in haste there in a cave by my god-brother from Anoyeia, Kosta Kephaloyiánnis, an affair which fiddled the foreign newspapers. As the bride's family was Venizelist and the bridegroom's royalist, it brought the whole island to the brink of civil war. [PLF]

some distance from the cave, two *andartes*[1] of Petrakoyeorgis mounted guard among the bushes.

Next day, while we were lying up and waiting for
sunset, an armed man appeared on a height a little way
off. The guerrillas from our party crept up to him, covered
him with their guns, and brought him a prisoner to our
cave. He was called George Savakis, from one of the
Messara villages. There was nothing for it but to take him
with us. We told him so and that it was useless to protest.
But he offered no resistance. Night fell, and, immediately
after the curfew hour of 8 p.m., we moved off in pitch
darkness to get across the plain. We reached Kapariana.
Moires, where a large German garrison was stationed, was
just next door. We approached the main road through a
little olive wood. When we saw it was all clear, we crossed
into the plain three at a time. Soon we reached the Geros
river which runs right across the plain. It was full of water
at this time of the year and there was no way across. One
of Mr Tom's best messengers, Manoliò Disbirakis, knew
it well, and led us to the shallowest part where we all
waded in up to our waists.

We followed no paths, but marched across the ploughed
fields straight to our destination. We were wet through
and our feet became so loaded with mud we could hardly
lift them. Passing Vasiliki Anoyia, we started up the low
mountain range that runs along the whole of the southern
edge of the Nome of Herakleion, and separates it from
the sea. As dawn broke, half an hour beyond the village,
we reached the winter pastures belonging to one of
Petrakoyeorgis's guerrillas called Dionysios from the village of Zaro. There was a little hill here covered with
large rocks and hollowed by deep caves and rifts; and here
we lay up. Dionysios slaughtered a couple of wethers, so

---

1 Guerrilla fighters.

we lit fires and put them on spits and roasted them. Sentries were put out, and the rest of us slept through most of the day.

When night fell, we were on the march again, and at dawn we were at the deserted village of Kapetanianà. This region including the whole south coast of the nome, had been emptied by the Germans. Neither man nor beast was allowed to move there without a special pass. We felt much safer in this empty waste, as there was not a soul there to see us. A patrol was sent into the village to see if there were any Germans there. It was quite empty. So, entering the empty village, we waited for dawn. We went into a few of the houses and, putting out sentries, lay down on the bare boards. But, in a second, we all leapt up in affright – we were being attacked by millions of fleas. It was impossible to stay there, so we left, shaking our clothes and our feet to get rid of them. Luckily day soon broke, and on we pushed. Suddenly, as it grew light, a precious ally rose up before us – a dense mist. All morning we advanced step by step, and in the early afternoon we reached the village of Treis Ekklesies.[1] There was a German guard post there consisting of three men. It was our plan to go down as night fell, cut their telephone wires and attack, taking them to Cairo as prisoners. When it began to get dark, and we could no longer be seen, we came out of the hiding-places from which we had been watching the post all afternoon, and scrambled down the mountainside towards the sea. We found some more caves; this was our last halt. We met some friendly shepherds and asked for information about the German post, but as soon as they heard of the plan, they begged Mr Tom, whom they knew from previous landings they had helped him with, that the Germans should be left unmolested, because

1 Three Churches.

it was not worth the odd five hundred of their goats and sheep that the Germans would commandeer afterwards as a reprisal. The action would have been in their pastures, and as it was an empty and forbidden area, they had only been allowed there after endless efforts to obtain the permission from the Germans. All the guilt would have fallen on them, and all their flocks would have been destroyed, and they would either have had to leave with the ship, or take to the hills that night.

Mr Tom saw that the shepherds were in the right, and that they would help in the future as they had done in the past; so the plan was changed and the Germans were left alone. He told the shepherds to guide us to somewhere where the waters were deep and without rocks. They took us to a suitable place, although it was no more than half an hour's distance from the German post.

We all waited on the mountainside above the sea, and Mr Tom, with our operator the airman Siphi, went down to the shore to give the signals. I went too to keep him company.

The signalling began.

About eleven o'clock we heard a noise like an aeroplane far out to sea. In half an hour's time the ship, like a dark monster, began to appear. It didn't come in very close, but turned eastwards, withdrew again and disappeared. 'Why did it go?' I asked Siphi. 'I don't know, George,' he said. Everyone was asking the same question. We went on signalling. After a long time, the sound could be heard once more, and the vessel reappeared. 'Ask them why they left,' I asked Siphi. 'It must come!' He flashed signals thick and fast with his torch. In a moment the ship began flashing signals back – a thing which was forbidden lest the Germans should see it from their post. Her signals said the sea was too rough to put the boats out. But the wind was north, and the coast was on the south, and there was no sea – except perhaps outside the cove, and this we signalled. She came in closer, and the boats were launched.[1] First came one boat, rowed by two sailors, bringing the end of a cable which was warped round a rock. They left another rope on which we were to haul as soon as they shouted from the ship. Mr Tom got into the first boat, and went back to the ship with them. When all on board was ready, they shouted to us and we began hauling, which brought two boats to the shore. The men got in one by one till they were full, and they were hauled back to the ship by yet another rope. This was done to save time, as oars would have taken much longer. When about thirty people were on board, the last boat came. In it were two Cretans coming from Cairo in the Service. It was pitch-dark, and I couldn't see who they were, but I heard them talking and one voice sounded very familiar. As I learnt afterwards, it was Pavlos Vernadakis whom Colonel Papadakis had taken with him in August last year; the other was Niko Lambethakis from Canea.

The two sailors in the dinghy were shouting for the last people to get on board. I was the only one left. Mr Michali was standing nearby, and I said to him, 'Mr Michali, I'm beginning to regret that I asked to leave.' 'Come on, George,' he said, 'jump in'; and gave me a shove on the back; and there I was in the boat. Mr Michali was staying on, so he threw us the rope, the cable was untied, the engines went faster, and the ship began turning. We were hauled alongside quicker and quicker, then we climbed up the rope-ladder, and the boat was hoisted on board. She had now turned about, and was sailing full steam ahead.

It was on the night of the fourteenth/fifteenth February

1 The Fairmile was commanded by Commander John Campbell, DSO, RN, who came ashore to conduct the evacuation. [PLF]

1943 at about four in the morning that we left enslaved Crete behind us and sailed away to the free lands of the Middle East. It was the first time in my life I had ever set foot in a boat or a ship. When I got on board I was led down to the hold. We threw ourselves into a great bout of eating and drinking, as we had had practically nothing for two days. Siphi, the airman who had come with us, turned himself into a regular waiter, constantly bringing us all we could wish for, and spreading it on the two tables, round which everyone was now seated on benches, eating and drinking away. 'What shall I bring you, George?' he said as soon as he spotted me. 'We're in England now. There's plenty to eat.' 'Bring me,' I said, 'something of everything and lots of it,' and white bread, tins of all kinds of different food, tea, rum and cigarettes were piled on the table. I ate and drank all I could hold.

The ship shook a great deal, and it looked as though we were going to have rough weather, and many of the passengers started throwing up all the food they had just eaten. I remained motionless in my place, to keep everything still inside me, hoping not to vomit like the rest. But I couldn't hold out for long, and suddenly exploded too.

We were in a sorry state for about two hours. Then I discovered a good way to counter the evil. They had brought army greatcoats for us on the ship, so I chose one that covered me from top to toe, put it on, and lay flat on my face on the deck. Day had broken and the sea had risen quite a lot; I lay there motionless in the same position more than ten hours. In vain they had come and given me a kick to send me below, two suspicious aeroplanes having been sighted, and the alarm given. The alarm was soon over. The planes were flying very high, and they were soon lost in the sky. It was not even possible to make out their nationality.

The day passed, night came on, and, between ten and eleven o'clock, we reached a harbour full of ships, both sunken and afloat. It was Mersah Matruh. The ship dropped anchor and we went ashore.

All were dizzy and our stomachs were worn out. On the quay, waiting to bid us welcome and take us under his wing, stood Mr Smith-Hughes. We sat down a bit to recover. Food was waiting ready for us, and they brought us a meal. Each one ate according to his powers, then we climbed into the two trucks that Mr Smith-Hughes had brought for us.

'Michali' (Patrick Leigh Fermor) and Vardi Paterakis (Manoli's youngest brother) in the gorge of Samaria a few years after the war

'O Tom' (Tom Dunbabin) seated on the left with moustache and beret and hands on knees, next to him on his left is 'Yanni' (Jack Smith-Hughes). Behind Tom slightly to his right is Manoli Paterakis and next to him with floppy hair and moustache is 'Pavlo' (Dick Barnes). The fact that Tom, Jack and Dick are all in uniform means that the Germans had already withdrawn to the Canea perimeter

Kyria Eléni, mother of the Paterakis brothers of Koustoyérako

'Kyria Pappadia', wife of Father John of Alones

Giorgios Doundoulakis who was Head of the Intelligence network in Herakleion and 'Michali' (Patrick Leigh Fermor) in Anoyeia, 1943

'Michalaki' (Ralph Stockbridge) in the centre with Levtheri Kalitsounakis, the nephew of Colonel Papadakis on the far right

The caique Porcupine which was used for infiltrating agents from Mersa Matruh

In the mountains above the Omalo and the Rotten Cliffs

Father John Alevizakis, parish priest of Alones

Father John on his donkey setting out for Argyroupolis

Nikoli Alevizakis of Alones
playing the lyre

Manoli Paterakis in his goatfold
after the war

Uncle George Robolas of Priné

Aleko Kokonas, schoolmaster of
Yerakari, and his wife Kyria Maria

Two old mountaineers of the Nome of Retimo

George Psychoundakis in later years

PART 3
Flight into Egypt

To Alexandria and Cairo

We set off eastwards, leaving Mersah Matruh behind us, of which, after all those bombardments, only the name remained. Arriving at Alexandria before midday, we entered the city in two army lorries closed on all sides with tarpaulin to prevent strange eyes from seeing us. So eager were we all to see the town that, in spite of strict orders not to show ourselves, several of my fellow-islanders cut huge holes in the awning with their daggers, and stuck out their heads. They leant half out of the vehicle, some even right out, standing there plain for all to see with their bandoliers and their silver-studded Mannlicher guns, their long silver-sheathed daggers, their purple sashes and high Cretan boots, their brows bound with black-fringed turbans. People must have looked at them with much surprise. They drove us straight to an English camp.

We were put into two barrack-rooms and given whatever we needed: blankets, towels, soap, plates, knives, forks and spoons – and led off to the washhouse where we all had the baths we so sorely needed. Then we went in to a meal. The cooks had orders to give us all the food we wanted.

On the third day we handed everything back, climbed into two more trucks (with orders this time not to tear the tarpaulin)[1] and left Alexandria without even a glimpse

1 A most necessary precaution against German and Italian espionage in Egypt.

of it, as nobody had been allowed out during our two days' stay. The road ran straight across a desert. The only thing we saw all day was an occasional gang of workmen clearing the sand off the highway, and, now and then, military camps that were the size of towns. At midday we stopped for a meal at a canteen somewhere in the middle of the desert. Reaching Cairo, we drove through the outskirts of the town to a suburb called Maadi, where we got out at a large military camp. After seeing the health authorities, we were taken one by one into a room where we gave up our arms. All the guns, pistols and daggers were handed over, and in the next we were medically overhauled. Then they asked us to hand over any documents we possessed bearing an official seal, also any newspapers, leaflets or orders distributed by the Occupation we might have about us. I went last, and when they saw I hadn't as much as a penknife on me, they asked where I had left my firearms. My answer was laconic: '*Where they are needed.*' Then they assembled us and told us not to worry about anything. We were to stay there several days till they knew where we were all to be fixed up. Everybody began asking for their guns and knives back but the answer was that they were not needed now – they would be looked after carefully and nothing would be lost. Our barrack-room had barbed wire all round, and land mines were planted six feet deep outside that. Our leaders were taken somewhere else and were with us no longer.

When we woke up next day we realized that we were in a camp full of German and Italian prisoners-of-war. This made a very bad impression on everyone and they began cursing the English. They greatly overdid it, for the English had several times told us not to misunderstand them for having billeted us there, as it was important for many reasons for us to remain hidden for several days, and this was the safest place for that purpose. But all their words were in vain, as when they left everyone broke out anew in a thousand complaints. The cuckolds, bringing us into a prison-camp! Taking our weapons away! Another declared that, in his own house, he wouldn't touch the kind of food they gave us even if he was dying of starvation, so there . . .

None of this worried me. I ate, drank and slept. The first morning we were there, the Italian prisoners in the next barrack-room wondered who we were, and one of them plucked up courage to ask us. At that moment the sentry in his tower saw and heard the Italians, rang his bell, and some police came along and fetched them one or two blows; so they didn't ask us again.

On the second day came an elderly English captain who spoke Greek well.

'*Yassas, paidia*,'[1] he said to us.

'Welcome to the Captain,' we all answered.

'Well . . . how are you all getting on?'

'Very well, sir.'

'Is the food all right for you? Do you get enough? Perhaps not quite enough bread? Do they give you any cigarettes?'

'We get cigarettes,' we said, 'but we'd like some more.'

'All right,' he said, 'and I expect you'd like something to drink.'

He left and in a little while came back with a truck-load of bottles of wine and cigarettes. He also brought glasses and bottles of beer, and started pouring out for all of us, and gave us plenty of cigarettes. Next day he returned with a fresh supply of everything. 'There's a good man,' we said among ourselves. But it almost seemed as if we'd put the Evil Eye on him, for he didn't come back next day.

[1] 'Greetings, boys.'

We asked a lieutenant who used to visit us what had become of him, and he said he was mad. At this we all took offence and nobody believed it for a moment.

The day after – our seventh in the camp – the elderly captain turned up once more, again bringing us lots of wine and cigarettes. He apologized for neglecting us the last two days, but he said his cat had been ill, and refusing all food; so he had had to take her to the doctor, and had been very upset.

Try as we might, we couldn't help laughing. We all burst out into helpless giggles. Trying to make up for this rudeness, one of them asked if the cat were better now. The Captain thanked him and said she had quite recovered.

All through that day we were taken one by one to a private office with a huge map of Crete on the wall, and asked quantities of questions. First they asked everyone what he was called, where he was from in Crete, and which regions he knew; which places the Germans were in and how many; which of these regions had plateaux, and how broad and long they were; what villages lay close by, where German garrisons were and of what strength. 'What beaches do you really know well, how many German posts are in the neighbourhood, what is their strength, what are the places called? What points do you know where ships or submarines could approach in secret? Is the water deep and calm?' You had to point out every detail on a map which covered the whole of one wall of the room.

Next day we were put into trucks once again. A Greek officer came too, also the English Captain from the Cretan office,[1] and we drove off to the Greek transit camp in Cairo.

This was outside Cairo at Mina Camp, close to the

1 The Cretan section of the Subversive Operations Executive, SOE, in Rustom Buildings, Sharia Kasr-el-Aini, Cairo.

pyramids. Petrakoyeorgis came with us, and as soon as we had got out, he assembled us without letting any of the Greek soldiers get near. Petrakoyeorgis, addressing us, said that all the soldiers would be longing to know where we came from and how and when and so forth. 'I need hardly tell you,' he said, 'that it is essential you should keep all that secret for security reasons.' Before he had even finished his speech, one of his *pallikaria* (who, like most of them had a passion to be addressed by the title of *Kapetanio*), wandered up to some soldiers. I watched him, wondering what he was up to and then heard him saying to the soldiers, 'Do you see that man in the middle there, talking? He's our leader, Petrakoyeorgis. We are guerrilla warriors, and we have just left Crete. We –' At this point I made him shut up by stamping on his foot; his leader was still repeating his admonition which had now ceased to be of any use to anyone. When he had finished, the English Captain called out the name Georgios Psychoundakis, and took me to the Greek recruiting office. Here they took all my particulars, and gave me a uniform. I got into his car with him, and off we went. He didn't let me sit on the seat with the Cretan clothes I was still wearing, but asked me to huddle on the floor to avoid being seen through the window. We drove through the whole city of Cairo like this till at last we reached another little town on the other side, called Heliopolis. We pulled up outside a villa at the end of the street called Sharia Asmoun. He got out first and looked all round him. When he saw nobody was about, he told me to get out and run into the house as quickly as possible. But inside there were servants and he didn't want these to see me either, so he went in first and sent them off to do something, then called for me and put me into a bedroom. Showing me the bathroom, he told me to have a bath and get into uniform and then join him in the hall.

When I was ready, he told me not to go out until the afternoon, when he would have brought me an identity card. This captain was called Dionysios – Denis Ciclitira, the same one whom we had later on in the Cretan mountains. There was another chap of ours there called Elias Milas from Herakleion, a sergeant in the Greek Army. His duty was to take care of the house, and look after the men who came there and do the shopping and so on. All the discarded civilian clothes were put by for other people when they were sent to operate in the same regions.

I got my identity card that afternoon and was free to go wherever I wanted. Vangeli Vandoulakis asked me if I felt like going into Cairo with him. That evening others of our people turned up. Most of them had arrived at the house a little earlier than me. Amongst others were Doctor Païzis and Petrakoyeorgis's brother, the doctor, the two Vandoulakises, Perikles and Vangeli, and the Paradeisianos brothers, Kosta and Yanni; also Mr Aristeides Kastrinoyannis, Apostolos Katechakis and some others, all belonging to the same evacuation party. But most of them left in a few days' time, and I was alone in the villa.

The Beauties of Cairo

The second day there, Captain Stockbridge – 'Michalaki' – asked me to go and see him. Mr Michalaki, as we used to call him when he was wireless operator there, had been back from Crete some time. Before that, we had lived together for eight months, and, as soon as he had learnt that I had come to Cairo, he had telephoned Captain Ciclitira to send me in to Cairo to meet him at the Café–Bar Trianon.

I went there with Vangeli Vandoulakis, and sat down to wait. The proprietor of the Trianon was a Cretan from Retimo by the name of Stelios Papadakis. You could meet any Cretan you liked there, from private soldier to general. Soon Mr Stockbridge turned up with Levtheri Kalitsounakis, Colonel Papadakis's nephew, whom he had taken with him when he left Crete in August 1942. We drank coffee, and I told them all my news from Crete, and asked for theirs. Levtheri told me all that had happened to him since he left with his uncle. This was during the German advance when the fall of Alexandria was dreaded, so the submarine *Papanikolis* had put them ashore at Haifa, in Palestine. The journey took them a week, under water by day, and on the surface by night. Since Haifa, Levtheri had not seen his uncle again. He had taken up his duties as a lieutenant-colonel and showed not the faintest sign of interest in what had become of his nephew, who had served him so faithfully up in the Cretan mountains, constantly carrying his children and his property on his back when the Germans were after them.

Fortunately, he said, he had been sent to the battalion of a very good officer, Christopher Stavroulakis, and all had gone well. Finally he met Mr Stockbridge, who took him on, getting him seconded from the Greek Army. I listened with interest, as who knew better than me what he had gone through with his uncle. Colonel Papadakis ought to have treated him as his own son – in Crete he used to call him, 'My child Levtheri.'

We had a few glasses there, and then got up to wander about and amuse ourselves till midday. With us was another English officer, Captain John Stanley, who couldn't speak a word of Greek. We took a taxi and went to the Zoo, as they were determined to show me all that was beautiful or strange in Cairo. We went all round the Zoo, and gazed and laughed at all the different kinds of animals there. They said it used to be one of the most famous zoos in the world before the war, but had now lost ground. These animals, both wild and tame, made a deep impression on me.

We ended up at a restaurant inside the Zoo on the banks of a lake with low mountains made of artificial rock and covered with tall trees and many-coloured flowers. The trees themselves seemed quite covered with flowers, and up in the branches flew many kinds of birds, so that the air was full of their singing. The lake was full of ducks and geese and other birds which played in the water without stopping, all quacking, drinking and singing in their own style. At that hour I could almost have deemed that I was in the middle of Paradise.

We ordered food, which was not slow in coming. Everything glittered with cleanliness; we ate with a growing appetite, and drank lots of beer. Whenever we wanted anything, we called a waiter, and there was always one standing nearby. '*Esma, tala hena!*' we cried.

First we had some soup, then some meat, and then Mr Stockbridge asked what pudding we would like, or if we would like some fruit. Each one began to say what he wanted. I said I would eat first and then think.

'Do you still want to go on eating, George?' Mr Stockbridge asked me.

'Indeed I do, Mr Michalaki,' I said.

So they called the waiter and I had a few fried eggs. When I'd finished, I asked: 'What else is there to eat, Mr Michalaki?' (I wanted to tease him and remind him of something in Crete).

'Holy Virgin!' he exclaimed. 'Can you *really* eat some more?'

'Don't forget I've just come from Crete, Mr Michalaki – don't you remember the Pyróvolo cave near Kallikrati? You can't have forgotten the grass and the snails we ate without any bread, and the saddles[1] of the snails all broken up among the grass?'

'No,' he said, 'I don't think I can ever forget that.'

'Well, I've just come from there, and food is the first thing I'm after . . .'

'All right, George, you eat as much as you want.'

'Well, let them bring the pudding now, and then I'll start all over again.'

He translated all this to Mr John,[2] who burst out laughing and went on a long time.

We left our table at last, and after going all round the garden again, returned to the Trianon.

We talked of Crete the whole time, about our villages and our friends and about the Germans. It was almost sunset, and time to part. It was hard for me to find the way home, without knowing where the tram left from,

1 Shells.
2 John Stanley.

so Levtheri came with me to put me on it. It was my first day out! I knew just where to get out in Heliopolis, and all went well. I went to sleep feeling very happy.

I went into Cairo every day, often meeting Levtheri, and going about the town and the suburbs. I wanted to see every single thing. Cairo had many strange and beautiful places, and, to me, all seemed strange and beautiful. I very much liked the gardens of Cairo, and the Nile with all its boats and all the places of amusement on its banks.

After the Zoo, the Gardens on the Gezirah were the most beautiful. They covered a vast expanse, all divided up. There was grass everywhere – fat short grass that looked like a green velvet carpet. There were lots of people there every day – some for fun, others to watch, and others to pass the time playing various games. One part of it, shut off from the rest, had some small artificial mountains with great caves inside and all shaded with different kinds of trees and flowers. Various staircases and pathways led through flowers and shrubs to the top of these hills. In the caves to left and right were little tanks with crystal-clear glass fronts, and inside, all kinds of different fishes. They said there was every sort there that swims in the Mediterranean. The rest of the garden is all flowers and high, towering trees, pines and date-palms and so on, and a little lake with fish. There was also a part of Gezirah devoted to bathing, and a big building opposite the bathing-pool, with restaurants, beer, dancing, music, a barber's shop and I know not what else. Sometimes the satirical press in Cairo wrote about Gezirah – I remember one Greek paper with a rhyme that ended

> the green grass of Gezirah
> is the place to start a family . . . *etc.*

One day, Levtheri and I went to see the pyramids. The tram stopped a little way off the biggest one, the pyramid of Cheops. We took a little path uphill, past the Mena House Hotel, which is said to be the best in Cairo. (It is where the Egyptians had made plans to entertain Field-Marshal Rommel. I heard that they had covered it with German and Italian flags when the Germans were advancing into Egypt.)[1] We reached the pyramid – an entire mountain! We had brought electric torches with us, in order to see inside. People were going up and down the east side of it. I wanted to go up too, so started the climb in great delight. A Greek soldier on the way down advised me not to go up as it was very tiring and tricky. I didn't listen to him. I went knee-over knee-over up those huge steps till I got to the top. From there, what a vision! The eye could see to its full extent in nearly every direction. The whole town of Cairo was spread out on the great plain. There was a narrow platform there where many visitors had cut their names in the stone, so I got out my stiletto and cut my name and fatherland there as well, and enclosed them in a square. Then I gazed at the scene once more: the Nile that divided the desert in two and passed through the city, the other pyramids south and west of me, standing up so strikingly. Farther on were other remains of the ancient Egyptian civilization, such as the Sphinx.

Then I started down again. Most people get dizzy when they turn round and look down from that enormous height. People often fall down the steps out of vertigo, so many avoid the ascent. I wasn't at all dizzy. When I got down, I could easily have gone up again.

Some men in *galabiahs* were standing at the entrance, selling lamps and offering to guide strangers inside. But we wanted neither candles nor guide. We lit our torches, and went in alone. It was very tiring, as you can't stand

---

1 This rumour was widespread.

up straight anywhere, and your knees soon start to ache. We reached the first chamber, where there is some story I can't remember about the daughter of Cheops. We went back a bit, and started climbing steeply.

The other chamber, where the King's tomb was, must have been almost at the summit. But the mummy is no longer there. An English archaeologist took them to a museum in London when he explored the pyramid I don't know how long ago.

The inside of the chamber was built out of square granite blocks, three by three. That kind of stone exists nowhere in Egypt, and the nearest place where it is found is the Sudan, I think six hundred miles away from Egypt. The echo of your voice inside this chamber lasts several minutes.

Next we went to the Sphinx and several other ancient places nearby; but night was falling and we had to leave. Levtheri was quartered in Cairo, so I caught the tram to Heliopolis. I already knew how to get about without losing my way.

I slept well that night, but when I tried to get up next day, I was quite powerless. I had completely seized up.[1] I had to stay in bed all day, and only got up the day after. My legs ached a whole week.

On the twenty-fifth of February, the Service organized a Cretan *glendi* for all of us who had just left Crete. In the Almaza Camp outside Heliopolis in the desert stood a beautiful little tavern kept by a countryman and near-villager of mine. It was called the Café Metro and the owner was from Kástelos in Apokoronas – he had settled in Egypt long years ago. He prepared a rich and luxurious banquet for us, and the whole place was taken over for the evening. Several English officers were at the banquet

[1] Literal translation.

– Mr Smith-Hughes, Mr Tom and the two airmen we had brought with us from Crete. There was a Cretan lyre-player, so we danced all the Cretan dances and sang many Cretan songs, especially those we had taught the English to sing with us up in our mountains: 'When will the sky grow clear', 'On a rock in the high mountains', 'My little swallow', 'An eagle was sitting', 'Risen from the flames of Crete', and so forth. We got 'fezzed up', as we say, with all the drink; it was a true Cretan *glendi*. Nothing but Crete itself was lacking, and that firing of pistols and guns into the air which is so frequent in Cretan rejoicings – indeed, in the mountain villages, quite indispensable. At last, after many hours, we broke up, and everyone went home all the better for it.

On other days my exploration of Cairo continued. I went nearly everywhere with Levtheri Kalitsounakis. We went to the Greek cemetery of Cairo, St George's, a little way outside the city. The church of St George is very old. It used to be an old tower, in the vaults of which St George was imprisoned. His tomb is there too, but I couldn't see it because excavations were going on all round in search of ancient remains. Then we visited the Archaeological Museum of Cairo, which impressed me profoundly. It was the first museum I had seen in my life. It had many marvellous and beautiful things in it, but I especially remember the representation of Cleopatra.

Another day we went to Maadi. It is one of the prettiest suburbs of Cairo, with lovely broad streets all planted with flowers and overshadowed by fine trees. It seems a very aristocratic neighbourhood, because it is full of most luxurious villas and beautiful gardens. I liked going there and practising bicycling. I didn't know how to bicycle, but Petrakoyeorgis's son Herakles taught me.

Another fine place near Cairo was Heluan, a small town one hour away by train.

Outside Heluan, mechanics of the Greek Air Force were in training. There was also a beautiful Japanese garden, adorned with a great variety of trees and little rivers and ponds in which swam many fish of every kind. Little bridges and rocks and pretty little Japanese houses were scattered about, and all was carpeted with deep green grass. On the banks of a lake stood marble statues of the god of Japan with his wife and his many daughters. Their god points to his ear with one hand and the five fingers of his other are laid across his lips, closing them: 'See, hear and be silent.' Because of the war of the Allies with Japan the garden had been commandeered, and I don't know to whom it belonged. Loud-speakers were dotted about this garden, playing music and giving news from the Cairo Broadcasting Station.

One day we went to the Greek hospital at Abbasia, on the edge of Cairo towards Heliopolis. The civil and military hospital. There were many wounded fellow-countrymen in the Greek hospital and we often went to keep them company and cheer them up.

I went to the Greek Command to get my enrolment fixed up, and was allotted to the guard company of the Greek War Ministry. But I never actually joined them as I was seconded from the fifth of March to 'Force 133', the espionage service of our Allies in Greece.

So I wandered about Cairo all day long, only returning to Heliopolis to sleep. Cinemas, theatres, bathing-pools, roller-skating, boating on the Nile, I tried everything, and when I wanted to hear Greek politics talked or, better, Greek songs, I went to the Café Trianon or Le Soleil.

This is how my first days in Cairo went by. But soon not a day passed without a feeling of slight melancholy. I couldn't help thinking of my family left behind in the darkness of Crete. The scales of the war were now dipping on the side of the Allies, and the Germans, driven yet

wilder by their evil fate, were ready to destroy everything
on the most unmeaning pretexts. Which of our villages
are they burning now? I wondered. Who and how many
are standing with bound hands before a German firing-
squad? Whenever we sat down to eat we said to each
other: 'White bread! Here we are with the best of everything, while over there, our own people eat wild herbs
and bread made of sawdust and acorns, with forced labour,
the whip and the execution squads for their only
pastime . . .'

We talked all this over one day with the English Captain
Ciclitira, and among other things, I talked about sheep-
theft which had spread considerably because of the hunger
and the anarchy. I told him too of the frequent killings
among ourselves, usually for old family feuds and ven-
dettas, but mostly because of sheep-theft. Woe betide us
for a while when the Germans are driven out, I said –
who will be able to put us straight again? 'There's only
one thing for it,' he said, 'Crete ought to be run by the
English for at least ten years.' I took deep offence at these
words and said I thanked him for his magnanimity and
we broke off the discussion at this point.

I went off with several of Petrakoyeorgis's men to the
New Zealand Camp at Maadi. We were trained in the
handling of all the latest English, German and Italian arms.
We had lectures on these from morning till night, leaving
for Cairo on Saturday and returning on Monday. I got to
know a New Zealand sergeant-major here who had fought
in the battle of Crete in '41, and got away to Africa eight
months after the island fell. He had escaped from Selino,
in southwest Crete, with three comrades in a rowing boat.

One midday, the Prime Minister of New Zealand came
into the canteen (he had come to greet the New Zealand
troops in Maadi). He went up to each group of New
Zealanders, shook them by the hand, asked how they

were getting on, and so on. He played games with some of them and came up to us while we were playing billiards, greeted us and then played a few shots. This struck me as extremely odd.

My friend left for Crete again at the end of April with Mr Stockbridge and Captain John Stanley, without my seeing any of them again. I was getting more upset every day at remaining inactive. I wanted either to go and learn something, or go straight back to Crete. Everything beautiful suddenly began to look ugly, and I wandered about restlessly all day long. Soon Mr Aristeides Kastrino-yannis came to our house. All the others had left soon after their arrival. We shared the same room for a few days, and one night he told me that he was going back to Crete, but asked me not to tell anyone. It was a golden opportunity to smuggle a letter to Mr Michali or to Mr Aleko who had stayed in Crete, so I wrote one and addressed it both to Mr Michali and Mr Aleko. I said that I didn't mind any danger, and asked them to summon me back formally, and on a suitable pretext. I also wrote that I loved and missed them, and begged them to do whatever they could for my sake. Meanwhile, I got a letter from Mr Aleko, saying all my family were well and asking how I was getting on in my new house.

At the end of May some more Cretans arrived, and among others, Uncle Petro from my village – Kapetan Petrakas. He told me about my family, and generally all the news of Crete.

A few days later Uncle Petro took me with him when he and some others were invited to the house of Mr Sophokles Venizelos.[1] I have forgotten the name of the splendid mansion he lived in; I only remember that it was

1 Son of the great Venizelos, leader of the Liberal party and Prime Minister of Greece after the war.

one of the tallest in the city, on top of at least fifteen storeys. The lift in this building was one of the latest American lifts. (I don't know how it works, because our blocks of flats in Crete are all reached by stairs and ladders.) There were more than ten of us. We opened the lift doors and all went in. We shut the door and pressed the button for the tenth floor. The moment we reached it, the doors opened by themselves, then shut again at once, and shot down to the bottom again without even one of us getting out. We tried to stop it in vain. It reached the bottom, opened and shut again and then sailed up again in exactly the same way. We pressed the buttons of other floors, but the same thing happened there. I don't know how often we went up and down – it went on until the Arab doorkeeper stopped it at last on reaching the ground floor. We all leapt out, some of us very alarmed. The Arab explained that too many of us had got in at a time, and only allowed half of us to go up at once. Mr Venizelos greeted us warmly, asked us all about the general situation in Crete, and about our life with the Germans. He spoke to one or two privately, then we all saluted and left.

A Pilgrim to the Holy Places

Before many days had passed, Mr Tom came to our house with a signal from Mr Aleko, asking me if I was ready to go back to Crete with him. I was very cheered up by this news, and told Mr Tom that I was ready to leave the instant he was.

'Not at once,' he said, 'but in about a month.'

'A month!' I exclaimed. 'In that case I have a special request to make, as it is an opportunity that I may never have again in my life: could I have leave to visit the Holy Places in Palestine?'

'I don't see why not, George. I'll give you your leave pass to go tomorrow.'

I felt very grateful and thanked Mr Tom, who then left for the office in Cairo. In a little while I went there too, and made my daily visit to the Trianon. Two days passed, and, on the thirteenth of June 1943 I went early to Mr Tom's office. He gave me a pass, a warrant, a return ticket, and twelve paper pounds; and off I went to the station. I caught the train, and set out for Palestine. The train was full of English soldiers bound for Haifa, but all I knew was that my ticket said Lydda. I thought Jerusalem must be somewhere near there. We got to Ismailia towards evening and crossed the Suez Canal as the sun was actually setting. Balloons were going up all along the canal, and countless ones were already in the sky. This was done to protect it against night attacks. I shall never forget those clusters of balloons high up there, glowing away in the light of the sinking sun as far as the eye could see. When we had crossed the canal bridge, we had a long wait at Kantara. There was a military canteen where they served all soldiers, on the strength of their tickets, with tea and sandwiches and other sweet tea-time things. We travelled all night, and woke up in Palestine, which at first seemed just a continuation of the Egyptian desert. Soon, however, the train was carrying us through an immense garden, for that is what it looked like. At about half-past eight, it stopped, and outside, I saw a board bearing the word LYDDA. I took my bag and got out.

Then I saw that there was not a town, nor even a village in sight, only a little shop, or stall, at the side of the road. Lydda was just a place-name. I couldn't understand a word of the language they spoke at the stall, nor did I know what language it was. I signalled to every vehicle that drove by in any direction, as I didn't even know where Jerusalem lay. If they stopped, I shouted one word: *Hierosolyma*: but I didn't understand the answers, so I gave it up. I sat there over an hour, until by chance a Jewish driver turned up who knew a little broken Greek. He said there was only one bus a day to Jerusalem along that road, at six-thirty in the morning. It was now nearly ten. I couldn't wait there till next day, so I asked where he was going, and he said to Tel Aviv, so I got into his car. 'I'll come too,' I said, 'and catch something from there to Jerusalem.' When we reached the main Tel Aviv road, I found a bus at once, and we drove off through unending forests of oranges and lemons. The ground rose in low hills covered with orange trees, and looked like a great ocean with jewelled waves, a true marvel to behold, after travelling through the desert with the dust rising in high pillars till it gets through even the smallest chink. But here was a clean, sunwashed air that sank deep into the soul bringing with it a divine intimation of true happiness. We reached Jerusalem and drove down a steep lane until the bus stopped in a public square.

The moment I got out a man rushed up and asked me in Greek where I wanted to go. Thinking he understood it properly I said, 'To the Greek Town Major's office.' 'I know,' he cried, 'I know. *Xevro, xevro!* Come with me.' I followed him, and we went to an hotel in the ancient city of Jerusalem. 'Here,' he said, 'they are Greek Christians.' I gave him a tip. It was called The Helle[1] – a moving name! I took a room there and left my bag. The first thing was to eat, as I was pretty hungry. A little way off, I found a Greek restaurant called The Olympus. Here I found well-cooked food done with olive oil, which I hadn't eaten for a long time – ever since I left Crete. I met some other Greek soldiers here from the Third Greek Brigade stationed near Haifa, who had come here as pilgrims to pray at the shrine of the Most Holy. We joined company – nine of us altogether – and, after eating and drinking, we headed for the Holy Sepulchre.

Jerusalem is divided into two halves, the Old Town and the New. The Holy Sepulchre lies in the heart of the old town, in the Church of the Resurrection, which was built by our St Constantine. The old town is girdled with strong walls pierced by five gates; the Gate of Herod, which leads to Bethlehem, the Jaffa and the Haifa Gates, the Gate of St Stephen which leads to the Garden of Gethsemane and the Mount of Olives, and the Golden Gate. It is called the Golden Gate because it was there that Jesus entered the town with his disciples when they spread palm branches and sheets along the path, on the

1 Name of the Greek warship sunk near Tinos without warning by an Italian submarine before the outbreak of the Greek-Italian war in 1940.

day we solemnize as Palm Sunday. But it has remained shut ever since then, and they say it will only open again at the Second Coming.

In the Church of the All Holy Sepulchre

We went to the Holy Sepulchre, where a monk led us inside and explained everything. Before the entrance, the entire front was propped with beams – it seems that it was about to fall headlong. On the left of the entrance high up in the belfry are eight bells which are all rung at the same moment by pulling on a single rope, except the one in the middle, which is one of the biggest bells in the world. It only rings once a year at the Commemoration of the Resurrection of Our Lord.

As soon as we entered, we were in front of the Apokathelosis, the place, that is to say, where Joseph of Arimathea lay the body of Christ and wrapped it in bands and anointed it with spices before placing it in the Tomb. This is marked by a marble slab with a large candle at each corner and nine sanctuary lamps hung across it. The monk told us that as we, as good soldiers, were fighting for the glory of our country, they also had often shed their blood here in order to uphold the name of Greece. For this reason the lighted sanctuary lamps are shared out, and we can be proud because we have more than the other Churches and the most important of the Holy Places. Out of the nine lamps burning above the Apokathelosis, six are Greek and three are foreign, discernible as such by their different colour. A little farther forward and to the left was a place like a cage with an Ikon of the Most Holy Virgin inside, and a lamp which is always burning. She stood here and wept when her Son was hanging on the Cross. A little farther on was the choir of the church under the highest dome of all, in the centre of which lay the Most Holy Sepulchre. This choir is circular and it has large windows all the way round, like doorways without doors, exactly the same in number as the heresies of the Christian Religion. Each year on Easter Saturday, at an hour past midday, the Holy Fire appears by itself, and the Patriarch takes it and gives it in turn to the waiting Christians. First to the Orthodox and then to the others according to their order in the heresies. We were told that a Greek mason had built part of the Church of the Holy Sepulchre, and had been forbidden to cut Greek inscriptions, for some reason. But he put them there all the same, camouflaged so that they should not show, and after a year he uncovered them; but they caught him and put him to death. We were also told that whoever does not believe that the Holy Fire is holy can take thirty-three candles – the number of years that Christ remained on earth – and twist them into a plait during the service on Holy Saturday, and the fire won't burn him at all, even if it is held against his breast.

Not a year goes by without some miracle, quite apart from the great and unquestioned miracle of the Holy Fire. That year, thirty-three candles, twisted together in the hands of a little girl, all kindled by themselves at the same moment that the Patriarch's caught alight. She was standing right at the end of the church, and thousands would have had to have passed on the fire before it could have reached her.

Then we climbed a stone staircase on the other side of the church, and in a little while we were standing by the rock of Golgotha. The great rock where the Jews crucified their malefactors could formerly be seen from all over the town. Now it is enclosed in the great church. The summit is the floor of a narrow church filled with the ikons of many and different saints, candlesticks, sanctuary lamps and so on. East of the rock is a marble table with a cross in the middle. Under the table on the rock, and in the centre of the table is the hollow in which they erected the Cross of Christ. To left and right of it are two more, where the crosses of the two malefactors were placed. On the right of the emplacement of the Cross of Christ the rock is split from top to bottom, and this is where, they say, the blood of Our Lord fell upon the skull of Adam, which lay in a little hole at the base, and washed away the sins of our ancestors. We later saw this place – the Place of the Skull – from below. Immediately beyond the split rock, there is another piece of it locked away behind glass. This is because it was washed by the blood of Christ when the soldiers pierced His side. They cut little chips off this rock to give to pilgrims, as they did formerly with the Holy Cross, of which now only a small piece remains, which they have kept for the Church.

Once, when we were delivered from a barbarian invasion, the Holy Cross became three large bits. One of them remained in the church, where it was bit by bit dispersed; the Christians of the West took another, and the third went to Russia.

'All these places', the monk said, 'are ours – Greek – but we made room for the Catholics to place an image of the Blessed Virgin there,' and he pointed to a carved statue of the Blessed Virgin a few yards to the right of the positions where the crosses stood. This statue of the Catholics was wonderfully adorned with different offerings of priceless value.

Nearby, in the same choir, there is a little room which was cut off by our Emperor Herakleios – he wrote an inscription inside which I have unfortunately forgotten. I only remember that the meaning was that before God, and inside His church, every man must humble himself. It was also written that he set free the Holy Places and went to Golgotha to pray and to glorify God and thank Him, and that, as he was about to prostrate himself in prayer in all his magnificence, his imperial diadem fell to the ground.

After Golgotha, we went on exploring, and saw some wells of enormous depth, with water at the bottom, where the inhabitants of the city drew their water in ancient times. Today it is holy water, and any Christian should pull up a little and drink it. Passing from room to room, we reached the lower part of the great rock of Golgotha. There was a little cave here where Jesus was imprisoned. They kept Him constantly bound to an upright iron stake (which is still there) in such a way that he was forced to lean constantly upon the sharp point. This room also contains a cylindrical stone about three feet high with a basin-shaped hollow at the top, which has a curious history. One year, about four hundred years ago, the Armenians told the Orthodox Christians that they would take the Holy Fire first from the Holy Sepulchre. But the Holy Fire always comes first, every year, to the Orthodox Patriarch, who happens to be a Greek. The Armenians turned all the Orthodox out of the church by force and waited by the Holy Sepulchre, while the Orthodox stood in the courtyard outside the church door, and all, with the Patriarch at their head, knelt down. The Armenians waited, believing that the Flame would come to them first, and, in their determination, they began to lay bets and to fill the stone basin with human dung. Then they told the Orthodox that if the Holy Fire did not appear to them first they would have to empty the basin by devouring the contents. But, in the opposite event, the Armenians would be compelled to empty it themselves in the same way.

At exactly an hour after noon on Easter Saturday, the time when the Holy Flame appears, one of the marble columns supporting the door shattered by itself and a great flame burst out of the heart of the marble. The Patriarch lit his candle at the flame, intoning the '*Devte, lavete phos*',[1] and all the Orthodox lit their candles. The Armenians, meanwhile, were waiting in vain by the Holy Sepulchre. When they saw the miracle, they were obliged to empty the basin which they themselves had filled. From that day forth the Armenians have always sought to pollute everything belonging to the Greeks, even putting dung into their coffee, their food or their wells. To this day, the marble column remains splintered and blackened with the smoke of the Holy Fire, as we saw with our own eyes.

We passed through several other rooms until we reached the last one at the end of the church and went down a staircase to find ourselves in a small chamber. Here we saw the well where St Helena discovered the True Cross. Wherever the True Cross might be presumed to lie hidden, the saint had dug. She searched many years, without losing hope, until one day she sat down in this very place and began to wonder where she should order new excavations. Noticing a beautiful perfume, she felt moved to find out where it came from. Then, seeing a little flowering plant pouring forth this lovely scent, she ordered her people to start digging. She watched them in silence, until, from the depths of the well, they drew the three crosses; and, as we all know, she recognized the Cross of Our Lord from those of the two malefactors. The little plant that guided St Helena to the cistern, where the True Cross lay hidden, then took the name of Basil – the royal plant. It is called so to this very day.

1 'Draw near, receive the fire.'

At Bethlehem

Taking the same monk with us, we set off for Bethlehem. To leave the Old Town and catch the bus, we passed through the Gate of Herod. The road we followed was a market: a narrow cobbled street, with steps almost all the way. The level part at the beginning was almost entirely occupied by goldsmiths working on various trinkets. But, farther on, stalls on either side were loaded with food and fruit. This narrow path was slow going because of the crowd. With all this variety of food and wares, it was just like one of our markets in a Cretan town. There was an abundance of all kinds of fruit. The only things that made it different from one of our markets were the bananas.

Leaving Herod's Gate, we took a bus to Bethlehem. In a little while, driving first downhill and then up again, we came to the hill opposite Jerusalem where Bethlehem stands, and stopped opposite the Church of the Nativity. Built on the eastern edge of the town, it is one of the most ancient of all Christian churches and there is room outside for thousands. The entrance is narrow and very low, and you have to stoop a bit to go in. We then found ourselves in the very large and beautiful interior, the high vault of which is upheld by two rows of pillars about ten yards high. In several places the floor opens in rifts, where, much lower than the present level, you can see the old floor, which is all covered with mosaic. At the end is the high altar, and the sanctuary floor is the roof of the cave where Our Saviour was born. We reached the point where the star kindled when Christ was born. They have placed a large star down there in modern times.

Farther down still, we came face to face with the Manger, the same marble manger where Christ was born. Several sanctuary lamps burn over it, and the whole cave is alight with lamps and candles reflected in the adornments and the votive gifts with which the cave is filled. We knelt down and prayed, lit some candles and then wandered through the other parts of the church. We found a baby and baptized[1] it all together, the nine of us, all soldiers. It was a little girl, so we christened her Maria-Elevtheria.[2] She was the Orthodox child of a Christian Arab family, and her mamma had brought her to the church to be baptized. It was five o'clock on Monday the fourteenth of June 1943.

When the Sacrament was over, we caught the bus back to Jerusalem. Here we said goodbye and separated, each going his own way.

That day there were parades of units of all the Allied armies stationed in Palestine, in celebration of the United Nations. Flags of all the Allies fluttered from the roof of the English Government House. I went to bed early in the Olympus Hotel, filled with enthusiasm and gratitude for my presence in that sacred city, the centre of worship of the whole of Christendom.

I got up early next day, and, after breakfast, hired a bicycle to have a quick look at the New City, for there are few parts of the old where you can go on a bicycle. I went all over it, and admired it very much. I found a lovely out-of-doors Greek inn, where all the Greek families of Jerusalem gathered at night to dance Greek dances. I went

1 i.e. stood god-parents.
2 Mary-Freedom.

here several times and thoroughly enjoyed myself. The whole of my second day I spent in the old town. Here I met a fellow-islander who had been there for years. We made friends, and went to the cell of a Cretan monk, where we drank some *tzikoudia* and ate a *mézé* of olives – things of which we have plenty in Crete, but which I had not seen since I left it.

On the third day I went by bus to Galilee to find Colonel Papadakis. It is by the Mount of Olives, three-quarters of an hour away on foot. There was an English cemetery from the last war on the left side of the road, and on the summit of a little hill stood a country house belonging to the Patriarchate, where the Patriarch had given Colonel Papadakis some small quarters.

I found the Colonel and his family, and we talked nearly all day about past times in Crete. All the while the words he had shouted at me in that fanatic rage on the mountain-ledge kept passing through my mind. 'Your work with the English is finished! If you don't leave within one minute, I'll kill you! . . .' We talked a great deal, and, when we had eaten together at midday, I went back to Jerusalem.

I prostrated myself in prayer again in the Church of the Holy Sepulchre. I wanted to get to know the church inside out, and wandered round it for hours.

Other Pilgrimages

Next day, my fourth in Jerusalem, I went to see the Praetorium, where Pilate sat in judgement over Christ. Unfortunately the monk who had the key was away, so I saw nothing but the outside, which is in the courtyard of a house, and looks like a cellar. I saw the Church of St Veronica next door. It is a Catholic church, and it is built in the exact position where St Veronica met Jesus labouring under the Cross and wiped His face with her kerchief. His face was imprinted on the cloth, and her parents put her to death with a thousand torments.[1]

All this – St Veronica kneeling to wipe the face of Jesus, her martyrdom and death at the hands of her parents, is represented by statues; and, the church being dark except for a faint glimmer of light, you would think you were looking at the real thing. They look so alive.

I went to the Praetorium again that afternoon, but the monk was still away. Some boys told me that, what with all the soldiers who came to visit the place, he had made enough money for the time being, and wouldn't be back again till he was short of cash. So be it, I thought, and left.

After visiting the Temple of Solomon, St Stephen the Protomartyr, the Garden of Gethsemane, and bathing in the river Jordan I set off with another Greek soldier for a monastery called the Holy Cross.

1 This is a private version of George's.

There were no monks, but many Greek refugee families had been installed in the cells. We heard that the biggest tree in the world – a cypress – had formerly grown there. Also that the only survivor from the destruction of Sodom and Gomorrah – I think he was called Lot – committed a great sin with his two daughters in the same place. But he repented, and asked somebody – I can't remember who – what he should do to be saved. And the angel of the Lord told him that he would only be absolved from his sin when he brought water from the Jordan and sprinkled it on three rods, which he then stuck in the ground. But nobody must drink any of this water first, and he was forbidden if he met a thirsty man or beast, to refuse the water. The distance from there to the Jordan was great, and there were no springs on the way. Thus Lot was carrying water for forty years, to sprinkle on these three rods, and only at the fortieth did he succeed in bringing any without some having been drunk on the way. He watered them, they grew and burst into leaf and then all melted into a single tree, which became the biggest in the world. When Solomon was building the temple, he needed enormous beams for the support of the dome; so he ordered the cypress to be felled. They felled it, measured it, took only the length they needed (for it was very large) and dragged it to Jerusalem. They took it to the temple, and stood it up on end. But they saw that it only reached half-way. So they threw it down and measured it again, and it was exactly the right length. When they stood it up again, it still only reached half-way. 'This wood has a curse on it,' they cried, and threw it out of the temple. And when the Jews condemned Christ to be crucified, the cross was hacked from the wood of this accursed tree, which was still lying outside Solomon's temple. That is why the place was known as Holy Cross, and why a monastery was built there. It is also why cypresses are the most hallowed trees in a cemetery.

I only saw one more church, that of Joachim and Anna, the parents of the All-Holy Virgin Mary. The church is the actual house where they lived and died. I got my leave-pass stamped again at the Town Major's, bowed down for the last time in the Church of the Holy Sepulchre and boarded the morning train from Jerusalem on the twenty-fourth of June 1943.

PART 4
Back to Crete

The Return

On the first of July a car drew up outside our house in Cairo. Inside were Mr Smith-Hughes and Mr Tom, to give us our last instructions. Already we had been given the clothes we were to wear on arrival in Crete (we had been wearing uniform up till then), also German identity papers filled in with false names, and some blank ones as well: our own pistols and watches had been returned to us and all had been fixed up – our papers, our finger-prints, our photographs, unrecognizable signatures, and real – almost real – rubber stamps from most of the villages in Crete.

We took our rucksacks and got into the car. A Mr Alexander Rendel[1] was to accompany us as far as the coasts of Crete. Mr Smith-Hughes came as far as the station to say goodbye to us. The car moved off, and goodbye, Heliopolis!

We got into the Alexandria train; as it started, Mr Smith-Hughes wished us good luck.

'Keep walking, George!' he said.

'Don't worry, Mr Hughes,' I said, 'I'll be the same as before.'

The train stopped half-way, and we went by car to another train, which was taking troops to Libya.

1 Major A. M. Rendel ('Sandy'), R A, author of *Appointment in Crete* (Alan Wingate).

Close to El Alamein the train went off the rails, and we had to wait five hours till another engine arrived. The derailing was due to sabotage. It was practically nightfall when we moved on. We approached El Alamein, and the entire desert was smothered with the wreckage of war: broken aeroplanes, tanks, cars, trucks, cannons – all of them blown to bits, or crumpled up or scattered, covered the entire wilderness. It looked like a vast graveyard ploughed up in every direction with trenches and bomb craters and shell holes and explosions. The night fell and we could see no more. When day broke I didn't know if we were still in Egypt or travelling through Libya. I only remember we left the train soon after the sun rose, and travelled on by military truck, passing through Tobruk. The harbour looked very like Suda Bay, except that it is smaller. It was full of ships – not temporarily, but for ever – and none of the houses standing looked as if they could remain upright much longer. Nothing but ruins and disaster.

We travelled across the desert all that day, and saw the trail of death and destruction everywhere. It was impossible to leave the road anywhere because of the extent of the minefields. We had a meal in a camp somewhere in the Libyan desert. The food was very good, but the scenery, if one can call it that, was terrible: quantities of sand, and all blowing so high that it filled your mouth the moment you parted your lips. It was evening by the time we drove downhill towards the sea. A little way below us lay Derna, where a little surface-craft was waiting for us. We went on board and threw ourselves on the food and drink with a great appetite.

Afterwards, Mr Alexis[1] took me into the town, where we went to a lovely bar and had a few. As Mr Alexis only

1 Sandy Rendel.

knew ancient Greek, he was trying to learn the modern sort. He had a manual and a lexicon with him, and he looked up and asked me to explain every word that came out of my mouth. We went back to bed on the ship, waiting the order to leave. We weighed anchor about midday and travelled for a few hours, then turned back as it was very stormy in the open sea, and, the Captain said, it would get worse and we would have been unable to make any headway.[1] Next day we all three went into the town for some beer at an army canteen.

'I don't believe that there'll be much more delay,' said Mr Alexis, 'but meanwhile, we've got to kill time somehow.' We borrowed a rod and fishing tackle from the canteen, and bathing-dresses. 'Besides which,' he said, 'we'll have three Greek lessons a day.' I was to be his teacher. When we went into the town, he said, 'What do you feel like having, George? You're my teacher and I must look after you.'

I didn't like Derna. But there were some vine-trellises over the roads near the harbour, and the grapes were getting ripe. It made my mouth water to look at them. I suggested trying to find some to buy, but we hunted everywhere in vain. 'I'll soon get some,' I said, as we returned to our ship. We were going along a broad street covered with trellises. Soldiers were billeted on most of the houses. I shinned up into one of the trellises like a cat and cut down two magnificent bunches, although not absolutely ripe. Mr Alexis, who hadn't expected this, took to his heels the moment he saw me, and tried to keep as far away as possible. I soon caught him up with a bunch in each hand, but he refused them, saying they were stolen property.

'You must have some,' I said, 'if only a few, and see

1 This very often happened.

how good they taste. In fact, as your teacher, I insist on it – it's one of the most important Greek lessons you could learn.' So he laughed and took some. When he had eaten some, he said, 'They are delicious, please give me some more. I'm sure I'd soon learn to steal if we stayed together much longer . . .'

He told me there was an ancient Greek city nearby, called Cyrene, which we ought to go and see. So we all three set off next morning in our army truck to Cyrene, which lies a few hours west of Derna. We reached the ruins of the town. Mr Alexis was an archaeologist, and he had a book on it with him, and insisted on examining everything. We went over the great temple of Apollo, also Apollo's well, where the water, spouting out of the mouth of a large stone frog, fell into a cistern round which were great marble lions. We wandered about all day, getting back to Derna in the evening.

Another order came for us to leave for Crete. According to the engineer our first ship had broken down, so we moved to another, leaving in the afternoon. The sea was perfect and we had a very good journey. By the time the sun began to set we were close to Crete and before darkness fell completely, we could see the peaks of the White Mountains through binoculars. Just then a Junker appeared high in the sky and began to circle above us, but without coming any lower. The crew were all at action stations, and the anti-aircraft guns were all aimed at the plane. We were ordered below, but the plane drew away without coming any nearer. When the alert was over, night was falling. We travelled on in the dark for several hours. Our arrival in Crete was due at midnight or 1 a.m.

Midnight came, one and two passed, and it was getting on for three. It was about 4 a.m. when I felt the ship slowing down, and then heard the ship's bell. 'We've arrived,' I said to myself. I seized my rucksack joyfully, and was about to run up on deck.

'I should leave your things down here,' said Vasili, the New Zealander.

'Why,' I said, 'aren't we taking them with us?'

'No,' he said, 'we aren't going anywhere.'

I left him there and went on deck filled with curiosity. To my great surprise I saw that we had returned to the harbour from which we had set out. The ship had turned back when the German plane appeared, and I hadn't realized it. I can't describe my feelings when I realized that, instead of the rocks of Crete, we would be setting foot once more on the sands of Derna. Every minute seemed an agony, and each hour eternal.

We got the order to leave that harbour, as enemy spies might have got wind of us. We left eastwards. We passed the headland beyond Derna and dropped anchor in a little desert harbour there, where we stayed that night and next morning, leaving for Crete at midday. We sailed for three hours, but still luck was against us, for a heavy storm had blown up. Waves were breaking over the deck and we were all sick with the motion. Back we went to Derna. We signalled all our movements back to HQ by wireless, and they sent us fresh orders. About midday Mr Alexis said a signal had come telling us to leave the ship and the harbour altogether and go back the same way we had arrived. We didn't know where for, but orders would arrive later.

A military vehicle came and picked us up with our stuff, but we were stopped as soon as we got near the aerodrome and Mr Alexis was handed an order to remain at the aerodrome till another order came through. The commandant gave us a hut for the night and arranged for us to eat in the officers' mess.

We went round the aerodrome next day and looked

at the innumerable destroyed German aeroplanes there. After supper we settled in the library of the mess, where there were a number of Greek books and periodicals. Mr Alexis put a few of them in his pocket saying, 'I'm going to steal these.' (He said it was the first thing he had ever stolen.) Before we got to bed, a signal came telling us to leave the aerodrome and return to the harbour, so we left in a truck. It was night and nobody saw us go on board. It was a different ship, and when we got on board we settled down to sleep. Next morning we were not allowed on shore, but had to remain in the hold until we moved off about midday. As soon as we were out of the harbour, we went up on deck. I recognized the ship at once – she was the same one that had taken us off the island on the fourteenth of February. It was the third ship in which we were to try to reach Crete.

I told the Sergeant that we were sure to return to Derna. 'No,' he said, 'we've got a first-rate captain, and nothing will stop him – submarines, aeroplanes or storms.' The sailors asked us what ship we had been on before, and when we told them they all laughed. They said the skipper was just about fit for sailing from Derna to Alexandria, and no more.

We took the direction of Alexandria, and when we were in the open sea, turned towards Crete. Before we had altogether left African waters, we passed a huge English convoy of at least a hundred ships. We stopped, and let them pass us on their way to Alexandria.

Nothing else happened all day, and the weather was very good. Towards evening we tried to pick out the high mountains of Crete with glasses, but could see nothing except a vague dark shape on the horizon. Between ten and eleven we passed close to the small islet of Gavdos,[1]

[1] 'Clauda' of the Acts of the Apostles, port to which St Paul was carried by 'A tempestuous wind called Euroclydon'.

leaving it on our right. Just then an enormous searchlight, probably from the Gulf of Messara, began raking the sea. Now and then it fell on us, but it was a long way away and looked very dim. I remained on deck all the time, hoping the same wouldn't happen to me as last time. In a little while the ship went in close, and we began sailing along the coast (trying to pick out the signal-flashes), and then back again, for about an hour. We turned back once more, and then saw an electric torch flashing from the shore. It was the appointed signal, and must have been coming from Mr Aleko,[1] who was in command of Western Crete. Mr Michali[2] was in command of the eastern half, and I wouldn't be seeing him now for Heaven knew how long. We would have to send him our news from the White Mountains to the far-off mountains of Lasithi . . . About a hundred yards from the shore, we lowered a dinghy and got in with our gear – the New Zealander, Mr Alexis and I. Two sailors rowed us in.

1 Xan Fielding.
2 Patrick Leigh Fermor.

From Free Territory to Crete in Chains

It was about one in the morning, at a place known as Kaloyéros, or the Monk, on the night of the twenty-ninth of July 1943, that we landed in a deep grotto (the sea went right inside) at the foot of an enormous, endless precipice beaten by the waves. From the depths of the cave a hole climbed upwards and out on to the mountainside, with the cliff falling away sheer underneath.

Mr Aleko was waiting for us in the grotto with Little Aleko the wireless operator (whom the boys had now nicknamed the Tinker), my fellow-villager George Phindrilakis, also Antoni and George Paterakis from the heroic village of Koustoyérako, and a few other chaps.

Mr Alexis talked to Mr Aleko for a few moments, handed over some things he had brought, and got into the dinghy to go back to the ship, as he was returning to Cairo. Soon the dinghy began to fade into the shadows of the sea, and we all sat down. What a heap of stories we had to exchange! They told me they had come down to meet us five or six times. The Germans had got wind of it, and had only just left that coast, having searched it thoroughly for two days. They had come with caiques, landing in force and making an entire warlike expedition along this very stretch; but without encountering a soul. Our people all lay up in hiding and watched them firing bursts of sub-machine-gun fire into every bush, shouting in Greek, 'Come out of it, you horn-wearers!' But, as they found nothing, they had left the day before, and our people came back at once.

The moment we arrived, some of the boys set off for the village to bring beasts on which to load all of our stuff which we could not carry. It was six hours from there to the hideout in the mountains, and all very steep and irregular. Dawn broke, and we spent the whole day in the cave. The beasts arrived at twilight, and we hoisted all the gear up to the strange back door of this sea-cave, on the steep mountainside, where we lashed the stuff to the wooden saddles; and the animals set out. They were to go a much farther way round, and we were to leave with the first light of day.

As soon as the dawn of the thirty-first of July broke, we shouldered our Cretan haversacks and hit the path. Mr Aleko and I were the last to leave the grotto. One of the boys, wanting to help me, had taken my pack.

'Haven't you got anything?' said Mr Aleko.

'No, nothing,' I answered.

'Well, you take this then,' he said, giving me his *sakouli*,[1] 'it's very light.'

It was so heavy I could scarcely get it on to my back. Inside were the gold sovereigns we had brought from Cairo for the Service.

We followed a winding footpath up the steep slope to the mountains, five or six of us, some walking fast, others slow. I came last because of the weight I was carrying, and also because my feet, with all these months' inaction, had got out of the habit, as you might say. Soon they were all a long way ahead, and, in half an hour, right out of sight. I got very tired and couldn't go a step farther, and at last sat down. I waited for someone to come back and find me. Antoni Paterakis halted and shouted to me from above.

1 Cretan haversack woven with bright colours.

'Come down here and help me.' I shouted back, 'I can hardly walk.'

He came down to where I was.

'What's up?' he said.

'Nothing's up, Antoni,' I said, 'I've just got tired, that's all. Do take that *sakouli*.'

He picked it up, and then seeing how heavy it was, cried out, 'O, what the devil's inside it, to make such a weight? It must be ammunition for pistols or something.'

Able to walk freely, I soon reached the others; they were sitting round a spring as clear and bright as crystal.

When I saw Mr Aleko and told him the *sakouli* had been too heavy for me, he said:

'Ah, George, George! What a wreck you are! You see what happens when people go to Cairo?'

'Yes,' I said, 'you just take your nice light *sakouli* and let's see how far you get with it.'

We got up to resume our path, and Mr Aleko shouldered the *sakouli* with the sovereigns. There was an iconostasis by the spring, where the Germans had shot four of our people in 1942.

The Germans had made a fierce raid up the White Mountains, killing whoever they found there – shepherds mainly, and frightened villagers in hiding – as well as the mass executions they carried out in several of the villages. A few stones and four wooden crosses marked the humble graves of those four martyrs to freedom. Only some wild flowers watered by their blood and dried up by the summer sun adorned the earth that shelters them. We felt a cold shudder as we passed, but also a holy duty towards them that flooded our hearts with courage and strengthened our will to do our duty.

Although we were only advancing at the rate of twenty minutes to the hour, Mr Aleko was soon done for – he told me I had been quite right in saying the *sakouli* was too heavy. So Antoni Paterakis, who has immense resistance to fatigue, took it and carried it all the way. We reached the hideout that afternoon, right up in the high mountains of Koustoyérako, at a spot called Pytharaki.

It was a steep mountainside thickly forested with enormous pines and hill-cypresses, with a well in the middle giving very little water but, what there was, clean and as cold as ice. The lair was about two hundred yards higher. The boys had built a hut of branches under the trees, and all the things were heaped inside. Near the hut to left and right were the beds they slept in: all round each of these was a row of stones, about fifty to the yard. This was the basis, and inside were strewn thickly-leaved branches, and on top of these, sweet-smelling twigs from various mountain shrubs as soft as down. Big shaggy branches were stuck in the ground on either side, meeting overhead and forming a low tent covering the whole bed, all so thickly and skilfully woven together that neither wind nor sun could penetrate. Only a little doorway was left for the owner to crawl inside on his belly.

The moment we arrived we all fell asleep to recover from the long climb. When we awoke, we started cooking tea and talking round the fire. Mr Aleko asked me how I had got on in Cairo. I told him the whole of my life there in few words, and also about Mr Dionysios, their officer there. Our conversation broke off, and our attention was diverted to the Tinker, our wireless operator, who was larking about with the rest of the boys. But his larks consisted of things like punches and arm- and leg- and head-twisting, and so on. They were angry with him but all in vain. He approached me, but I at once said I refused to join in. So he started on my fellow-villager George Phindrilakis, punching him in the stomach so that he fell down winded. I told Mr Aleko that I didn't consider this a joke at all. George got up in a little while in tears and the crazy operator chased all the others behind trees by throwing huge stones at them. If he had hit anyone, it might have killed him.

'Do you call that a joke?' I said to Mr Aleko. 'What would happen if he hit one of them?'

'But Holy Virgin!' he said. 'What about all the people killed and wounded in the war?'

'Yes, but we're not at war, and things like that ought not to happen in a game.'

'But, good God, when I was at school I was always getting thumped over the head.'

'You may like it, Mr Aleko, but I can't believe it. Anyway he doesn't hit you over the head, but only us, and I don't want to get mine bashed in . . .'

Crossing the White Mountains

Next dawn was the beginning of the first of August. We spent all day talking and telling stories. In the evening Mr Aleko said that next day I was to accompany Vasili (as we all called him), the New Zealander, over to the Nome of Retimo and introduce him to all our people there. Mr Aleko was going to use him as his assistant, which meant he would have to get to know everybody in the Service.

As soon as the second of August began to dawn Vasili, George, Stelio Vernadakis and I set out. We traversed the forest of cypress and pine at a slant, and reached Akhlada, where the Koustoyérakiots have their cheese-huts, a little distance from the hideout. We struck north-eastwards here and reached the high peak of the White Mountains, below which is stretched out the plateau of the Omalo. The Omalo is a plain right up in the White Mountains where, among other things, they grow the best potatoes in Crete. There are any amount of cheese-huts there where they make cheese of many different and rare sorts; and it played a great part in the days of the Turkish Slavery. It is the same Omalos which is mentioned in the mountain song:

> When will the sky grow clear?
> When will the spring come round?
> So I can take my gun again,
> (My beautiful patroness),

> And go down to the Omalos,
> And the path of the Mousouri . . .

Now the Germans had a guard post in the Omalo, and they often lay in ambush in the passes to observe and waylay the movements and doings of the National Resistance of Crete. They also took all the fruits of the labour of the people of the Omalo.

We took a downhill path south of the plateau, to avoid the Omalo, and climbed down the precipitous path that leads thence to the Gorge of Samaria, the wildest canyon of Crete. We had to watch out here at every step – it was the most dangerous place of all by reason of the frequent German ambushes. We approached with stealth and spied out the land thoroughly. But there was no movement. We went through the cleft one by one and the descent began.

After climbing down for an hour we reached a place called Poria, where the Viglis family from Samaria have their sheepfolds. Before we reached the *mytato*,[1] we noticed some men moving about. We became suspicious at once and hid, and then, approaching under cover, we looked at them through our binoculars and saw that they were Germans. The question was: what were we to do? There was no other path. The only thing was to stay hidden until they went. Fortunately they left after a few hours in the direction of the Omalo. Then we went to the sheepfold, where they looked after us well, giving us yoghurt to eat and a fresh cheese for the journey.

We had to get a move on, as the appearance of the Germans had put us back a lot. Night caught us in the foothills of Mount Venizelos, so we had to lie down there. It was the hottest month of summer, but so bitter was the

---

1 Cheese-making hut.

cold that we could not shut our eyes all night. We didn't wait for full daylight to be on our way.

We reached the peak which will symbolize for ever the name of that never-to-be-forgotten artisan of Greek happiness, Elevtherios Venizelos. Our thoughts winged back for a minute to the early years of his life, to his great struggles, and the shining moment when, seated on this peak, he wrote, with the flame of patriotism burning in his heart, his symbolic poem beginning:

An eagle sits upon a high mountain . . .

The breath of his influence strengthened our souls – it was as though it flooded the air, and we felt it deep in our very entrails, cool and free and filled with sweetness and the voice of harmony; such thoughts, in those difficult days, found a path into our bones and our very souls.

We headed downhill, while bit by bit the high peaks and steep mountainsides fell behind, and we reached the outskirts of Kampoi. We were heading for the group of houses called Tsakistra, but, the moment we were among them, we suddenly saw Germans very close. Fortunately they didn't see us and we turned back and cut the mud. Hiding behind a hillock, we watched them. As they still didn't leave, we changed our route and went on to Kyriakosellia, where we found our good old friend Levtheris Kourakis. He led us to some open caves in a valley behind the village.

After an early start, we headed straight for my village of Asi Gonia, passing outside Pemonia and Phré and stopping at Uncle Nicoli Vandoulakis's vineyard outside Nippoi. The grapes were ripe and others of the Vandoulas brought us a meal from the village. Here Stelios Vernadakis branched off to Vryses and the three of us pushed on. In four hours' time we were climbing up the Asi Gonian peaks. Night overtook us, so we slept at Drapana, one of the highest peaks of my village. Next day George went on ahead, while Vasili and I waited in a cheese-hut belonging to my cousin Marko till it was dark. (I didn't want to appear all of a sudden in the village and endanger my family.) We took the path as soon as evening fell, and were at my house in an hour. When I suddenly came on them like this, unawaited and unannounced, the joy of my family cannot be described. We sat and talked for hours, then I went and slept outside the village. It was the sixth of August.

Next day we asked Mr George Alevizakis of Argyroupolis to come to the village. Vasili had a letter and money for him from Mr Aleko. He was one of Colonel Papadakis's first collaborators up at Vourvouré, and the most flattering man of all the Service; especially eager to assist us in anything to do with supplies and clothing whenever we needed it – always, however, with our money. We were wonderfully looked after whenever we went past his house; wonderful wine, food, *tzikoudia*, walnuts and so on. He now had an execution squad which he had managed, I don't know how, to organize, and for which he received subsidies from the Service. It consisted of twelve members in all. Their first duty was to assassinate the German agent Komnina, the man who had deceived Andrea Polenta and had him captured and shot with our other people in Ayia Jail. He was executed inside his own house.

Next day George went back again to the Eparchy of Selino, and I remained on a few days in my village.

Much had happened there during my absence in the Middle East. After I had left to catch the boat in February, the underground hideout in Kampoi had broken up and moved to my village. They had spent the first ten days in the mountains west of the village at Rodaré. Meanwhile, the villagers had built a house for them on the other mountain that rises steeply from our village. To get across that mountainside meant passing terribly steep bits and dangerous sliding rocks, where one man could bring down half the mountainside. But it is more level higher up, with small hollows surrounded by peaks and trees. The little house, built out of stone slabs at a place called Gypselota, had been Mr Aleko's lair all winter. For the Service, it has been the hardest winter of all, because the Germans had a good idea of what was going on, and, with the aid of traitors, were hot on our trail. Fortunately there were no bad Greeks in my village and the Germans could get no positive information. Although we had frequent alarms and many German raids and searches and much oppression – more, indeed, than in any other village in the island – they never managed to pull off anything serious. Life up at Gypselota was very hard, largely because the earth on the roof[1] was the wrong sort. Water dripped through unceasingly and their clothes were always wet. Mr Aleko often took them all off, saying it was colder with all his damp clothes on than stark naked, and he was right.

But bit by bit, and from mouth to mouth, the news spread, *via* passing refugees from strange places, to the nearby villages, and finally to the ears of a villager of Kourna called Kytros. He was being pursued by the Greek police for something, and, in order to escape them, he went to the Germans and received an amnesty as the price of betrayal. This evil and unworthy Greek well knew the lie of the mountains of my village, because we are neighbours of his village. So, towards the middle of May, he took two or three Germans, by night to avoid being seen by anybody, and led them up into the mountain where the hideout was perched. They had a wireless-spotting apparatus and an aerial with them, and they hid inside a half-ruined sheepfold sometimes used by the

1 The usual roofing in Crete.

shepherds, in a spot called 'the Fields of Nikolas'. Meanwhile a similar apparatus was in use in Argyroupolis; they were both trying to pin-point the exact location of our transmitting set. The chasm where Kytros and his Germans were hiding was only twenty minutes' distance from the set. Luckily God looked after our people, and, as usual, in the most suitable way. The set had broken down for several days and was completely out of action. Vasili Daskalakis had been summoned from Canea to fix it up, and had stayed on. Meanwhile, two little boys, having spotted the Germans, informed everyone in the hideout and suitable precautions were taken. When the Germans saw that they had been observed, they took up their apparatus and left.

Kytros paid for all this a bit later, when a patriot – George Grylos, one of our people from the start – stabbed him to death with a dagger in the middle of his own village. So all through the spring they moved about from one place to another in the neighbourhood, and under the protection of our village. In April an aeroplane came and dropped stores to them at Kalolakko, up in the mountains southwest of the village. They fell a little off the mark, but they found and collected them all. Most of it was clothing, some of it medical stores, the rest food, guns, Sten guns and pistols. What was needed was kept for the lair, and the rest distributed by Mr Aleko and Uncle Petraka among the villagers.

At the end of May, Uncle Petraka left the village for the Middle East, leaving Pavlo Gyparis in his stead, whom Mr Aleko knew well and who was always ready and eager to help him. Mr Aleko moved over to Selino, when, on the second of June, a serious event happened in the village.

It was at the time when the flocks are grazed from folds in the high mountain summer-pastures. The Germans were passing through Koumara, a mountain south of our village, where some of the villagers had their sheepfold. They were moving quickly, and by the time the shepherds got wind of them, they were right outside. Uncle Petraka was there – he just managed to get away, but they saw him. They said nothing at the time because there were very few of them, but they acted later. On June the second, Schubert (the butcher of Crete and criminal tormentor from the Gestapo) went to the sheepfold. Four Cretan traitors were with him, the Tsouliadakis family from Krussona in the Nome of Herakleion, and another from the Apokoronas village of Embrosnero, Manousso Thymakis.

Thymakis had been in prison with a life sentence, and the Germans had amnestied him after he had made a jail break during the Battle of Crete. The condition of the pardon was the usual sort – that he should serve the Germans by betraying his fellow-countrymen. He came to our village as a refugee claiming sanctuary and, as he was a distant kinsman of a family there, he was taken in as a guest. In this *mytato*, where he now appeared with Schubert, was a young acquaintance of his – one of the ones who had befriended him a few days before. He left the others a little way off and went up to the fold with Schubert. 'Welcome to Manousso,' Marko Gyparis said, as soon as he saw him. In they went, greeting everybody. Schubert was in disguise, and Thymakis introduced him as an English officer. He told Gyparis that he had just arrived from Cairo, and wanted to meet his colleagues in the hideout. They told them there were some others, but, as they were armed, they had thought it better not to bring them up to the *mytato*, in case there was anyone there who ought not to see them. They were very skilful – well used to deceiving guileless people – and poor Marko Gyparis was easily taken in; he told them all that had been happening in the village – all about the English, the hideouts, the set, the arms, the explosives, the drops, and a lot besides. The butchers summoned their comrades, who joined them, and when they had got all the information they needed, they asked Gyparis to guide them to the hideout where the English were now. He refused, pretending he had work to do, and then, with dramatic speed, he was executed at the door of his sheepfold. Ioannis Psychoundakis, who shared the *mytato*, was seized by another who ran behind him, while the first emptied his pistol into Marko's breast. Like lightning, Psychoundakis broke away from the traitor's hands and took to his heels. They fired bursts of sub-machine-gun fire after him, wounding him slightly in the forehead. But he carried on, and got clean away. Then Schubert and the four traitors fled to Myriokephala, and from there to Argyroupolis. The event was soon known all over the village. Several armed villagers set out to catch them up and kill them, but they were too late. A few days later a large force of Germans arrived and overflowed the village. They searched every corner of it in accordance with the information now in their hands, but in vain. In vain, too, they pressed the Goniots, as they had often done before. They didn't succeed in getting a single word, even out of the last and the simplest in the village. A party of villagers got away as soon as the search began, and ran in the dark to the Khainóspilia, seized the explosives we had hidden in the cave, and hid them in various other places where it was impossible to find them. After a search lasting several days without finding the smallest guilty fragment of evidence, the Germans returned helplessly to their base.

I had heard about this in Cairo from Uncle Petraka, but without the details.

Two months had now gone by, and the village had quietened down. All was quiet and normal when I arrived. I hid for a few days, then, thinking I couldn't hide for ever, appeared quite normally in public. Everybody knew where I had been and what had happened, but nobody asked me and I told nobody. I stayed there till about the twentieth of August, and then left for our lair in Selino, along with Manoli Gyparis.

We went through Apokoronas, as we always did, then climbed up into the White Mountains and in two days we were among the peaks of Selino at Akhlada. Our lair was very close.

Not many days passed before, one night, an aeroplane came and dropped stores by parachute. We were waiting for them in Akhlada, where we had prepared the ground signals. But all except one or two of the parachutes fell on the steep slope where our hideout was, in the pine and cypress forest. During the night we only found the containers that had fallen at Akhlada – with, among other things, a wireless set, some pistols and some money. When day broke, the whole forest seemed to be garlanded with parachutes, which had settled like great white doves on the tree tops gently beating their wings and making the tall woods look still more beautiful in the light of daybreak. Before the drop, we had shifted the lair a little below the well among some small caves in a gully.

We started collecting the parachutes, climbing the trees and unhooking them, then, when they fell to the ground, opening up the great barrel-shaped containers. They were full of all kinds of English clothing and of arms. The last were all German, except for the Bren-guns, Tommy-guns and Stens. There was some food as well, some ammunition, boots and plenty of bullets of all calibres. The assembly and transport took all day.

Not a thing was lost. In a few days' time, Mr Aleko called a meeting of the Selino Kapetans and distributed the stuff. They brought their bands with them, and each *pallikari* was given a complete new uniform, an Australian hat, a rifle and plenty of ammunition. Besides the Kosto-yersko band, with the Paterakis family as leaders and Kapetans, another Kapetan, Kosta Basiàs, turned up with his band and drew arms.

About the twelfth of September, Mr Aleko gave me several letters and one hundred and thirty gold sovereigns to take to Colonel Tsiphakis at Priné. I left our hideout very early, passed Mount Venizelos in the afternoon, near Yephyria. Suddenly hearing some shooting, I broke off and hid. But I soon saw that it was only some shepherds blazing away in the Cretan way[1] and went on. I reached Kyriakosellia late at night. Levtheri Kouris and his wife were at home. I gave him a letter and twenty sovereigns. His wife took the letter and read it, whispering it audibly to herself out loud, so I was able to hear it all. It was only a few words from Mr Aleko: 'I am sending a little present to your wife and children.' They were overjoyed with the present, and thanked Mr Aleko again and again. I also took a bundle of subversive leaflets[2] out of my *sakouli* and gave them to Levtheri to distribute in Canea.

---

1 Even in peacetime there is a constant sound of shooting in the Cretan mountains – usually solitary shepherds practising, or just blazing away for fun.
2 This was an important part of our work in the island.

A Small Incident in the Samaria Gorge

Leaving for Selino before daybreak on the eighteenth, we climbed up into the White Mountains and headed for the Omalo, reached the Poria, where the Viglis sheepfold lies. There we found Roussos Viglis, who told us a troop of Germans had just left there, heading up the winding path to the plateau – exactly on our route, in fact. But if we delayed, darkness would overtake us in the Seliniot crags. We asked if there was any other way through the gorge. 'There is one,' Roussos said. 'Come with me and I'll show you.' We followed him to the lip of the canyon.

He showed us the path of the wild ibexes climbing the opposite cliff, which meant descending first to the darkest depths of that steep gorge. He said we might meet some 'wind-boys'[1] there, and if they said anything to us, we were to say that the Viglis family had told us to pass that way. We thanked him, and started down towards the depths of the gorge. Though they are very wild, these are spectacular regions: enormous trees, planes, cypresses and pines with strong and gigantic trunks, and crystal springs streaming down on all sides. Right at the dark bottom, we met the wind-boys Viglis had told us about; so we greeted them and went on our way. When we had gone on about two hundred paces, two of the wind-boys overtook us at the run and sped on ahead. I saw what their

[1] 'Wind-boys' – outlaws, robbers or sheep thieves on the run.

215

intentions were, and called to them to stop in a friendly tone of voice. They stopped and we approached. We offered them cigarettes which they accepted. I told them if they were running because of us, not to worry, because we were good men, and there was no question of sheep-rustling or anything like that. I told them too, why we were going that way and also who had sent us. 'We weren't running because of you,' they said, 'but because of some work we have.' We went with them right to the bottom, till we crossed the Omalo-Samaria path. To camouflage our destination, I asked if that were the way to the Omalo, and we moved off in that direction. When they were out of sight, we changed back into the right direction, aiming for Linoséli, a little pass high up leading out of the canyon.

We had gone on for about a mile when a powerful voice[1] from a long way off summoned us to stop. At first we pretended not to understand who they were addressing. Then the shouting grew angry.

'It's those wind-boys,' I said to Yanni. 'They probably want to rob us.'

Then they opened fire on us. 'Stay where you are,' they shouted, 'or we'll kill you.' Bullets were whistling past us thick and fast and hitting the trees all round us, and our position, clambering up the steep slope, was very dangerous and exposed. I said to Yanni that we had better stop and hide among the rocks, or we would be killed for sure.

'No,' he said, 'let's run for it, and try to reach the peak.'

I saw that it was still a very long way above us, and quite impossible. They would have killed us. I stopped and shouted back, 'Are you shooting at us, boys?'

---

[1] The Cretan mountaineers have very strong and carrying voices and a particular articulation which makes them comprehensible when conversing at immense distances.

'Yes, at you,' they answered. 'Stay where you are or we'll kill you.'

'All right, but why didn't you tell us what you wanted when we were with you? It's not right to delay us like this on our road. I told you we weren't bad men and that the Viglis family told us to come this way. So what do you want?'

'Stay where you are! Stay there!' was all they answered.

'Run for it,' said Yanni, and ran on ahead. The firing burst out again.

'Stop, Yanni,' I shouted, 'or they'll kill us both. We've got our pistols, so let's hide among the rocks and kill them when they get close.' He said something about Germans that I didn't understand, and again told me to run for it.

'I'm not such a fool as to run now and get shot in the back,' I said for the last time, and 'Stop! I'm staying here.' So I stopped and hid among the rocks, while Yanni ran on, and I lost sight of him after fifty yards. The shooting went on, and then stopped. In a few minutes the robbers had arrived and began searching among the rocks.

I had moved over slightly in their direction, to the bottom of a cliff. They passed just overhead, and soon headed downhill. I saw them very clearly as they passed in single file. There were seven of them – all very young except one of about twenty-five, a sturdy fellow with a fair moustache – the others under twenty. The eldest had a German rifle and binoculars. I let them get past me, and then summoning all my courage, stood upright among the rocks.

'What's going on, boys?' I said. 'What's all this about?'

'There they are! There they are!' they all shouted. 'Look at him!'

'No need to look at me,' I said to the armed one, 'come over here.'

'Herakleiot traitors, that's what you are,' they said, as a pretext.

I was wearing riding-breeches with slanting pockets in front. I had one hand in a pocket with my pistol ready and my finger on the trigger. I watched the armed man carefully. If he had made the slightest suspicious move, I think I would have got him . . .

The two we had encountered came up and told me to show them my identity papers to make sure, as they said, that I was not a Herakleiot.

'Identity papers don't mean anything,' I said, 'perhaps I'm not using my own, perhaps I've got ten. I can only tell you that I am a Khaniot from the Eparchy of Apokoronas.'

'From which village?'

'From Kourna' [a lie].

'What's your name?'

'Dramilaris.'

'Where are you going?'

'I'm going to Selino,' and I repeated the story about the Germans up at the Viglis sheepfold.

'Who do you know in Selino?'

'The Paterakis family.'

'The cuckolds! Now we know what sort of a man you are, who's to blame if we kill you?'

'Who else but you?'

We went on like this until they asked me what had become of my companion.

'You ought to know,' I answered. 'You could see. I couldn't see anything from here.'

One of them said he could see him reaching the peak of Linoséli.

'I shouldn't think so,' I said. 'He has never been in these parts before and doesn't know the way.'

'Well, if he doesn't know,' they said, 'he'll fall over one of the precipices and get killed anyhow!'

'He's not the sort of boy to get killed like that. If he finds he can't go on, he'll either wait or come back.'

'This is a very bad region,' they said, 'he'll either fall over a precipice or go to some sheepfold at night where they'll kill him.'

'No, he won't. He'll neither fall nor get himself killed. Are they all such cannibals hereabouts?'

I started to move in the direction that Yanni had taken.

'You won't get through easily in that direction,' they said. 'It's better along here,' and they guided me a little to the right.

I shouted for Yanni in case he was hiding somewhere. The talk of this gang had made me suspicious.

'Yanni!' I kept shouting, and the echo of my voice went howling down that wild gorge. I reached a bright, clear spring on the edge of a chasm a little before Linoséli. I only sat for a moment, for evening was coming on. I drank some water and set off at a quicker step. By the time I got up to Linoséli, night had fallen everywhere. I lay down against a rock, because the place is such bad and dangerous walking it was impossible to continue. I decided to wait till the moon rose, and spreading some branches, tried to sleep. I needed sleep badly, but how should sleep have come to me? For every moment, a thousand pictures kept passing through my mind. What had become of Yanni? To chase all evil thoughts away, I decided that Yanni must have continued uphill, but he might be lost and surrounded by precipices . . . At the slightest sound I shouted 'Yanni!' but only the echo of my voice went rocketing through the limitless dark.

At last the moon began to rise, and her rays to illuminate with silver the high mountain crags. I jumped up and took the path again.

I walked slowly and with care. I was horribly hungry.

It was a little before dawn when I got to the hideout. All the boys were asleep in their little caves.

I woke them up and told them the whole story, and

asked one of them, who knew the region well, to go and have a look for Yanni. Not one of them had the decency to get up and go. I woke up the cook and asked him to get water and boil some tea, and then decided to go back myself as soon as day broke. Even he turned over on the other side and went to sleep again. Then sleep overcame me too in the corner where I was sitting. It was already daylight when the cook went to the well for water, and what should he find? There was Yanni, wounded and groaning with pain. The cook drew some water and led Yanni back to the cave. Everyone jumped up. He was in a tragic state, drenched in blood from top to toe. A bullet had gone through his arm just above the wrist, making a big hole where it had entered, and a still bigger one where it had gone out again. He had bound his arm up tightly above the elbow, to stop the bleeding and his forearm had swelled enormously and turned blue.

We had varied and plentiful stocks of medical supplies and surgical instruments from the last drop. We untied his arm and started to clean the wound. Not far away there was a hideout of Cretan patriots with a wireless set at a place called Sphendílopo. The best surgeon in Selino, Doctor Pentaris, was there, so one of our party ran to fetch him. He looked at the wound and told Yanni there was nothing for it but to cut off his hand. 'All right, Doctor,' Yanni said, 'if it's absolutely necessary, cut it off.' He cleaned the wound thoroughly and gave him something to take the pain away. The doctor bandaged it and told us to undo it every hour for twelve hours and let a little blood flow.

All this was because his arm had been tightly bound up for the last twelve hours. He would have to have his hand off or die. When he got over his pain and his tiredness a little, I asked him how he had got lost, and why he had not heard me shouting to him. He told me the bullet had hit him a hundred yards farther on, and that he had fallen. He went on a few paces then, and crawled into a little hole in the mountainside. He thought the pursuers might be Germans, so he opened his camera and burnt the film inside. Then he bound up his arm, and remained in hiding for hours. He managed to get to a well, and when the moon rose, made his way here with the utmost difficulty, arriving by daylight. He said he had not heard my shouts. The wind-boys must have gone past the place where Yanni was hit, seen the blood, and, thinking they had killed him, and not knowing who he was and what might happen to them, turned back without trying to find him.

Vasili the New Zealander[1] turned out to be an excellent nurse and looked after the patient until the afternoon when the doctor returned, who said his hand looked much better, and perhaps he wouldn't have to lose it. He got better with difficulty, but most of the fingers have remained useless.

1 Sergeant-Major 'Kiwi' Perkins.

The Fight at Tsilívdika

A few days passed. Then one morning Mr Aleko, the New Zealander (Vasili as we called him), Paul Vernadakis, Manoli Gyparis and I left the hideout for the Nome of Retimo, where a boat was due. We went by our usual path over the White Mountains to the Eparchy of Apokoronas. At the Viglis sheepfold we met Roussos Viglis, who had directed Yanni and me on our way just before Yanni got wounded. He said the man who shot Yanni was his own nephew and that he wished we had killed him.

We split up into two parties on reaching Apokoronas. The New Zealander, Manoli Gyparis and I went on ahead, bound for Asi Gonia. Mr Aleko gave me a million drachmas to leave with Paul Gyparis to buy food for people going through the village on duty. The password for such people was to be '*Black Carnation*'.

Vasili and Manoli left for Alones. From there Vasili was to take one of the Aloniots to guide him to the seashore at Rhodakino, where the boat was expected, and I was to await his return. Mr Aleko arrived there on the first of October, and sent me to Alones to await a band of men with whom he had a rendezvous at Argyiades outside the village. When they arrived, I was to put myself at their orders and bring them, probably, to my village.

I went to the rendezvous point, and in a little time Mr Alexis arrived – Captain Sandy Rendel, the officer who had conducted us from Cairo, and who had recently arrived in Crete and settled in the Lasithi Mountains over in the East. He told me the others had changed plans, and would not be coming, so we climbed up to Tsilívdika, whither the others were bound. Kapetan Manoli Bandouvas had arrived there with some of his band. They were trying to leave for Cairo, because, after the battles with the Germans in the Lasithi Mountains near Apano Siphi and the burning and slaughter of the whole Eparchy of Viano, it was best for him to leave the island for a while. The Germans had got to lose all trace of him, for, with the losses he had inflicted on them during the last battles, they were in the mood to plunge any area where he was lurking into deep mourning.

TRANSLATOR'S NOTE. *This was two weeks after Badoglio's surrender in Italy. Lasithi, the easternmost of Crete's four provinces, was occupied by the Siena Division under General Carta. Shortly before I had organized a large arms drop for Bandouvas, the most powerful of the Cretan guerrilla leaders, and told him to stand by in the eastern mountains to take over the Italians' arms before the Germans could occupy the province and disarm them. To negotiate this I visited Neapolis, the capital of Lasithi, and secretly discussed the matter with the General and his staff; there was even a question, at one moment, of the Italians holding the Lasithi passes against the Germans. Bandouvas, thinking the island was about to be invaded by the Allies (the Cos and Leros battles were in full swing) decided without any orders from Tom Dunbabin (who had landed from Egypt meanwhile) or me, to attack the Germans on his own. He ambushed a German column with a heavy force in the Eparchy of Vianos, killing over a hundred. The German general, Müller, immediately went through Vianos with fire and sword, burning villages and massacring several hundred of the villagers. Bandouvas's force was put to flight and dispersed and he was forced to ask Tom Dunbabin to evacuate him and a remnant of his band to Egypt. Meanwhile, I had managed to persuade General Carta and some of his staff to desert to Egypt as well, and smuggled them over the mountains to the south coast, where we joined Bandouvas and Tom. When the boat arrived from Egypt the only people to leave were the Italians, and, by mistake, me, owing to the bad weather which stopped me landing again after seeing them on board. So Tom Dunbabin was left with Bandouvas on his hands with his stragglers, all on the run, whom it was essential to evacuate. They were pushing westwards along the south coast, in hopes of a new boat being laid on by Tom and Xan in the Rhodakino area. – PLF*

That night, groups of the same band arrived in twos and threes. By next night, all the English officers in Crete had assembled there – Mr Tom, Mr Alexis, Mr Stockbridge (Siphi, his name having been changed from Michalaki to avoid confusion with Mr Leigh Fermor, Michali), Mr Stanley (Yanni) and Mr Fielding (Aleko). Mr Michali had left for Cairo a few days before, taking the Italian General Carta, commanding the Siena Division in Eastern Crete, with him, whom he had persuaded to desert. A unit turned up from Photeinou under the Peros family, to reinforce the mission. There were also the Rodakiniots with their band, the Aloniots, the Vilandredo villagers with the Loukakis family, Yanni Katsias and several others, all armed. You would have said the whole of Crete had risen in rebellion. The camp where we assembled was the same place where we had had the set the year before, in the days of Colonel Papadakis.

Food was prepared for everybody in a huge cauldron. The Aloniots and the Vilandredians told Bandouvas that they had one of his shepherds hiding in the village, in flight from the Germans.

'Who is he?' Bandouvas asked.

'George Ergazakis of Kastelli Pediada.'

'Him?' Bandouvas exclaimed. 'He's one of the worst of the traitors. He is down on our list. Fetch him here at once.'

Nikolas Alevizakis and Stathi Loukakis[1] set off at once. Arriving at Vilandredo at nightfall, they caught him at the sheepfold, bound him and brought him up to the mountain.

The examination began, and, as it was impossible to hide the truth, he confessed nearly everything. He said Polioudakis, the Quisling chief of police of Herakleion, had enrolled him into the service of the Gestapo as a spy; and much else besides. He also gave away the names of the other German agents in his area (and they were not a few) and a whole string of other information, all of which was copied down on paper. The interrogation lasted far into the night, and in the end the report was read out loud and given him to sign. He confessed that he had been a traitor to his country, and asked for his pardon, as he had repented. That was why he had left his area and settled in our district, he declared, so that the Germans might lose his track. But it was proved conclusively that he had come there expressly to spy for the Germans. He was sent off for the night under armed guard.

Then the fourth of October dawned. I went up early on sentry-go to a lookout post, as a unit led by Pavlo Gyparis was expected from my village, bringing old Andrea Polentas with his two sons, Christo and Pavlo. They were being hunted by the Germans and were due to leave for Cairo. But before the sun was up, I heard a shot in the hollow behind Tsilívdika, immediately behind the hill where I was standing. Then, after a few moments, a second, a third and a fourth. I ran back to the men like lightning and roused them with a long loud whistle. They all leapt to their feet and asked what was afoot. I shouted 'To arms!', ran back to my place, and saw the band arriving

---

1 Stathi Loukakis's little daughter was baptized by Xan and me the year before and christened Anglia (England). [PLF]

from my village. In a moment all our men were gathered
along the height, opening fire on a party of Germans and
Italians in the hollow of Tsilívdika, who were turning and
running like hares. It was a reconnaissance unit heading
straight for our hideout. But Manoli Gyparis, from my
village band, was coming on ahead of the others behind
the hill, to see if we were there, as agreed. The enemy
party caught sight of him as he was climbing up. An Italian
fired at him, but missed, and Manoli fell flat on the ground.
He saw the Italian aiming again, so fired back, and shot
him dead. The others turned to run away, and Manoli
went on firing. Then the others of our party reached the
top of the hill, and anyone would have thought a large
battle was in progress. An Italian *carabiniere* NCO put up
his hands, but the others had fled a long way by now.
The rest of the enemy unit were even farther off, sheltering
behind hillocks. Our people took the dead man's gun and
brought back the prisoner. Yanni Katsias shouted to me,
telling me to run to Kali-Sykia[1] and warn the villagers to
clear out, lest the Germans, returning in force, should find
them there and kill them all. I did so at once, and took
Mrs Katsias and her two children and left the village. We
were half-way back when the sounds of fighting broke
out afresh. We hastened on to see what was happening,
but by the time we had got up the mountain, it was over.
Yanni Katsias, who had come to meet us at the sheepfold
of Tsilívdika, told us another German unit was coming
down from the west.

The Italian *carabiniere* prisoner told us yet another unit
was coming from the opposite direction. Our people had
already seen them and were waiting for them behind
cover; and, when they got close, they opened fire. All of
them were killed except the leader who managed to get

[1] The nearest village.

away. A Greek was captured, wearing German uniform and armed with a German rifle – the only thing missing was a German cap, which he had probably thrown away. Finding himself face to face with Pavlo Gyparis and Petro Petrakis, two Asi-Goniots, and seeing there was no hope of flight or safety, he put up his hands and shouted, 'Hey, boys! – I'm a Greek, too, and from here!'[1]

'Who are you?' they shouted. 'Throw down your rifle.' They took his gun and handed him over to Mr Aleko, who was a little farther on. His name turned out to be Alexiou, and he was on the run from Retimo, and worked as interpreter at the German post at Plakia, just along the coast.

Mr Katsias asked me to take his wife and children to Vilandredo, to the house of Stathi Loukogeorgáki. This I refused to do until I had seen Mr Aleko and received the order from him. George and I took one of the children apiece pickaback and set off. The moment we turned down hill and broke cover, three bursts of sub-machine-gun fire came rattling past us. It sounded like some kind of signal. I ran back, shouting to Yanni Katsias. He came running up to us and I told him what had happened. 'They're here! Look!' said George. It was the leader of the advance guard who had got away, some distance from us. Katsias leant on a rock, aimed his English rifle and fired. 'He's still running,' George said. Yanni Katsias fired again and he fell. 'Go on now,' he said, 'he's done for.'

Some of the boys ran out and took his things. Andrea Peros from Photeinou got his Schmeisser sub-machine-gun, and also brought back a leather letter case, which Katsias took to where the officers were. Mr Siphi[2] took the leather case and examined the papers inside, as he

1 i.e. from Crete.
2 Ralph Stockbridge.

knew German. Searching through them one by one, he found one which was written in Greek. The letter was one informing the Germans about the assembly of guerrillas at Tsilívdika on the height above the ruined church of St Constantine, and it was signed 'Kouvakis'. He was from Selia, not far away. So it was decided to interrogate Alexiou at once for further information. But Alexiou denied all knowledge of him. He declared that he himself was only a poor interpreter, a job he had taken in order to earn a little bread. Theocharis Saridakis and Antoni Zoïdakis, both from the Amari, soon discovered a means of sure and conclusive examination.

It was this. For some time past, Mr Siphi had had with him a German deserter called August. He was as bright as a button and had learnt fluent Greek. They made a plan, then Antoni led him at the pistol's point, with insults and feigned blows, to where Alexiou was. 'Get up, you dog,' he shouted, 'and come and die too.' He led them to a ditch, and aimed his pistol at them. At that moment Theocharis appeared. 'Antoni! No!' he cried. 'Don't execute them yet. The colonel is in command, you must wait till he gives the order.' Antoni lowered his pistol, and started swearing at both Theocharis and the colonel for not letting him get rid of them both on the spot. A sentry was placed over them with a tommy-gun, and the others left. Alexiou immediately asked August the German, in Greek, who he was. 'I don't understand,' the other answered in German. So they both began talking in German, and August asked Alexiou who he was, saying he himself was a German officer captured in the Viano fighting. He went on to say that, with all this shooting, their captors would be afraid to take them about as prisoners and would certainly shoot them both. He cursed the Germans bitterly, saying why didn't they send a large force, if they knew Bandouvas was there? 'The Germans aren't to blame,' Alexiou answered, 'but the man who gave us the information – all he told us was that there were fourteen *andartes*[1] here, with Manoli Yanás from Rhodakino.' The present party had been sent forward to verify this, and, if shots were exchanged, a signal was to be sent to Spili to summon a whole battalion which was stationed there. Alexiou told the German to cheer up, saying that as soon as the Germans who had got away informed the Command HQ, the tables would be turned – the great thing was to delay their execution as long as possible. He had given valuable service to the Germans for three whole years he said, and they would move heaven and earth to save him. When August had learnt all there was to know, he made a sign to the sentry, and was led away.

Then Alexiou was brought forward and questioned again, but with no result. 'I'm a poor man,' he kept saying, 'and I just do my day's work with them for a crust of bread. That's all I know.' Then August appeared, and began to speak to him in Greek. 'Do you deny all you have just told me?' he said. Alexiou, seeing what had happened, shouted at the German: 'Ah, you dog! You are just trying to save your own life!'

'He saved it a long time ago,' Mr Tom said. 'Because even if he is a German, he's got some sense.' Then Theocharis formed an execution squad to shoot him a little way off. They led him away, and as he walked, Nikolas Manouselis from Kallikrati shot him twice in the head with his pistol; he fell, and, leaving him for dead, they came back.

Passing the same place a little later, they saw him sitting up and talking as if nothing had happened, saying he wanted to speak to Bandouvas. Bandouvas went, and he started complaining about being killed, and asked for his

1 Irregulars.

wounds to be bandaged. 'Come,' they said, 'die quickly,' and several more shots were fired into his head. His last words were: 'If anybody goes to Selia, give my greetings to Maria Kouvakis.' The other traitor was taken and shot and thrown down a hole.

Then everyone moved off from Tsilívdika, and, in the evening, went down to the beach at Rhodakino, in case the ship came to carry them away.

Georgie and I set off to a village nearby with the two little children on our backs. We put them down a little way outside the village, and I went in to find somebody there. But our man had taken fright, and didn't want to hear of hiding Mrs Katsias and the children; so we set off with Mrs Katsias and the babies to the tiny village of Nisi.

I had an aunt there, my mother's sister, the widow Katina Romania. She accepted Mrs Katsias with kindness, and said she could stay as long as she wanted, and we went back to our village. The Germans, having cut off the upper villages, were streaming south from every direction. They went to Tsoúndaka, but, when they reached the scene of the battle, they couldn't find any of their dead, because our people and the Aloniots, before setting off, had thrown them all down chasms among the rocks, so the Germans thought they must have been taken prisoners.

They burnt Kali-Sykia, and, when some of the old women tried to escape, they threw them alive into the flaming houses. Alones they looted from top to bottom, and a strong force advanced on Kallikrati. A large number also headed for Rhodakino, but the village had been emptied. They shot everybody they came across.

Next day, on the fifth, they reached Kallikrati. Our people, meanwhile, had gone down to the beach, but no boat turning up, they went into hiding in the Skaloti gorge, and, climbing up to Manika, laid their plans.

That morning, the Germans shot and wounded Manoli

Disbaraki, one of the best boys in Bandouvas's unit. He was also one of Mr Tom's best runners. He was from the village of Kamares, and we used to call him Manolió. He managed to take cover and then, slipping away, went to Doctor Papadakis in Levkoyia, to have his wound seen to and bandaged. This good doctor handed him over to the Germans, who, when they recognized him, shot him dead out of hand, to stop him getting away yet again. (He had been captured a year before during a raid on Mount Ida, with a charging-engine in his hands, having hidden all the other gear in the hideout. He pretended to be daft and the Germans took it in, and, dressing him up in German uniform, they set off for the Amari, in order, they hoped, that he might guide them to the secret wireless station. He slipped away from them at Ano Meros and rejoined us in the hills.)

The Germans burnt down a number of houses in Rhodakino. When they reached Kallikrati a half-mad old man told them to clear out, or else Bandouvas would come and see to them. They started beating up the village, and, in the next couple of days, shot thirty of the villagers who had handed over arms.

When the Germans said, 'Whoever refuses to hand over his arms will die,' an old woman, addressing her husband, said, 'My poor old man, give them your gun and don't let us be killed.' 'Be quiet, wife,' her husband said. 'We haven't got any arms.' 'Hand it over, my poor old man, they know you've got it.' What was the old man to do? All this went on in front of the Germans. So he handed over his beautiful Mannlicher and was executed along with the others who had surrendered guns. They burnt down nearly every house in the village, letting some of the old and bed-ridden, who couldn't get out, be burnt to death inside.

This was Schubert's battalion, which also burnt

Kali-Sykia. Alas! some of them had once been Greeks, from the village of Krussona, in the foothills of Mount Ida in the Herakleion Nome.

I was at my village that day with Phindrilaki and our operator from Selino. There had been a lot of trouble at Koustoyérako on the twenty-fifth of September. The Germans, after repeated reports about Koustoyérako, went there and surrounded the village, but they found only women and children as all the men had remained outside the village. So the women and children were assembled and the interrogation started. Where are the English? Where is the wireless? Where are the arms? Nobody talked, but the Germans had positive information. They lined them all up, and, as they refused to speak, prepared to execute the lot. But, before they could press the trigger of their heavy machine-gun, ten Germans fell dead. For some of the village men – about ten – had taken up position along the top of a sheer cliff above the village, from where they could watch every detail, and, at just the right moment, had opened fire. Not a bullet went wide.[1] Terrified, the Germans took to their heels leaving all their gear, their machine-gun and most of their rifles. But it didn't rest there, for the Koustoyérakiots gave chase and fired into the gristle.[2] Meanwhile their little irregular force received new recruits and the hunt went on for two days. A large number of Germans were killed, and others, hiding here and there in small groups, straggled back to their base. So all the men from the little villages of Koustoyérako, Leivadà and Monì collected their women and children and took to the mountains, some settling at Akhlada and some at our hideout.

1 Costi Pateraki actually fired the first shot which killed the machine-gunner, at a distance of over four hundred yards. It still seems to me one of the most spectacular moments of the war. [PLF]
2 i.e. to kill.

Next day a heavy German force descended on all these villages and all their anger exploded over the empty dwellings. With the help of fire and dynamite, not a single stone was left standing on another; but they did not dare to go into the mountains where a hundred gun-bearing men were waiting for them in readiness. Expecting a head-on clash, the villagers waited there for several days, and then decided to send away the operator and his set lest they should come to harm. He was brought to my village by one of their boys, reaching the district right in the middle of our own brush with the Germans. On the second day Georgie and I installed him in a good cave not far off, at a spot called Aphroim.

As the sixth dawned, we made our plans.

Not knowing if the German beat-up would reach our village, we thought of hiding the operator – Little Aleko the Tinker – somewhere else, for greater security. So I left him with Georgie and my first cousin Ioanni Psychoundakis, and went to Argyroupolis, where I found Mr Alevizakis and explained the situation. His orchard was a perfect hiding-place. I was astonished when he refused to hide him there even for a few days. I went back to the cave of Aphroim, but Georgie and the Tinker had left.

I waited for news in the village, and in a little while, Mr Aleko turned up. Bandouvas had gone to Kalo Lakko in Sphakia, Mr Tom and his party had left for the Amari and the rest of the English to Askiphou, which was where Georgie and the Tinker had gone – they were looked after by our old friends the Karkanis family. They all wanted to go on to Selino, but, learning of the troubles, the plan came to nothing. Bandouvas would not stay on in Sphakia, as the inhabitants were terrified after the recent troubles. So they split up into small units and turned back. Mr Aleko came back to the village with the Tinker, and Mr Siphi went to Kourna, to the Katsokhírina farmstead belonging to the Phindrilakis family. After two days there, Levtheri guided them to Kato Vasamonero, where, after resting a few days, they left for the Eparchy of Mylo-pótamo.

Vasili the New Zealander left for Selino and began to organize the villagers of Koustoyérako, Monì and Leivadà, which had now been burnt to cinders. A strong and well-armed band grew up, recruited mostly from these villages, but with a few from other villages and eparchies, like the three Tsirandonakis brothers from Zourva in Kydonia. Every now and then an aeroplane would come and drop them what they needed.

Mr Pavlo [Dick Barnes]

Bandouvas and his men returned towards Mount Ida, and, at the end of October, left the island from Ayio Sava, in the Apezanoi district. Uncle Pétraka came back on the boat that took them off, having been absent in Cairo about five months. A new English officer also arrived, called Mr Dick Barnes.[1] The wireless operator who came with him was the regular sergeant-major we had all known a long time called Harry.[2] He was one of the English that got left behind in '41, and he had only left a few months before.

They reached our village early in November, when Mr Aleko was living in some caves nearby, at a place called Vervílidon. Mr Barnes, who was known as Pavlo, was due at the village of Kalonykti, where his operator Harry would be waiting for him. Harry, while he was wandering about the island after the capture of Crete, had become great friends of the Galeros family there, and above all with George Galeros and his brother Charalampos. Mr Aleko told me to guide Mr Pavlo there. Charalampos lived at a little farm at Metochia, a small distance from the village of Limnes. So I guided Mr Pavlo to Charalampos's house in his vineyard. But Harry had moved off to Kalomitsi in Apokoronas, where he was friends with the

---

1 Captain, later Major, R. C. Barnes.
2 Sergeant-Major Harry Brooke, DCM.

Marinaki family, and had not yet come back. I left Mr Pavlo there and returned. Mr Aleko had left the village for Kastelo with Pavlo Vernadakis.

Mr Aleko lived near the village at a place called Rhodaré till late November, then returned in December to Kastelo. One of my journeys took me to Kastelo on the sixth of December. The church at Kastelo is dedicated to St Nicholas, and it was his feast-day. I arrived as they were beginning to ring the church bells, and went to Pavlo Vernadakis's house, but only found Stelio there, who said he would take me to Mr Aleko's and Pavlo's hideout.

There was continual rifle and machine-gun fire going on at some distance from the village. Rather anxiously, I asked Stelio what it was. He said it was German firing practice between Kourna and Kastelo, in the direction of Mr Aleko's lair. I didn't want to stay in the village with all this shooting going on, as it seemed to be getting nearer. Stelio said he would go and see what it was. But I only waited two or three minutes, then, taking a young cousin of the family, who was there for the feast-day, I said, 'Let's get out.' It was lucky we did, for just below, a number of Germans were running in open order, rifle in hand. Before we could say anything to each other, others appeared up above, and then some more below. They encircled the village and closed in. Whatever happened I had to get out. 'Run!' I told Stathi, the young cousin. So we ran to the east side of the village, where there is a cliff that is only low enough to jump down in one or two places.

We were at the cliff in a moment. Fortunately it was one of the low parts, but there were thick thorn bushes all along the edge, which made it more difficult. 'Jump!' I shouted, but at first he was scared by the height of the cliff. Then he said, 'Wait a moment. Why should I run? I haven't done anything . . .'

'Go on, get down,' I said. 'They're not the people to ask whether you have or you haven't,' so I gave him a shove. When he had jumped, I followed him, and got caught up in the thorns, and before I could get free and drop, cut one of my hands very deeply. But it was no time to bother about that.

I got up and ran for it down the slope. The other side was exposed to view, so we turned right, crossed a brook, and found ourselves on a path that could only lead to Patima. As we started along it, several bursts were fired at us from the top of the cliff. It wasn't far, and they could have got us by throwing a stone.

'Lie down,' Stathi said, 'or they'll kill us.'

'What are you talking about? Wait here and get caught? Keep running along the right of the road, stoop double and don't be afraid.' The right side was sheltered from fire by a low wall. Soon we reached a wide stream flowing down from Patima, and followed it uphill. We were out of danger. Stathi made off for Phlaki, and I for my village, where I told Uncle Pétraka what had happened. Then I went to Argyroupolis for more information, and to wait for Mr Aleko, if he got away. I found him there with Pavlo Vernadakis. They were hiding in a cave near Mr Alevizakis's orchard.

The Germans from Kourna had been practising shooting a little below the place where they slept at night. Woken up early by the noise, they remained motionless among the bushes and waited. Suddenly, lying flat, they saw the bushes opposite beginning to move. 'Who can it be?' they whispered. Pavlo raised his head a little to see, and there was a German pushing his way through the undergrowth. 'Draw your pistol,' Pavlo said to Mr Aleko. 'I see a German.' They waited with both pistols cocked. He was coming straight at them, and, the moment their eyes met, Pavlo fired. The German fell behind a rock.

But, only being wounded, he started firing into the air and shouting for help. Mr Aleko and Pavlo got up, firing hard at the rock that hid the German. Climbing another large rock, they started off, when suddenly Mr Aleko remembered he had forgotten his *sakouli*, which was full of important things – letters, money and so on. They went back for it. But the German was on his feet and running to pick it up as well. Mr Aleko fired at him, Pavlo made a dart for the *sakouli* and snatched it up. Then they both ran for it, and, taking cover, made their way to Argyroupolis.

The Germans, wild with anger, dropped their exercises and headed for Kastelo. Rounding up all the men they could find, they carted them off to the horrible jail at Ayia. Many of them were strangers who had come to the village for the feast of St Nicholas.

At Dryadé

Our talk was interrupted by Marko Stavroulakis running up with the news that Germans had suddenly appeared at the top of the orchard. Mr Alevizakis soon followed him, bearing the same information. Mr Aleko thought it was a bogus alarm to put the wind up us and make us clear out. Our presence had scared everyone there. Very gently and wearily, and, in a bored and ironical fashion, he listened while Mr Alevizakis went on. Then, turning to us, he said: 'All right, we must be on our way . . .'

He sent me off to Uncle Pétraka to tell him he was all right. Then I was to pick him up at Dryadé, some way off in the direction of the northern coast, between the villages of Karoti, Kouphi, Kato-Vasamónero and Meto-khia. It was a winter grazing place, and several shepherds were there with their flocks.

After I had told Uncle Pétraka what had happened I left for Dryadé at dawn. I found our people opposite Karoti, above the cliffs at the entrance to the Petré gorge, through which the Loumbiné river flows towards the sea on the north coast. The Mantàs shepherds had built Mr Pavlo – the last officer to arrive – a little hut here. There they all were, with the wireless installed in a cave on the very edge of the gorge. Mr Aleko and Pavlo Vernadakis stayed with them a few days, but Mr Pavlo soon complained that they were eating his food, and asked them to go. The food was supplied by the hospitality of the Mantàs family; and Mr Aleko, who had been two years in Crete, and well knew the limitless hospitality of the Cretans and also their present difficulties, suggested to Mr Pavlo that he ought to buy food. Mr Pavlo frowned and answered that he had heard much of Cretan hospitality and thought there was no need to buy anything. Mr Aleko explained the whole situation, and said it was not right to be a weight on the people in their present poverty and that, as he had some money, he ought to buy food from Retimo. So Mr Pavlo called Stelio Mantàs to send him into Retimo for supplies. He wrote out a list. When he saw it, Mr Aleko burst into a fit of ungovernable laughter. The quantities written down were so small that Mr Aleko asked if he might make a few amendments. Where two *okas* of beans were entered he added a nought and turned them into twenty. All the numbers were in single digits – one and two at once became ten and twenty, and, I well remember, at the end was written 'five sweet cakes'. Mr Aleko put the word '*okas*' above the five, and Mr Pavlo frowned still more. They had been talking Greek up till now, in order that Mr Pavlo should learn it (as he only knew ancient Greek, and had had few lessons in the modern). But at this point they broke into English. Mr Pavlo gave Stelio the list and he returned from Retimo that evening with a heavily laden mule; and among the other supplies were five *okas* of cakes, most of them *kourabiedes*.[1]

* * *

Mr Pavlo and Harry had been asked to spend Christmas with Colonel Tsiphakis, and had gone to Priné. We all met again at Dryadé after Christmas, but in a new lair.

---

1 A small round Greek cake made of flour and dusted with icing sugar.

The Mantàs family had given the alarm one evening, and next day had built them another little hut just above the first. It was so small that there was only just room for four men lying down. And we were exactly four: the two English – the officer and his operator – and two of us, the cook and the runner.

The kitchen was outside: two stones, that is, with the fire between them, on which we balanced the pot. If anyone turned over, he ran into a knee or a shoulder. So the poor cook, when I was there, and when it was not raining, had to lie down outside. Fortunately we all had good thick cloaks, of the rough white homespun kind the shepherds wear, which we had got from my village. But when it rained, we had a pretty bad time at night, as we had to remain sitting upright. One evening, when it was raining hard with a cold wind blowing, the wind tore open the tarred cardboard we had as a roof, and water came streaming in everywhere. One hole was exactly over Mr Pavlo's head, and the water poured down on him, so he piled all the clothes he could find on top of his head – his *sakouli*, his jacket and I don't know what besides. Suddenly a stone weighing more than an *oka*, which had been constantly rocking in the wind, tore through the paper and fell plumb on top of Mr Pavlo's head. He let out a shout, and woke up all of us who had managed to get to sleep.

'What's the matter, Mr Pavlo?' we asked. And he answered, 'This f–g hut is a public highway for water, wind, stones and everything else.' He was holding the stone in his hand, and, flashing his torch so that we could see it, he said it was lucky indeed that the rain had made him put all those clothes on his head – otherwise it would have killed him. In spite of all this, we couldn't help laughing. The rest of the night was torture as the entire hut was coming to bits. We repaired our villa later by spreading another sheet of tarred paper over the top and blocking the gaps in the walls with stones.

We had to limit our movements to and fro, because the Germans had set up an artillery observation post in Karoti, which was exactly opposite. We also had to cut down the arrivals of messengers. So we gave orders to all our friends to leave everything with Manoli Kallitsounaki in Kato-Vasamonero.

There was a deep cave – unknown to almost everybody – nearby, which came in handy as a hiding-place. We could take refuge there in the case of any acute danger, and we installed the battery-charging engine inside, where it could work without a sound being heard. We also stored all our gear there, leaving out only what we could carry on our backs.

On New Year's Eve, Uncle George Robola took Mr Pavlo to a *glendi* at Dimitri Bebis's house. He was wearing Cretan clothes and as his Greek had made great progress, it was not easy to spot him as an Englishman. Two Germans from Atsipópoulo turned up at the *glendi*. But as none of the girls wanted to dance with them, one of them took offence and got up and left. The other stayed on some time. Greeting Mr Pavlo, he asked his name.

'Pavlo,' he answered. 'Pavlo!' the German said, 'that English name!'[1]

'*Po, po, po,*'[2] Pavlo answered. 'What are you talking about? Pure Cretan!' The German said nothing, but got up to go – he left through one door, Mr Pavlo through the other.

I went there on the third or fourth of the New Year. The *glendi* was still going on – this always happens in Cretan villages. Each day of the first week of the New

---

1 I don't know where George got this idea from. [PLF]
2 Familiar negative.

Year the party moves to the house of a different villager, and on that day it was in the Mayor's house, at the top part of the village. I went there with Dimitri Bebis. We greeted the company, exchanged New Year wishes and sat down. The owner of the house – taking me for an Englishman – came over and greeted me by the name of Harry. I insisted I wasn't English, but all in vain – he said he knew me well, and remembered me from Christmas time. One by one, everybody came over and greeted me as though I were English. I didn't like this at all, and wanted to leave, but Dimitri insisted on our staying. The best of it was when the girls came and asked me if I knew any Cretan dances. Willynilly, I had to become English. I had wonderful attention and great kindness from everybody, and finally, to tell the truth, I really wished it were true!

Somebody whispered to the girls that I knew all the Cretan dances, and they all came and asked me to perform. I insisted in vain that I didn't know any, but they had me on my feet in the end. They wanted me to dance in front, but I said I didn't know how to take the lead, so they put me in the middle. The music and the dance began. Everybody clapped and shouted 'Long live England!' Someone else shouted 'Long live Russia!' There was a row and blows at once, and heaven knows what. I found Dimitri and we got up and left. It was all very tricky, but no fault of mine.

New Bands of Guerrillas

It was now January 1944. The fighting on all fronts was going well. All the world had begun to believe in the victory of the Allies, and even those Germans who had not been turned into cattle by Hitler could see that they were losing the war.

Everybody plucked up courage and hastened to enrol in some organization in order to belong somewhere. Irregular bands of guerrillas, apart from the ones which had always been in existence – those of Petrakoyeorgis and Bandouvas, of Uncle Petraka Papadopretrakis in Asi Gonia, and, a little later, the Rhodakino and Selino bands – began to spring up. These new units had a political as well as a patriotic purpose, eagerly fostered by their organizers. They took various names and began to exert themselves in the task of influencing the public. The population of the island was split into two political ideas: EOK¹ and EAM², they were called. But so far, nobody

1 *Ethnikē Organosis Krētēs:* The National Organization of Crete was Liberal, anti-communist and pro-Western Allies. This was the first in the field in Crete and much the more powerful of the two.
2 *Ellēnikon Apelevtherotikon Metopon.* The Greek Liberation Front was largely communist run and part of the left Resistance organization of the Greek mainland, where (unlike Crete, where, except for some parts of the Canea Nome, EOK was more influential) it had managed to absorb the bulk of the Resistance rank and file. It was EAM which was later to cause the December Troubles and the Civil War, both of which Crete was spared, owing to the heavy preponderance of EOK.

in them except the leaders knew anything about their political character.

The first armed band of EAM was that of Yanni Podia.[1] He had formerly been a member of Bandouvas's unit, but had split away after the fighting in Viano. Other units began to appear and one of them was in the Eparchy of St Basil, where they started oppressing all who refused to join them.

Colonel Tsiphakis, who was head of the Retimo section of EOK, asked the English to give him arms to equip a counter-balancing force in that eparchy. Cairo agreed, and the arms were eagerly awaited.

That month a new English officer came to our lair, Mr D. J. Ciclitira. It was the captain who looked after the houses of the Service in Cairo, so I knew him very well. His name in Crete was Dionysios.

About mid-January, Mr Dionysios passed our way, accompanied by Pavlo Vernadakis. They stayed a few days at St George's Farmstead with the Papalexakises, where we also often went. One afternoon when they were trying to get the news on a pocket wireless, two Germans arrived. As soon as they saw them they drew their pistols and the Germans put up their hands. They had managed to hide the wireless, but the Germans had seen the aerial outside and the earphones on their heads. They put the Germans under guard, and ran out to see if there were any more coming. They saw nobody and the two prisoners said they were alone. They were, almost certainly, merely on a scrounging expedition, so they made them sit down,

---

1 Of Asia Minor refugee origin, he was a youngish man of forceful, unstable and vicious character. After the war he appeared in the mountains with a communist band, and was defeated on Mt Ida by Right Wing guerrillas with Bandouvas's unit at their head. A guerrilla who shot him later walked through the streets of Herakleion displaying his severed head as a proof of his elimination.

and gave them something to eat and drink. Then, after talking to them, they decided to let them go and gave them some money to keep silent. The moment they had gone, our people cleared out in haste; all except one. They strung wire and flex all over the courtyard, and they twisted tendrils round them from the vineyard there. The one who remained, if he were taken by the Germans, was to explain it all away. He would say he was working in the fields for the Papalexakis family.

It seems that the two Germans said nothing at first; but when their colleagues saw them buying chickens and whole lambs, they asked where the money came from, and they told everything. The same evening a large number of Germans surrounded the farm and then, shooting signal flares, closed in, firing fast.

Inside, they only found the one who had remained behind on purpose, whom they arrested and interrogated. He said the people with the pistols were total strangers to him. They had entered suddenly and forced him to kill a lamb for them, and cook it, which they then ate, keeping him covered all the time. He was only waiting for them to go before running to inform the Germans, when two Germans had suddenly turned up by themselves, so he had not bothered about it any more.

'Where is the wireless?' they kept asking.

'I don't know anything about a wireless,' he answered, and he flatly contradicted the Germans when they said they had seen earphones and an aerial. He took them out and showed them the wires and the flex, and said perhaps the soldiers had mistaken that for a wireless, although he only had them there to hold up his vine. They took him to Retimo and locked him in the jail, where they interrogated him again and again, with many threats and blows, but he didn't change his testimony by a syllable. So, after a few months, they let him loose.

After all this, Colonel Tsiphakis took serious steps. He changed his hideout to a place above Khalepas, and then kept it on the move. For a while it was impossible to find him, even for us in the Service, as I discovered when I tried to find him soon afterwards.

'He was afraid of the Germans, George, and he went away,'[1] Mr Pavlo said.

'That must be it,' I said.

'But where?' he said, 'to Lasithi?'

He mentioned Lasithi ironically because it was the part of Crete farthest from Priné. That was how frightened he was supposed to be, according to Mr Pavlo.

At the end of February we both left for the Amari as Mr Pavlo wanted to meet Mr Tom. We ate and drank with great *keph*[2] at the houses of various friends on the way, finally reaching Khordaki near Ano Meros, the last village up the slope of Mount Kedros. Mr Tom had his lair thereabouts, and thither we were led by Nikoli Kamaro. It was about ten minutes from the village, at the spring of Yero. He had a fine hut there with a sheet of corrugated iron on the roof, probably used by the shepherds who pastured their flocks there in winter-time. When they had had their talk, we all sat down and began singing. Mr Tom's hideout, unlike ours, was very handy for food and drink, and the wine in those parts is like the wine at the marriage of Cana in Galilee. Also they had such a large supply of oranges that some of them had gone bad. Everyone began to drink deeply, and by and by, we were all very merry and this soon turned into a rag. We started with the oranges, picking out the rotten ones and throwing them at each other. Mr Pavlo didn't like this at all, and said it wasn't right. But before he could finish, he

---

1 This is explained later on.
2 A Turkish word meaning pleasure, high spirits, enjoyment, appetite.

caught several on the head at the same moment, the attack being led by Mr Tom. When the oranges were finished, it was the turn of sticks and stones. Mr Tom had got hold of a long stick, with which he charged down on the others pretending it was a rifle with a fixed bayonet. I had never seen him in such high spirits before. Then it was the turn for water – whole bucketfuls were thrown about, until we were all drenched to the skin. There was shouting and horseplay until nightfall.

In the evening, Niko Souris turned up from the coast, where he had been in charge of a landing which had taken place the night before in the Gulf of St Paul in Sakhtouria. I think it was the seventh of February. The other boys who had gone there to help arrived about daybreak, having stayed behind to organize the transport of the stores. This time the ship had also brought a representative of the Greek Government in Cairo, Air-Commodore Emmanuel Kelaïdis,[1] the backbone of our Air Force. He was the first and last representative of our Government to come to Crete. A Cretan from the Nome of Retimo, he had passed through our village in 1941, and, after climbing up to Vourvouré where our hideout then was, he left for Cairo.

It was now March 1944. Our presence was becoming generally known in the surrounding villages, which was dangerous. This was the fault of Harry, our operator, who had made lots of friends, with whom he used to wander about and make merry, in the surrounding villages. He stood godfather to a child in Episkopi, and also had a number of girl friends. I told him this was all wrong, and that he was putting the whole region and also our security in danger, but he loved rows. He answered a number of

1 He is now (1954) an Air Marshal and Commander-in-Chief of the Greek Air Force and Master of the Military Household of the King.

insulting things. I was so furious at all this that I went off into the rocks and remained there till nightfall. From that moment I began thinking of going back to Cairo and rejoining the unit from which I had been seconded. I didn't want to stay with them any longer. It was just a question of waiting till there was a ship and then asking Mr Pavlo to let me go.

An Alarm in the Hideout

It must have been about the middle of March when we were all in the hideout that Yanni Mantàs came running in a great fright, saying, 'Quick, they're on top of us.'

'What's happened?' we all asked, jumping up.

'Two hundred yards down the hillside – twenty Germans heading straight for us!' We seized our stuff and put it on our shoulders; then with Mantàs following a little way behind, we headed straight for the deep cave five hundred yards away – Mr Pavlo, Harry, the cook and I. I remembered Mr Pavlo's words, said as a joke, about Colonel Tsiphakis being frightened of the Germans. Each time he sent me there with a message he would say: 'Did you find him, George? Hadn't he run off to Lasithi?' While we ran, bowed down under wireless sets, batteries, rucksacks and so on, trying to make the cave before the Germans could see us or catch us, I stopped all of a sudden and turned to Mr Pavlo, who was running behind me and shouted, 'Mr Pavlo!'

'What is it?' he answered.

I answered in a low serious voice.

'Four more for Lasithi!' and he laughed.

We reached the cave and hid inside. From there we observed all that was going on; and nothing was happening at all. It was not hard to make out what it was all about, however, as the same trick had been done before. The news was pure imagination, and laid on to frighten us so that we should move to another area. They thought that our position there was no longer safe, wanted us to go, but couldn't make up their minds to tell us so outright. But all this was our fault, Harry's that is, who strolled all over the place making our refuge common knowledge in the district. I brought the subject up with Mr Pavlo, and went through all the reasons why we ought to move. But he stubbornly denied them all, and said we would never find such a good hideout again. And in a way he was right, it was wonderfully fitted for our work. Close to the Germans and all the main communications and the sea. We had whatever information was needed at once. Any special point we wanted to know from Canea or Retimo was cleared up with the greatest ease and speed. When one of us didn't go into Retimo for information, one of Colonel Tsiphakis's messengers would do it, and news from Canea would be brought by one of our people by any Greek car or bus – and quite often by a German vehicle – or by bicycle, as far as Episkopi, where the policeman brought it on to Dryadé straight away. We had wireless schedules with Cairo as many times as we wanted and every item was tapped off as soon as it arrived.

Those days we had been carefully watching the loading of a cargo into a ship of seven thousand tons which lay at anchor in Suda Bay. It was taking on military stores and a quantity of German and Italian troops. We learnt the day and hour of departure, and signalled it to Cairo. And we saw her, early next morning, moving out from among all the other shipping, and then sailing away from the Gulf of Suda. We watched her through binoculars, and at exactly nine-fifteen, the submarine's torpedo hit her. All the other shipping at once gave her a wide berth, and about twenty aeroplanes arrived on the scene and began dropping depth charges all round into the sea. Exactly three hours later, at twelve-fifteen, during which time she had remained motionless (stopped by the first attack), the second torpedo struck. Then she began to break in half, and finally sank.

The sinking of this ship had a powerful effect on the spirits of the Germans, who realized that none of them could count on leaving by sea in safety.

In spite of all the advantages there were several reasons for our departure, and one of these, according to one of our sources in Retimo, was that the well-known traitor and German cat's-paw, Alexomanólis, had learnt of our stay in that region, and was offering twenty *okas* of rice – an almost unheard-of thing in those days – to anyone who would guide the way to our lair, or to the people hiding us. And other informants of ours – notably Maria and Calliope Petrakis, the schoolmistresses of Kouphi and Episkopi – had warned us that everybody knew exactly where we were hiding.

But in spite of all this, Mr Pavlo didn't want us to move.[1]

---

1 As I have George's permission to append notes and comments, I must state, with all deference, that I find that his judgement, usually so sound, has slipped up in the case of Dick Barnes and Harry Brooke. His attitude was certainly not shared by the other Cretans and English on the island. Tiffs and misunderstandings were bound to occur between people living in a confined space on top of each other for months. I think this is a case in point. [PLF]

In Search of a New Lair, and the Capture of our Cook

When he admitted, at last, that we were right, and that it was time to go, I suggested we should ask Colonel Tsiphakis, and if he knew of no likely place, then I would find one. So we all left for Priné, where we went to Uncle George Robola's bee-garden outside the village, which was one of our haunts. I left Mr Pavlo there among the hives and went into the village, where I found Vangeli Robola, and told him Mr Pavlo was waiting for Colonel Tsiphakis among the hives. Soon we were setting off along the main road, to inspect a new hideout at Mikri Gonia. But two hundred yards before the entrance to the village, we met the Chief of Police of Atsipopoulo with two policemen, leading Yanni, our cook, in chains.

We both knew the Chief of Police well, as we had met him at a baptism in his village at which Colonel Tsiphakis was presiding. He had invited Mr Pavlo and we had both gone. (It had been very entertaining to see how Mr Pavlo watched every detail of the sacrament of baptism. It was the first time he had seen a sacrament celebrated like this, for, he said, a baptism in England was a very serious business. When the priest asked if the water were warm, or, say, when someone brought the anointing oil, Mr Pavlo would repeat the same rigmarole: 'Do you believe all that stuff? Pour in the oil! Do you believe in it? Is the water hot? *Do you believe in all that?*' – It had become almost a proverb. We were always saying, 'Do you believe all that stuff, Mr Pavlo?') So the moment the Chief of Police saw us, he recognized us. We took him to one side and asked him where he was leading Yanni and why? He told us the whole story. Visiting Metochia to make some enquiries about a recent sheep-theft, they had seen this boy in the village square, and he had looked suspicious. They called him, covered him with their guns, and told him to approach with his hands up, and searched him. The first thing they found in his pocket was a Beretta automatic pistol; then a pair of binoculars. 'There,' the Chief of Police had said to the villagers, 'so you are sheltering sheep-thieves in your very midst!' They took him into the schoolhouse to make a more thorough search, and found a military compass. Yanni told them outright that he was no cattle-thief, but was with the English, and, if they were patriots, they should let him go. The Chief had already suspected something of the sort, as sheep-thieves rarely carry compasses. (They can get anywhere on the darkest nights without compass or map!) But they could not let him loose without going into it. It was in vain that several of the villagers, friends of Yanni's family, had implored the Chief to set him free. Even if he had wanted to, it was impossible, as he had been caught armed with a pistol in front of everybody, and there might have been a bad Greek in the crowd who would have betrayed the whole thing to the Germans. They decided to take him to the station to find out from Colonel Tsiphakis if he was really in the Service, and, if so, let him free.

We told him there was no need to ask anyone, as he was our cook. But, said he, he couldn't trust one of his policemen, because he was a newcomer to the station – a Greek from Above,[1] and it was impossible to say what

---

1 i.e., the mainland.

sort of a man he was. 'I'll call him over and tell him what's going on, and then I'll know from his behaviour and his attitude what sort of a chap he is – but if he doesn't react as we should wish – what then? We'll let him go, and I'll join you as an outlaw.' So he called up his two policemen, and told them the whole affair, and the newcomer said he was ready to die if the Chief gave him the order. 'Well done!' the Chief said, 'I felt sure you were a good patriot, but I wanted to hear it from your own mouth.' He said we could go on our way with the absolute-certainty that, a little farther on, Yanni would be given back all his stuff and told to run for it. They would fire a few shots into the air, pretending he had escaped. And so it was done.

The Mission

We were back in the little hut among the peaks of Dryadé; days passed, and soon we were at the end of April.

A signal came saying a ship would be arriving at the beach near Rhodakino, and Mr Pavlo and I set out for the south, I think on the twenty-ninth of the month. When we reached the high crags overlooking Rhodakino, we lay down and gazed out over the shore and at the expanse of sea which the ship would sail across the night after. I thought that would be the best time to ask Mr Pavlo if I could leave. So I said that when the ship arrived I would like to go away with her.

'But what will you do down there, George?' he asked me.

'I would rejoin the unit from which I was seconded,' I said.

'You mean, you'd go to the Greek Army?'

'Why not? After all, I'm a Greek soldier already.'

'Yes, but what would you do there?'

'The same as everyone else – what my officers tell me; whatever the country demands of us.'

'Well? Your country is here, and here is where your services are needed. Where else could you do more? In Cairo?'

His words caught me by the throat unexpectedly. Having nothing else I could say, I went straight to the truth I had wished to hide from him, and which Mr Pavlo well knew.

'Don't forget,' I said, 'that we both agreed once that we ought to separate.'

'But, George, why? What complaints have you got against us?'

'No complaints, but I want to go.'

'But why do you want to leave? You must have some complaint, so please tell me what is it?'

Once more I had to confess what my complaints were, which he knew.

'I can't stay on with you,' I said, 'when you have Harry there saying there are no patriots in Crete, and that no one would fight if there should be a need of it, and that we are all thieves. Harry forgets so much and so much . . . At any rate, he seems to forget all the help and care and kindness he received for over two years in Crete when he was straggling from one village to another, and felt himself so secure among the unpatriotic Cretans . . . When have I ever stolen anything from you? Theft is an evil custom that has remained on here since the time of the Turkish slavery, and it is a scourge among us today. But we are not all thieves, most of us are very ashamed of all that and Harry ought to have better judgement. Whether we are fighters or not is a thing we have amply proved in the past, and will prove in the future.'

Mr Pavlo remained silent a little while after these words and then said: 'Perhaps, George, Harry lost his temper for a moment about something, and that's why he said all that.'[1]

He kept repeating what he had said at the start: asking what I would do in Cairo, and saying it was a pity for me to go back to the Greek Army, and so on. Then I put it

1 This, considering Harry's fondness for the Cretans and his popularity with them, is almost certainly the explanation.

from a different point of view – that I came from a poor village and a poor family, and that, if I went to the army, I might have a special bent in some direction, and learn something that might come in useful in civilian life. I produced a thousand and two reasons and arguments! In the end he said he could not let me go until he had found someone to take my place. He said that he too was planning to leave for Cairo soon, but he would send me on first, and see to it that I received training in whatever I showed an inclination for. But first he must find a boy whose work he could rely on, who knew all our people, and the paths and the mountains.

I told him there was a fellow-villager of mine, Aleko Barbounakis, who would be entirely suitable, and he might take him on right away. But, he said, he must see first that he was able to do his work properly, for which reason he could not let me go for a month. Our discussion lasted a long time, as we sat there among the thyme-bushes in the hot mountain sun, with the calm Libyan sea stretching away into the distance from the rocky shore below us. We had still not come to an agreement by the time we rose to go. He thought he had persuaded me to stay on, but I planned to jump into one of the boats secretly, and leave.

The sun began to slope towards its setting as we made our way to Rhodakino. This village had been evacuated by the Germans who had blown up a number of houses there, which was why we found (I think) Emmanuel Kotsiphi up in the hills. He took us down to a house of his, which was still standing, in the top part of the village. Here he cooked a hare he had shot and gave it to us to eat. We went off with numberless friends from the house, and I can't quite remember where we slept that night. All I remember is that at dawn on the thirtieth of April we were in the middle of about eighty heavily armed men belonging to the Rhodakino and Asi Gonia bands who had arrived there during the night. We lay encamped all day about half an hour from Rhodakino and fairly close to the sea. We had no food, so we sent Aleko Barbounakis, who was with the Asi Gonia band, to go inland to buy us a goat or something, get it boiled and bring it back to us.

All day long we watched a couple of aeroplanes which flew low along the shore from the Gulf of Messara towards the western coasts of Crete as far as we could see, and back. They came and went, each time in an opposite direction, all through the day. We were very disturbed about this, and many different conclusions were reached.

When it began to get dark we abandoned the rocks where we were lying up, and moved down to the beach. It was a steep descent, but we were soon there. Mr Ciclitira had come there with Pavlo Vernadakis, who was sending his fiancée and his sister to Cairo, as the Germans were after them. I took the signal-torch and went to a point Mr Pavlo chose. He told me what signal to flash and, to begin with, there was to be a quarter of an hour between each signal. We were on a steep cliff-side about a quarter of a mile above the shore, and here I sat in a cleft under a wild olive tree. Mr Pavlo went down to the sea, and I remained with Pandeli Troullinos from Karé to keep me company and stop me from nodding off and forgetting to give the signals. I started flashing on and off, pointing far out to sea: Da–di–di, Da–di: — · ·, — ·; these signals had to be repeated five or six or ten times every quarter of an hour. About nine o'clock we heard something that sounded like a caique out in the dark. Soon we could hear it better, and I started shortening the intervals between the signal-groups. They sent my fellow-villager Georgie Phindrilakis up to tell me to flash every five minutes. I did as they said and the same noise, the same low hum, continued without either approaching or fading. I had suspicions from the start that it was not one of ours, with the queer noise it made, dookoo, dookoo, dookoo . . . They never made a noise like that, not being caiques. Ours, each time that I had heard them, had made a noise more like an aeroplane, with little breaks in it, and we should have heard this one coming in alongside at least half an hour ago. Then, those aeroplanes all through the day . . .

Putting all this together, I had no further doubts that we had an enemy craft on our hands, or some fishing caique with Germans on board. But none of our people seemed at all worried, so I sent Georgie down to see what was going on and come back and tell me. I told him to say that I felt a hundred-per-cent certain the boat wasn't one of ours. Georgie was back in a moment with orders that I should flash the signals every three minutes. So I flashed almost without stopping, but feeling very frightened. Two hours had gone by since we first heard the ship's engine . . . Now it sounded as if it were getting nearer, for the sound of the engine grew louder. In a little while it had come in very close, and down below everyone was getting ready to embark. Some were even changing their jackets and taking off their boots[1] and getting rid of anything they might leave behind for the others. The ones remaining behind were collecting them, to eke out their own rags.

The sound grew quieter now – a sign that it had reached its stopping-point, and was preparing to put down the boats. I flashed my last signal.

Just as I was pressing the switch, I saw the ship flash out two signals. This was startling, as no signals were

---

[1] This rite of discarding footgear – the most precious commodity in occupied Crete – was always performed before leaving for the Middle East.

expected from the ship. But before I could say anything, I saw lights like flaming tongues coming towards us. Phindrilakis was standing next to me, and, curled up on the other side, Pandeli was snoring hard. I seized him and shook him hard, shouting, 'Wake up, Pandeli, they've eaten us!' The first burst of machine-gun tracer bullets were mowing the leaves down in the wild olive tree over our heads.

Pandeli, waking with a terrified start, rushed downhill before we could stop him, while we ran uphill and fell flat until the ship should stop firing. Some mortar bombs were dropping and bursting quite close. When the firing stopped I told Georgie to get up. 'We'll go a bit higher up and wait for the others, because soon they'll all be up here.' When we got to the path, we sat down and waited.

In a few moments we heard hurried footfalls approaching, and realized they were our friends from the beach.

'What's happening?' we asked.

George Yanà of Rhodakino, Manoli's brother, was the first to arrive.

'Run uphill,' he cried, as quick as you can, and get out of the cordon, or they'll get us.' We took fright and began running beside them in the dark. We let Yanà go in front as he knew the way backwards. I soon noticed that nobody was following us, and that we must have been fewer than ten. I asked Yanà where the other ones were, and he said they would go to Argoulé by a different road, and we must make haste until we reached the foothills.

When we got up to the foothills, we lay down to sleep till morning. As soon as dawn broke we descended a litle way and found all our fellow-villagers and a few more besides, so we all headed uphill, and assembled at the Rhodakino sheepfolds and cheese-huts. From there we could look down on any German movements, and see what happened in Rhodakino. They would certainly burn some more houses. Mr Pavlo and I headed for our hideout again, as the operation would be postponed for a while after all these doings.

The Capture of the German General

Marko Stavroulakis came with us as far as the village of Argyroupolis. When we arrived there we learnt that all the Germans in Crete were in an uproar because their commanding General, Major-General Kreipe, had been kidnapped outside Herakleion on the night of the twenty-sixth.

As soon as the abduction of the General was known, the Germans had flung a cordon round Mount Ida, where they thought the General might be hidden.

The truth of the story was that Major Leigh Fermor and Captain Moss and several of our people – Manoli Paterakis from Selino, Stratis Saviolakis from Anopolis in Sphakia, Antoni Zoïdakis and George Tyrakis from the Amari and several others from Herakleion – had left the hills and lain in wait by the road for the General to pass. Some other units had been told to stand by in case of need. The operation had been planned in Cairo by Mr Michali a long time before.

When I got back from Cairo at the end of July 1943, Mr Michali had been in the mountains of Lasithi, where he had managed to abduct the Italian General Carta of the Siena Division with some of his staff at the time when Badoglio made a truce with the Allies. He took them off with him to Cairo, then dropped back into Crete by parachute, landing in the Lasithi Mountains. The aeroplane that brought them came on a night when the sky was not very clear, and Mr Michali jumped first. If the jump was a success, he was to signal to the others to follow. His drop was in fact very smooth, but the plateau in the meantime had become swathed in mist, so the others could not see the signals and jump as well. After a time the aeroplane was forced to return to Cairo with the other boys, Manoli Paterakis, George Tyrakis and the Captain. Several evenings the aeroplane came back, but the weather continued to be cloudy, and it was all in vain. Over two months passed before the others could reach the island by sea. All the details of the abduction were planned and tested until at last the moment came when the men were all in their arranged positions. Some of the Herakleiots, however, fearing reprisals, wished to bring the operation to nought. And indeed, this might have happened, had not Paterakis had the courage to say to the Major:

'Mr Michali, we have come here to do this work; let us not go till it is done.'

'Bravo, Manoli,' he said. 'Off we go'; and the work went forward.

Mr Michali and Mr Moss, in their Gestapo uniforms, with their pistols and all the rest of it ready, stood in the middle of the road. The car arrived in front of them. They gave a signal for it to stop. One went to one side of the motor-car, the other to the other. Mr Michali asked for their identity papers in German, having saluted smartly. 'General Kreipe,' the General said, and at that very moment, one of Mr Michali's hands grasped him by the bosom and the other thrust his Colt ·45 pistol against his heart, followed by the words: 'If you love your life, General, do not resist.'[1]

1 George's version of this operation is obviously a collection of several different hearsay accounts, and many of the details (e.g., these dramatic words) are later additions, or time has been at work on them. But as he does not pretend to have been present at the time, his version is perfectly legitimate folklore. The main lines are correct. Wherever George himself was an eye-witness, the recording is surprisingly accurate. For a detailed account of the actual physical facts of the operation, the reader may refer to Billy Moss's exciting account of it, *Ill Met by Moonlight*. [PLF]

At the same moment, Moss had done the same to the chauffeur, who, however, offered resistance. At the same moment the other boys had leapt from their hiding-places and run to the car. The chauffeur was bound at once by one of the parties whose responsibility this was, and, without wasting time, Paterakis, Tyrakis and Saviolakis and the two officers got into the car. They bound the General's eyes with a cloth and the stilettos of the three boys were against his chest, ready, at the slightest motion, to pierce his heart. The two Englishmen sat in front and the car continued along the road with the Captain at the wheel. It was evening when they passed through Herakleion, and the Germans, all coming out of the cinema, practically blocked up the streets. When they saw the General's distinguishing marks on the car, they saluted without stopping, and the car passed through the whole town and took the uphill road towards the Nome of Retimo. During this drive through the town they met twenty-two check posts, and only at the last one, by Konoupedes, did they receive the signal to stop.

The car slowed down, and putting his head out of the window, the Major said in an authoritative voice, 'stand to attention, the General is passing.' The sentry leapt to attention with a bang of his heels and the car was speedily lost in the dark. They reached Yeni Gavé, halfway along the Herakleion–Retimo road, and, as soon as the village was passed, the car drew up. They took the General out, and the Captain with two of the boys struck uphill with him in the direction of Anoyeia. The car with the Major and another boy continued along the road. They took it close to the seashore[1] near the village of Panormo, and left it there. They scattered empty cigarette tins of the

---

[1] It was some miles from the sea, at the head of a gorge leading to a likely beach.

English Navy,[1] and fag-ends and made footmarks in the sand, and stuck a letter to the windscreen of the motor-car which said, 'This operation was conducted by an English Commando aided by soldiers of the Greek Army in the Middle East, so all reprisals against civilians are unjust and in defiance of International Law. We are sorry we cannot take the motor-car with us. We shall meet again soon. Major Leigh Fermor.'[2] They left the shore, and climbed up on to Mount Ida.

The Germans found the General's car next afternoon. It had been noticed since morning, but nobody bothered to go and see what car it was, as Mr Michali had broken off the flags to keep. But apparently the Germans did not believe the General had left the island, because at once Mount Ida was surrounded by thousands in search of him and his captors. But the men who had carried him off so boldly knew how to hide him as well. They conveyed him from cave to cave and from hole to hole, laying their plans carefully in advance. Meanwhile the Germans sought everywhere, shouting 'General Kreipe!' at the top of their voices.

In our lair at Dryadé we learnt the whole tale of the capture, and every few hours fresh details kept coming in.

There was another episode the day Mr Pavlo and I left the Rhodakino Mountains. The Rhodakiniot bands that remained high in the crags saw the Germans advancing on Rhodakino and beginning to burn down the houses. Then, separating, one party took the mountain path, the other retired along the shore. Descending from their heights, the Rhodakiniots placed an ambush for the mountain party,

1 Player's Navy Cut.
2 See note I (p. 264). The letter was signed by both officers.

and waiting until they were close up, opened fire. Not one of them escaped and two prisoners were taken.

Five or six days passed – it must have been about the sixth of May – when a signal from Cairo reached our hideout, addressed to Mr Michali. It said that a vessel would be putting into shore at Sakhtouria to take the General off the island that night. It came at about nine in the morning, so I had to take the signal to the Amari at top speed. Mr Pavlo said I must run to Yerakari, faster than ever in my life before and give the envelope to a boy there who would know where Mr Michali was in hiding and run the rest of the way and deliver it.[1]

I took the envelope, and, in spite of the enormous distance, reached Yerakari early that evening. I found Dimitri Koutellidakis there, and told him it was vitally urgent for him to get the letter to Mr Michali without the slightest delay. He despatched a boy at once to Ayia Paraskevi, as that was where Mr Michali was. The boy was back first thing next morning, saying that Mr Michali was not there, but at Pantánassa. He had sent a runner with a signal from there informing GHQ Cairo, that the beach at Sakhtouria was now being guarded by a large German force, and it was impossible for a ship to approach it. He had already sent off two or three runners to our hideout, but none of them had managed to arrive, so he had been obliged to come some of the way himself, and send out other messengers.[1]

However, Mr Michali had learnt that evening in Pantánassa that one of Mr Pavlo's messengers had passed through Yerakari, and he came to meet me just as I was off to find him at Pantánassa. I told him about the telegram, and that the ship must have come the night before. 'Never mind,' he said. 'We couldn't have gone there, because

---

1 I had gone forward to try to find a beach free of Germans from which the party might be evacuated. [PLF]

the Germans moved in yesterday morning. I'll send you straight off to Mr Pavlo,' and we went from there to Pantánassa and on to Yeni. He wanted to get in touch with Yanni Katsias and fix up a rendezvous-point with Mr Pavlo. I went into Yeni to find out where Uncle Yanni was. Mrs Katsias said he was at the sheepfold of Tsourbovasíli from Karines, so Mr Michali and I went there and found him. Then Mr Michali asked me if it would be possible to bring our wireless there, to accompany him for a few days. I said I thought it would be difficult, but we must see what Mr Pavlo would say. He also asked me about the beaches of Preveli and Keramia, and whether a ship could approach either of them now.

'Not at Preveli,' I said, 'because there is a permanent German post at the only good beach. I don't know the Keramia beach, but we've got a man from that district, Levtheri Papayannaki of Akhtounda, and he'll tell us all we want to know. He's in Retimo, but I'll go and get him without losing a minute. But I think, Mr Michali, that the only place you will be able to leave from is our beach at Rhodakino. That's where it will be in the end.'

'Come on, George,' he said, 'you go and get Mr Pavlo at once. Only don't go like a tortoise!' He also said: 'I've got my Cretan costume in Argyroupolis – is there any way of getting it without holding you up?'

'Mr Michali,' I said, 'it needs exactly the same amount of time for me to go and get Mr Pavlo as quick as possible and Levtheri Papayannakis from Retimo and your Cretan clothes from Argyroupolis. Don't worry.'

'My child,' he said, 'if you manage to do all that, you're a great man.'

'Your words flatter me, Mr Michali,' I said, laughing. 'I'm off. *Yassou!*'[1]

---

1 'Greetings.'

'Go with good fortune, and quickly!'

I left him in the afternoon and sped to Karé, where I found Pandeli Troullino in his house. 'Pandeli,' I said to him, 'go to Retimo at once and take Levtheri Papayannakis to Mr Michali, who is waiting for him in Yeni. Tonight if possible.' Pandeli left immediately in one direction, I in the other. I reached our lair in the evening, told Mr Pavlo all my news, and sent a runner to Argyroupolis to fetch Mr Michali's clothes. So next morning Mr Pavlo and I set off to Yeni, where we found Mr Michali with Uncle Yanni Katsias. We sat there till the evening, and, when the sun set Yanni took us to the east side of the village, where they brought us some food and first-rate wine, and our *keph* was great. The four of us were soon singing. Mr Michali sang a sheep-thieving couplet to the tune of the Pentozali[1] which went:

> Ah, God-brother, the night was dark for lamb and goat and dam, sir,
> But when we saw the branding-mark, we only stole the ram, sir.

– the Ram – the head of a flock – meant the General. It was a couplet he had made up, in the style of the old Cretan *mantinada* which runs:

> Ah, God-brother, we couldn't see, the night was black and dirty
> But when we saw the branding-mark, we only rustled thirty.

(It is a satirical couplet about a sheep-thief, suddenly finding out that the sheep he plans to lift in the dark belong to his god-brother. But, seeing his god-brother's ear-mark, he only steals thirty, instead of the whole flock.)

[1] The quickest of Cretan dances.

Then a runner came from the boys with the General, saying the Germans had put a cordon round Ayia Paraskevi, and they had been forced to break cover by daylight to get through. The last few days, with the Germans searching for him everywhere, he told his warders, 'I no prisoner; in a little while, you all prisoners.' The Germans, shouting 'General Kreipe' all over the place, had given him greater courage still. They went to Khordaki and waited for orders from Mr Michali where to move. Early next morning, Papayannakis came back from the beach with the results of reconnaissance at Keramia. Germans had just arrived there too, and Mr Michali's suggestion that we should take our wireless along with him did not work out, as I had thought. It was a difficult thing.[1] But I promised to carry every message to and fro between him and the set at the rate of lightning.

With the telegrams for Cairo that Mr Michali wanted us to send, we returned to the set, Mr Michali heading for Yerakari to rejoin the party with the General – or rather, with 'Theophilos', as they called him. (Mr Michali had given him this name, forbidding the use of the words 'General' or 'Kreipe', for security reasons.) Mr Tom's wireless and also the one on Mount Ida[2] had gone into hiding because of the German drive, so Mr Michali had lost touch with them, which was why he had come in search of us, who were much farther away from him. Mr Siphi's wireless also had been shifted four or five days earlier to Monopari, a hamlet near Kato Vasamonero. When we got to our lair, we too shifted a little way from the peaks of Dryadé to about half a mile south-west of them – to a crevasse built up with rocks all round, like a

1 Done, nevertheless, on one or two journeys across the Messara plain, to meet ships.
2 It was out of order.

sheepfold. It was a wonderful hiding-place. We could work our motor there without a sound being heard outside. Aleko Barbounis had joined our party a few days before, and we kept him with us. I told him I was due to leave, and that Mr Pavlo would take him on in my stead.

In two or three days' time a signal came saying a torpedo-boat would put in to shore at Rhodakino for Kreipe and his escort, but Mr Pavlo never told me, knowing I would again ask if I could leave with her. So he took Aleko Barbounis with him, and headed for Vilandredo, where they had arrived by then with the General.[1] They had taken him *via* Patsos, where they were helped and fed by our old friend Evthymios Kharakopos, and from there to Karines and Photeinou to the shelter of the Peros family and other friends.[2] The signal about their evacuation caught up with them here. When Mr Pavlo returned with Aleko and said they had met the General, I confess I dearly wished I had been there too.

The torpedo-boat came on the night of the fourteenth of May, and the landing-point was closely guarded by the armed bands of Asi Gonia under Kapetan Petraka, and of Rhodakino, under the Kapetans Yanà, Kotsiphi and Khombiti. General Kreipe left that night, and the entire operation – that operation which so astonished the world, including the General himself – was successfully completed. In the end, seeing so many armed warriors moving freely to and fro, and guiding him fearlessly and willingly across the mountains from one end of the island to the other, the General said to Mr Michali: 'I am beginning to wonder who is occupying the island – us or the English.'

1 They were looked after here by Stathis Loukakis.
2 Notably the Tsangarakis family.

The Theft of the Gold

Soon, a new young officer arrived called Lieutenant Hugh Fraser. He fetched up at our hideout, where he had come to help Mr Pavlo. We called him 'Levtheri'.

On the tenth of June, Mr Pavlo told me to guide Mr Levtheri to Priné. He also gave me, in little sealed bags of twenty-five and fifty each, two hundred and fifty gold sovereigns, that Mr Levtheri had brought, to take to Uncle George Robola or Colonel Tsiphakis for safe-keeping, so that we could draw on them later on.

We found a large company with Colonel Tsiphakis at Priné. Sheltered by rising ground on either hand, they were sitting in a ring in the shade of a carob-tree. We joined them for a while, and before leaving, I led Colonel Tsiphakis away from the carob-tree, and asked him about the handing over of the gold. He said it was better for me not to go to Uncle George Robola, as the Germans had had his house under close observation of late. So I took off my *sakouli* and handed over the two hundred and fifty sovereigns for him to give to Uncle George Robola. 'I'll leave them here,' he said, 'to avoid flaunting them in public, and come and get them later.' He took several of the stones out of a wall nearby and put the sovereigns inside. We said good-bye and he rejoined the company.

At the hideout next day we were told the money had been stolen from the place where Colonel Tsiphakis had put it. Mr Pavlo set out at once to find out what had really happened. The money had indeed been stolen, and they openly suspected[1] (one of the most trusted of the guards of Colonel Tsiphakis's lair), for the deed had been very clumsily done. It seems that he had been on guard above the lair when I handed over the gold. He must have overheard and seen us, and, as soon as we had left, taken the gold and run away. He sent his brother to the lair to collect his rifle, and then both of them vanished. It was hard not to suspect them, but everybody held his tongue until it could be proved. Colonel Tsiphakis was beyond words upset; but so were we all. I don't know what his conversation was with Mr Pavlo; all I know was that when we left, Mr Pavlo was not at all satisfied.

We returned to our lair, informed Cairo of what had happened, and in a few days' time went back to Colonel Tsiphakis's lair. On the road Mr Pavlo again asked me what I thought about it, and I said more or less the same as the first time. Then he told me that Aleko Barbounis had all sorts of strange suspicions. 'What do you think, George?'

'Mr Pavlo,' I said, 'I'm glad you told me, but I warn you never to say it to anybody else, because it is a shameful suspicion. The thief will be found sooner or later and you will get the money back. So beware, and say it to nobody else. Don't believe everyone you talk to, and don't suspect people.' And so it was, for in a few days Colonel Tsiphakis informed Mr Pavlo that the thieves had been discovered. He suggested he should go and speak with the boys' papa, in case the latter could persuade his sons to return the money. We went together, and met him in Kyparissé. We talked a long time, but the old man could not believe his sons would do such a thing.

1 Name omitted for obvious reasons.

A Quick Visit to the Underworld

One day I was alone in the lair with the operator and
Yanni Kapetanakis, our cook. Above the deep tomb (as
you might say) in which we were living, and at the crest
of the hillock, was a deep hole down which we often
threw our rubbish. It was so deep that when you threw
a stone down it, you could hear the noise of it striking
against the sides on its way down and slowly growing
fainter and fainter. Nobody knew how deep it was. Yanni
and I explored all the holes and caves near our lair, and
finally came upon a cave with a very small opening which
grew much larger inside, and joined another chasm. The
floors varied in level and it was a vast necropolis of animals'
bones. It must have been a goat-thieves' hiding-place and
slaughter-house from ancient to modern times. In one
part of the cave, we found a way to penetrate far into the
depths. 'What fun it would be,' we said to each other,
'if we found ancient treasure!' I went in front with a
huge signalling-torch, but as we got farther in, the
beam grew dimmer. At one point there was a light coming
in from high overhead, and we were astonished to find
that it was the hole down which we had been throwing our
rubbish. It was impossible to penetrate farther horizontally,
but the way continued downhill. In the end, we said to
each other we would reach the centre of the earth. We
ought to have borrowed the famous clew from Theseus,
said one, to find our way out again. 'It wasn't his,' said

the other. 'It's Ariadne we should have had to ask . . .'

The downward climb went on, until we found ourselves in a very narrow place, with yet other chambers lower down. Throwing stones and hearing them travelling down farther still, we determined to go as far down as we could. I was in front, and just ahead of me was a large round stone blocking the way into the next chamber. It just fitted, but, thinking I could roll it down, I put one hand on the stone, the other on the side of the narrow entrance. I twisted my body to the left and, leaning forward, put my leg against the side of the stone and started shoving hard. All of a sudden it began to move and then rolled away below. At the same instant all the right side of that part of the cave collapsed, and fell far into the depths.

I remember nothing more of that terrifying phenomenon, after the moment I set the rock moving with my leg, but how it suddenly fell away under me. My other leg, which was resting on the right side, went over the edge as well and I thought I was about to follow the rocks into the bowels of the earth. I only managed to say 'All-Holy Virgin!' Then I don't know how many minutes passed. I only know that in a little while I discovered I was still in the same place. The inside of the cave had completely collapsed, and I had not heard a sound. Perhaps some unseen power saved me, for I had called the All-Holy Virgin's name, and not even a pebble had struck me. I lit the torch, and tried to discern what lay below; and I saw, shuddering, that I was on the very lip of Hades, if I may put it so. I turned back and shouted 'Ill-fated Yanni!' 'George!' he shouted back – he was filled with terror as well, thinking that I was already buried deep in that frightful abyss. He had halted a few yards behind me, out of the danger.

Quickly, quickly we abandoned our exploration, nor did we need the clew of Theseus and Ariadne to find the way to the Upper Air again. When we got outside, we were trembling all over.

'It made a noise like a huge explosion and an earthquake combined lasting nearly five minutes,' Yanni declared. 'I thought the whole mountain was coming to bits.'

'I didn't hear a thing,' I said. 'The only thing I felt was that I was going over the edge at the same time as the rock – and then, there I was in the same place, with everything changed all round me: I felt as if I had been to sleep. It must have been the most dangerous moment in my life. I have never felt Charon so close.'

The Dark Cave and Sabotage

One moonlight night we loaded all our gear on animals and left the region of Dryadé to settle in a large cave twenty minutes' march to the south-west of the village. The cave is called Skoteini,[1] and it runs into the flank of a little gorge near the Mousela river which severs the Nomes of Retimo and Canea. It goes deep into the side of the precipice, and there is a large dark chamber in the centre where millions of bats hang in immense clusters from the roof. A few days later I took the wireless set to the hideout of Mr Dionysios, up in the high mountains west of Asi Gonia. He and his party had all nested in a chasm enclosed by enormous rocks, full now of armed men and messengers, as it was on the direct way to our other hideouts in Selino and Canea and Apokoronas, and was also responsible for the beach at Rhodakino where the boats came, and for the distribution of the various stores from Cairo – arms, explosives, clothing, food and the rest of it. There was a constant going and coming and fetching and carrying. The wireless operator was an English lieutenant we called Manoli, a noble and generous man, though a little daft. He spoke no Greek and had an interpreter with him called Niko Xira, from the town of Canea.

In a few days Mr Pavlo set off with Aleko Barbounis.

1 'The Dark One'.

I realized they were going to meet a ship, but pretended not to. When Aleko got back, he told me Mr Pavlo had left for Cairo, enjoining him not to tell anyone as he would be back in twelve days. 'So he has given me the slip,' I thought, 'never mind.' The same vessel brought a party of commandos which was shortly to go into action in our area. They were looking out for a good place to lie up for a few days, and, until they were fixed up, they stayed in Mr —'s orchard in —, while the owner looked for another place for them. He soon declared that he had found a good one, but they would have to pay him fifty sovereigns.[1] It was obviously one of his usual schemes for exploiting people, and the English left his orchard in a rage and came to our hideout at Skoteini.

The day of the sabotage was approaching – it was due to coincide with similar actions all over Greece, and the commanding officer of the party went for a last reconnaissance on the plain of Armenoi, where they were going to strike. They had Mr —[2] with them, to supply the information about the German petrol and supply dumps at Armenoi, the biggest supply centre in the whole nome.

But he was unwilling to risk the area, and, a few days earlier he had started sending daily reports of the systematic evacuation of the stores. Finally, bit by bit, he presented a picture of the plain of Armenoi as almost stripped of its dumps, and finally suggested that the sabotage should be cancelled as not being worth all the trouble and the danger, and succeeded in persuading the English to drop the whole scheme. The night of the twenty-second arrived, when the general sabotage was to be launched, so the unit set off with their commander and for the bridge at Kouphi. There they lay in wait for a German motor-car, opened

[1] This is the only case I have heard of such a preposterous proposal. [PLF]
[2] Name omitted.

fire on it and blew it up. They killed some soldiers who were inside, and left some things lying about to show that it had been done by the English, also a black beret that — had borrowed from me. At the same time a party of our people cut the wires of the telephone exchange at Episkopi.

The Drop at Arkadi

On the way back we spent the night in the heather clump just outside my village. It was past midnight and bein very tired, we lay down and slept at once.

When dawn began to break, I was woken by a voic close by. It was a girl from the village shouting at the to of her voice, '*The black cattle are among the vine-shoots!* which was the village alarm for the arrival of Germans The vine-shoots, however, were very close to us, as i happened, and here we were still lying down. So I got u carefully and looked round, and just below us, among th same heather clumps, I saw a German waking up an shaking his greatcoat. A little farther on, three more wer climbing towards a garden. I woke Mr Levtheri gently saying: 'Wake up, there are Germans all round us.' H awoke – and I stopped him from standing up, as the bushe were low and sparse. Stooping double, we sneaked awa in the opposite direction, leaving the heather for som rocks and olive trees. Some more Germans were stretche out there all fast asleep. We hurried past them and away stopping only when we had reached Myrioképhala on th opposite slopes. They were wandering all over the place Then we left for Arkadi,[1] where a parachute drop wa due.

1 The most historically important of the Cretan monasteries, the 'rent Arka dion' of Swinburne's poem, Arkadi was the scene of the firing of the powde

As usual, it was a mixed success. After we had distributed the arms, whatever clothing remained was handed over to the Flock-Master of the Abbey, Father Gabriel, to be hidden away. We put a few bits of clothing into a sack for the use of the lair, also the parachute, and handed that as well to Father Gabriel to keep until we sent someone to collect it. He took me with him, so that I would know the hole he had hidden it in among the vineyards. The remaining things were given to Colonel Tsiphakis. The most important item was about fifty rifles.

When nearly the whole party had broken up, Mr Levtheri and I took the road to Amari. We were bound for Ano Meros, to meet Mr Tom there, who had just got back from Cairo. We climbed up as far as the old Turkish Tower, and down the other side until the Abbey of Arkadi was out of sight. As we entered this new territory, a noise that sounded like a battle with rifles echoed from the gorge on our right. We hastened on as fast as we could, thinking our bands, on their way home from the drop, had run into some Germans and come to blows. Hastening our steps, we left the noise far behind, and headed for Ano Meros. There we found Mr Tom with a cheerful company, and ate at noon next day in Doctor Katsandóni's house, then moved along to Yerakari, where we spent the night. We rested there all next day, as Mr Levtheri took a great fancy to the village. There was good wine, good company, sweet grapes and the gramophone playing in the shade of the cherry trees.

---

magazine in 1866, by the Abbot. Rather than surrender to the beleaguering Turks, he destroyed himself, along with the Abbey's defenders and the villagers who had sought asylum there. The present Abbot – the Archimandrite Dionysios Psaroudakis – and two of his monks – took up arms and played an active part in fighting the parachutists in 1941. Though the Abbey was closely watched by the enemy, the monks were always willing and eager to help in Resistance work.

We got to Alones on the last day of the month and installed our lair once more in the crevasse near Dryadé.

On the eighth of August, a party of our people – Levtheri Psaroudakis and the gendarmerie warrant-officer Stratidakis and Mr Tom, led by Antoni Zoïdakis[1] from the village of Ay-Yanni in the Amari – was heading for Priné. Mr Tom was on his way to meet the leaders of EOK and EAM to discuss the differences that separated the two organizations and come to an agreement about co-operation with each other, because things had reached a dangerous pitch between them. Mr Tom and his companions were about to cross over from the foothills of Vrysina where a path cuts across the main Retimo— Armenoi motor-road. This stretch of the journey was dangerous because of the Germans, for they had guard posts, trenches and machine-gun nests all over the place. There are some vineyards close to the foothills, and somewhere near the road there, two Germans were sitting. Both parties feigned indifference on both sides, and our people continued on the way in single file at wide intervals. Antoni Zoïdakis came last. The Germans must have got wind of something, for as the last of these strangers passed they fired at him with their pistols. He stopped one of the bullets, but did not go unavenged, for with the first report, Mr Tom, who was last but one among those bushes, turned round and emptied his pistol at the Germans. One was killed there and then, and the other seriously wounded. The ones in front doubled back on their traces, as there was danger ahead. Poor Antoni was left there wounded: perhaps his wound was not a mortal one, and perhaps he might have been saved.

Some more Germans soon arrived. They tied Antoni

---

1 A cheerful, fearless, enterprising man, a great friend, one of our best and oldest helpers, and one of the main figures in the capture of General Kreip.

to the back of their car and dragged him behind them all along the road to Armenoi. There they threw his unknown corpse, unrecognizable now, on the side of the road, forbidding anyone to bury him. When a couple of days had passed, they threw him into a hole and filled it up.[1]

I was there when Mr Tom arrived at Kyparissé next day and he said he wanted me with him, so I guided him from there to Melidoni in Apokoronas, where all the leaders and Kapetans had assembled, and also the representative of the Greek Government in Cairo, Air Commodore Kelaïdis. It must have been about the twentieth of August. I don't know what they discussed, I only know that they reached no agreement. So Mr Tom, Kapetan Petraka and two others from our village (Marko Drakakis and Joseph Petrakis) returned by the path along the foothills of the White Mountains. All of a sudden we were in the middle of an ELAS[2] unit of over fifty men. They wanted, they said, to have a talk and to ask Mr Tom whether agreement had been reached with EAM. 'Unfortunately not,' Mr Tom answered them. They wanted to know the reason, but he said they would have to ask their leaders, and find out from them. Their attitude to us was a bullying one, and they tried hard to force us into argument. I don't know what they wanted. Mr Tom and Uncle Petraka avoided it carefully, and we left them behind and went on our way.

1 He was a terrible loss to everyone.
2 ELAS: *Ellenikòs Laïkòs Apelevtherotikòs Stratòs* = Greek Popular Liberation Army, the left-wing 'army' of EAM.

The Burning of the Kedros Villages

It was night by the time we approached the village of
Meronas. We found a friend of ours called Aleko who
took us to a little solitary garden between Meronas and
Yennà, quite close to the motor road that runs through
Meronas to Yerakari. There we were told that the Germans were burning all the Kedros villages of the Amari
and shooting all the men they could catch. When dawn
broke, we got up and tried to head for Nevs-Amari
and Monastiraki. But suddenly, as we reached the brook
flowing down from Meronas, we saw a friend – a boy we
knew – running as hard as he could; and when he saw us,
he waved for us to run too. So we pelted downhill
alongside the stream, and stopped a little way above
Meronas, where he joined us. It was Niko Kalomeno-
poulos from Nevs-Amari. Then, coming down from
above, some Germans passed our hiding-place driving a
large herd of cattle stolen from the villages they had set
on fire. They were taking them to the school at Asomatoi,
and Niko had managed to steal a few back, and hide them.

We stayed in hiding there several hours, with the
Germans passing us continually, driving animals of all
kinds and dragging cartloads of variegated loot they had
plundered from the houses before setting them on fire.
They had looted them down to the very door-nails, as
we say.

Seeing that it was hopeless that way, we had to find

another. So we went to Bistayì, passing between the school and Yennà. There we found our friend Mr Manoussaka, and, after a meal with him, we continued our way, climbing up the side of Mount Ida to a cave above Nithavri, where Mr Tom now had his lair, in a cave where General Kreipe had recently been a guest for the night. I stayed there two or three days before leaving, watching the Kedros villages burning ceaselessly on the other side of the deep valley. Every now and then we could hear the sound of explosions. The Germans went there in the small hours of the twenty-second of August and the burning went on for an entire week. The villages we could see from there and which were given over to the flames were: Yerakari, Kardaki, Gourgouthoi, Vrysses, Smilès, Dryes and Ano Meros. First they emptied every single house, transporting all the loot to Retimo, then they set fire to them, and finally, to complete the ruin, they piled dynamite into every remaining corner, and blew them sky high. The village schools met the same fate, also the churches and the wells, and at Ano Meros they even blew up the cemetery. They shot all the men they could find. Finally, when they had burnt them all, they dropped leaflets by plane saying they had burnt Anoyeia, Kamares, Yerakari, Gourgouthoi, Kardaki, Smilès, Vrysses, Dryes, Ano Meros, Krya-Vryssi and Sakhtouria, because, they said, those villages had sheltered General Kreipe and his captors, until they set sail from Sakhtouria.[1] But the German leaflets were not telling the truth. They were not burning the villages after all these months because of the abduction of the General, and even if, as it seemed, they had learnt the outlines of his capture and flight from the island, their purpose was quite different, as we all grasped

1 Their information was incorrect, as the party, as we have seen, left from Rhodakino, about twenty miles west of Sakhtouria.

later. As they were making ready to evacuate the whole of Crete except an area round Canea where all their forces were to be concentrated, they were determined to take preliminary steps, fearing that bands of patriots and the Cretan people in general might fall upon them as they withdrew to avenge all the evil they had suffered. So they launched this cruel campaign to terrorize the entire island, and to show us all that the Germans in Crete still had the power to destroy and overthrow, as barbarously as ever, all that still remained standing.

At the end of August and the beginning of September, Mr Pavlo returned after two months' absence. Among the new arrivals there was an officer whom we called Mitsos,[1] who trained our boys in various types of heavy weapons. He had set up near our village, and the mountains resounded day after day with reports and the rattle of machine-guns and the bangs of bursting mortar-bombs and the explosion of limpets and mines.

At the beginning of September, all the English officers met in conference with our leaders at the Abbey of Arkadi. Mr Mitsos passed through our hideout, guided by one of the Pendaris family from Selino. We had some splendid company at this time, and roasted a pig, weighing twenty *okas*, on a spit. There was another officer, Captain Steve Verney (whom we called Stephanos), who took a boy from our village called Marko Drakakis as guide. Stephanos worked inside Canea itself. He also was heading for Arkadi with Mr Mitsos. In Canea he used to live in Sintrivani Square, just next to the harbour. Mr Pavlo and I left the hideout on the eleventh, but we started late, and were benighted by the time we reached Patsos. Here we were the guests of our friend Evthymios Kharakopos. We were in no hurry to leave next day, as the distance from Patsos to

[1] Major Bruce Mitford.

Arkadi is only four hours, and the Germans had bombarded Pantanassa the day before, so we had to be careful. Passing Apostoloi, we heard a lot of shooting, so swerved aside to Meronas to find out what was up. We learnt that an ELAS unit had opened fire on two German vehicles near Apostoloi on their way from Retimo to the Amari. The fight was still going on, so we changed our route and headed for Mr Tom's lair on Mount Ida and spent the night there. All through the night German machine-gun tracer-bullets fell like hail on Nevs-Amari, in the neighbourhood of the school. A Doctor Yeneralis of Yerakari, a well-known Germanophile, was killed in this bombardment.

At dawn, Mr Tom arrived with Granpa, as we called Mr Emmanuel Papadoyannis, later a minister in the government.

Mr Pavlo and I started back in the afternoon. Descending towards Phourphoura, we found men, women and children streaming up the mountain. They were frightened lest the Germans, after these new incidents, would burn down all the surrounding hamlets. The villagers had emptied their houses of all that was portable or precious, and then left, in order to avoid the fate of the Kedros villages. Many of the women we met were climbing up Mount Ida barefoot, heading right for the summit to pray in the little chapel there, and beseech the Holy Cross (to which it was dedicated) to prevent the Germans burning their houses down. We descended to Phourphoura, walked through the abandoned streets and made for Vyzari, and there was not a living soul in either of these great villages. We went through Kaloyerou and then through Monastiraki opposite. Only in the last of these did we see anybody – half a dozen, only, and all in flight. Seeing us going straight ahead, they shouted to us to turn back, because many German troop-carrying trucks had driven to the school packed with soldiers, who were now burning all the villages down. We feigned indifference and said we would carry on, hoping the Germans wouldn't trouble us as we had done them no harm. They said all they could to turn us from our purpose, but we shouted '*Yassas!*' and pushed on. But when we were out of sight, we swerved to the left again and started climbing up Mount Samito, which stands right in the heart of the eparchy. When we got higher, we were able to count more than sixty vehicles heading for the school. We couldn't see whether or not there were troops inside, as dusk was falling and all their headlights were on. We hastened across Samito to get to Mesonísia before night fell. It is a little hamlet not far from the burnt-out shell of Yerakari.

But, between Nevs-Amari and Kardaki, night overtook us. A light rain had begun to fall some time ago, and, under that cloudy sky, darkness had fallen earlier than usual. We tried to go on, but it was impossible on that jagged path in the dark. A strong wind blew up, and we searched for a corner to shelter from the wind and the drizzle, if it went on. Fumbling blindly, we found a rock one side of which, shielding us from the wind, was almost bearable. But we were damp and soaking with sweat, and very cold all that night. We couldn't shut our eyes for the cold, so we huddled up close, back to back, to try to get warm. Now and then Mr Pavlo asked me: 'Are you cold, George?' 'No, Mr Pavlo; what about you?' 'A bit, just a bit. Come a little closer and see if you can put your back over more of mine.' The night seemed to last a whole year, until at last dawn began to glimmer. We didn't wait for it to get much lighter before we were on our feet. What depressed us more than anything was that a few yards away stood a little empty, watertight house. We got to Mesonísia and found the house of a friend, a boy called

Manousso. His mamma quickly boiled us some eggs, and gave us a meal. When we had broken our fast, we set off, getting to Alones that night.

During our absence, they had captured the two brothers from Priné who had stolen the two hundred and fifty gold sovereigns. From the twentieth of June, when they had stolen them, till now, they had stayed inside Retimo town, where their capture would have been difficult and dangerous. As they denied having done the deed, we had let them think we really believed them and were looking for the gold elsewhere. So they took courage again and came out of hiding, coming to the village of Kato Poro to find work (they were builders), where their father had accompanied them. Some of our people caught them there – I don't quite know how – and led them off. They told them they would be executed if they didn't return the gold. As they saw their captors were in no joking mood, they returned two hundred and nineteen sovereigns, and said they no longer had the thirty-one remaining ones. So they took the two brothers, telling their father they would send them to Cairo. But their father did not want to be separated from them; perhaps he was filled with foreboding. They did not succeed in persuading him to remain, so they took him as well. Thus the father and the two sons were executed somewhere in the region of Rhodakino.

All this happened while I was away. I confess I was sad, terribly, terribly sad about those two boys and their papa; but what could I have done for them?

The time passed quietly and we had no more serious misadventures: nothing but endless journeys to Alones, to Asi Gonia, to Rhodakino, to Argyroupolis, to Priné. We often went to Kyparissé as well, for that was where the Greek Government representative, Air Commodore Kelaïdis, had his hideout. A duplicating machine had been set up, and they published a newspaper called *Elliniki Phoni* – *The Greek Voice*. A very good boy and a fellow-worker of ours, Stavros Biris from Zouridi, worked the machine and turned out our little newspaper. I had often gone to their house in Zouridi with Mr Pavlo and others of our people, and the hospitality we received was wonderful. Stavro's papa, Uncle Yanni, was always eager to see us in his house. Among other things, he had a cask of marvellous *retsina*, so we were often there.

At the beginning of October, the Germans began to retire in a body from the Nomes of Lasithi and Herakleion. We learnt that they planned to concentrate their entire strength in Canea in order to put up a more effective defence in the event of attack. The creation of the Second Front in Europe seemed to have struck them with total paralysis, and they began to withdraw from all the countries where they had spread themselves, and assemble again in Germany, their own country. But how would they get out of Crete? They were transfixed with fear that just vengeance and punishment would overtake them when they fell into the hands of the people they had soaked with blood. Their recent measures were characteristic of this fear. Moving from village to village and from town to town, they rounded up numbers of girls and put them into the troop trucks with the soldiers. Thus they knew they were safe from the attacks of the guerrillas, who were growing in numbers every day.

Next to our lair at Alones was a band of guerrillas in the National cause, of company strength and commanded by Kosta Matsaro from Episkopi.

With this new thickening of the Germans in our end of the island, we set up our lair once more at Vasilè, the better to follow the German movements and to keep Cairo informed by signal. The main road was only a little way off, and we watched the endless motorized columns of Germans passing below. There were frequent meetings between our leaders and with Mr Kelaïdis, the Government representative. All one afternoon, from his lair in Kyparissé, we watched the fighters and bombers of the RAF attacking a German column all along the road from Retimo to Canea. A number of German trucks were burnt out just below us with tracer bullets fired from machine-guns in the air.

Mr Pavlo, in Mr Kelaïdis's headquarters, said he had received a telegram from Cairo asking about the industries of Crete; what could he answer? 'What is there?' he said with an ironical laugh, 'unless sheep-theft can be called an industry?'

Every day the Germans were streaming past in interminable columns: first stores, then troops. Lieutenant Fraser (Levtheri) and Yanni Kapetanakis went and placed three mines on the main road to blow up some German transport. They planned to photograph the explosion. When they had withdrawn to an observation point, a Greek vehicle passed over them, full of civilians. Fortunately, it did not touch any of them, but they were afraid of what might happen next time so they dug them up again. Immediately afterwards, a whole column of troops from Herakleion drove past.

There was a last meeting of our leaders in our hideout, and when Mr Pavlo and I went to Priné, we saw a great many people assembled there, all of them armed and with the letters EOK sewn on to white armbands, and merchants of Retimo deep in discussion with guerrilla captains. We met other *andartes* on the way with the word ELAS written cross-wise on their caps and their chests. Both were preparing to enter Retimo the moment the Germans cleared out. The situation in those days was very unsteady: who would get into Retimo first? Who would take over the offices of the town command, and so on? Mr

Nikos Daskalakis and others came to Colonel Tsiphakis's hideout on behalf of EAM, and the two parties fell into agreement.

A German deserter who was brought to us asked us to give him an EOK armband. Other Germans who were heading towards Canea met a few guerrillas on the road, and threw them some rifle ammunition out of the truck, because, they said, they were '*Nazionalisten*'.

All the Germans in Canea

On the fourteenth of the month word came to our cave that the Germans were all leaving the town of Retimo. Mr Pavlo and Aleko Barbounis set off at once. Mr Levtheri, Yanni Kapetanakis and I went to take photographs of the retreat along the main road. We took several. When the last of them had passed they blew up the Loumbini bridge. They were abandoning the whole of the island and concentrating in the north-western part of Crete, in an area running roughly from Georgioupolis to somewhere near Rhodopou.

I didn't have the luck to see and describe the celebrations for the liberation of Retimo, for I only got there a week after it became free, having remained behind in the cave with Yanni to watch over all our gear, the wireless and so on. I confess that, during the whole of the occupation of Crete, I was never more depressed and on edge than during that week. At last, one afternoon, our people came and took us, and we found all the others installed in the clinic of Doctor Dandolo,[1] which had been taken over. Yanni and I celebrated that evening, but we were sick at heart at the thought of having missed that first free day of explosive joy and enthusiasm: the precious moment we had been awaiting for three and a half years!

1 One of the many Venetian names that still survive in Crete.

But Canea still remained, and we made a vow not to miss that.

The Dandolo clinic was a spacious and very suitable building for our work. We had a cook called Koukinos, whose daughter had been an interpreter to the Germans, but working all along for the National Resistance, in order to learn the names of anyone the Germans were after so that they could be warned in time; and generally to supply whatever other information we needed. Four of us slept in a room and rather late next morning, we went downstairs and the cook gave us each a little cup of tea. I emptied mine and asked for another. I was dumbfounded to hear him say I was only entitled to one.

'Come on!' I said. 'Who told you we were only entitled to one cup?'

'Those are Mr Aleko's[1] instructions.'

'*Mister* my foot. Give me some more please.'

'But it's true!' he said. 'I can't give you any more — come and see how little sugar I've been given to last a week!'

I went into the kitchen and he brought me a bag with almost three *okas* of sugar in it. I took hold of it, and asked to see how much tea there was. He showed me a pot. I took a spoon and began to fill up my cup with tea from the pot, and when I had drunk it, filled it again and then once more. Then I shouted to the other boys: 'Anybody want any tea? Come along!' I drank five or six cups, while the cook kept beating his forehead saying: 'What will become of me, now? The officers haven't had their tea yet.'

'I'll tell you what will become of you, Mr Koukinos,' and without further ado, poured the whole sack of sugar into the pot.

1 His fellow-guide and runner, Aleko Barbounis.

'Now,' I said, 'pour on as much water as you like, and it will be sweet enough. Give the boys as much as they want, and some for the officers, and there'll still be plenty.'

The poor cook's eyes were sticking out of his head by now.

'Mr Koukinos,' I said, 'let go of your hair and your forehead. Don't worry, I'll fix everything, but bear in mind that the same thing will happen each time you say I'm only entitled to one cup of tea.'

Then I went into Mr Pavlo's room, and asked him if there were any rules about how much tea we were allowed, and if I was entitled to a second cup.

'You can have as much as you like, George,' he said. 'There are absolutely no rules at all.'

I told him the whole story of the cook, and he laughed. I asked him to tell Aleko, to whom he had given the keys and the job of supervising the stores, to give the cook enough sugar and food, as there was plenty. Why should we have enough food and tea in the caves, and the opposite now we were in a town? Then I went and calmed the cook down, who, when he saw the results of all my goings-on, became very fond of me.

I had another row with Aleko Barbounis that day. He wanted to oblige Yanni and me – or rather to order us – to help the cook with his work, and the cook started shouting for us. I was furiously angry with Aleko. But I said nothing then, except that anyone who wanted servants could hire them and have as many as he wanted, but that I was not going to be a servant to anyone, least of all to anyone as junior to me in the Service as Aleko. He went straight to Mr Pavlo with a thousand and two complaints and I don't know what false accusations. He tried to persuade Mr Pavlo to cut out army pay in the Service. He could have cut Yanni's if he had wanted to, as he received his from the English service. But there was nothing to be done about mine, even had he wanted to, because it came from the Greek Army from which I had been seconded. All these may seem trivial and laughable to whoever might read this, but for us at the time the importance was great.

I learnt that Manoli,[1] the English lieutenant, had been taken prisoner on the eighteenth on the way out of occupied Canea in a small car. This happened because the car was a German one, which he had bought for the Service from the Germans through the agency of Papayannakis, the commander of a security battalion in Canea. With him in the car were Perikles Vandoulakis, Siphi Petrakis and a driver. They were stopped outside Stilo, and led off to Neo Chorio. There they were examined, and it was soon clear what sort of people they were.

Seeing they had been properly caught, they said to themselves that whoever could do so should make a break for it if a chance came. Siphi Petrakas made a dash, and took to his heels. They started off after him firing quantities of bullets, but he got away. The others they took to Canea. They all had bogus identity papers and kept their real names secret. But it was hard for the Englishman to deceive the Germans, as it was obvious what he was – to a Greek, at any rate.

'Where do you come from?' a German, who spoke Greek well, asked him.

'*Apo tous Kampoi* (from Kampoi),' the Englishman answered.

'But the Kampians,' the German said, 'don't say "*Apo tous Kampoi*"; they say "*apo tous Kampous*".'[2]

'To the devil with all that,' Manoli then said, flinging his cap on the ground, 'I'm an English officer.'

1 Lieutenant Geoffrey Barkham.
2 '*Kampoi*' (the village is called 'Fields') is nominative plural, '*Kampous*' is in the accusative. The latter is correct after the preposition '*apo*' ('from').

He was taken off and sent to Germany, but he managed to escape on the way in Yugoslavia, when some partisans held up the column by sabotage and attacked it. He was soon back in Crete. But Perikles Vandoulakis and the driver were kept on in Ayia Jail. Luckily Perikles kept up the disguise provided by the false name on his papers – woe betide him if they had recognized him as the one that had been taken prisoner in Vaphé in 1942, and who, escaping to the Middle East, had later been dropped by parachute in the Peloponnese and captured by the Italians with a smashed leg; who had then vanished from the hospital and now reappeared in Crete, in disguise, with an English officer, and in the capital!

In Retimo we had frequent parades and celebrations and torchlight processions; also rival demonstrations by the two parties. I went to several gatherings and celebrations, and read out loud some poems I had written in the mountains. On the twenty-eighth of October when the whole of Retimo was assembled in the school, I read one about the burnt village of Yerakari; painting a picture of the beautiful village as it had been once, and then as it was now, after its destruction. I will copy it down again here in honour of that heroic village:[1]

> What muse should sing, what voice could tell the long
>   and bloodstained story
> Of how the chains of serfdom bound our country in its
>   glory?
> Who has the power to tell the tale of bloodshed, death
>   and pillage,

---

[1] I have put George's lines into the decapente syllabic metre in which they are written. The jaunty doggerel lilt, half Macaulay, half Byron, is a pretty fair equivalent of the original run of the lines. The translation is almost word for word. [PLF]

The power from God, the grace to sing, the wonders of
the village?

Of Yerakari's vanished pride? Not mine that tongue, the
fingers

To weave a garland for her grave, her sepulchre that
lingers

Cold on the hillside now. But yet – what other voice
shall raise her

Ghosts from the shades? My unskilled tongue, my lowly
quill shall praise her.

The earliest beam from Ida's peak a-wakened Yerakari,

Highest in Crete, on Kedros peak, chief of the high
Amari.

Nature endowed with teeming gifts the valleys of the
county,

But on *your* leafy vales and hills, she scattered all her
bounty:

So many trees to shade your lanes and flowers to star
your mountains,

Whose stony breast ran bright with streams and flashed
with crystal fountains.

Beneath your trees quiet waters flowed; above their
branches woven

White houses lay like doves asleep along the sill of
heaven.

When happy Spring awoke the woods and fields and
glades, unfolding

Your flowers in Mount Kedros' lap, your rocks and
pastures holding

In spells of scented breezes bound, she hung the twigs
with berries

And summer bowed your vines and trees with clustering
grapes and cherries.

While girls with baskets sent their laughter running
through the meadows;

Under the cherry-branches, then, deep in the leafy
   shadows,
The Cretan lyre struck up beside the brook, the green
   woods ringing
With Cretan rhyming couplets and with village voices
   singing;
And each day dawned a holiday, the kindly sun's
   advancing
Marked by the clink of glasses while the forest shook
   with dancing!
True Paradise it seemed! When August beat on our
   Cretan mountains,
Ah, then we came from far and near to lie by your cool
   fountains!
Cool blew the breeze of summer there. What trick of
   Nature's scheming
Gathered such store of grace and blessing there, and
   heap'd such teeming
Abundance of all goodly things? How often have your
   bowers
And shades and songs and wines and fruits and waterfalls
   and flowers
Strewn blessings on our warriors, and hope and
   consolation?
Who sought thy refuge from the fight for our enslavèd
   nation?
Who fought through all those bitter years under the
   tyrants galling
And dwelt in lonely mountain tops, where rain and
   snow were falling;
When black despair hung in the air, when tyranny was
   master,
When blood was shed 'neath the tyrant's tread and Death
   reign'd and disaster?
You were the secret shelter for each Greek and English rival

Of tyranny, who grasped a gun for liberty's survival!
But when the Dark Hour came at last, the storm clouds
broke asunder,
Barbarian tempests flung their fire, high mountains
crashed with thunder.
And now you lie there, cold and dead, ruined and black
with burning,
Empty and silent in the hills and dark with fire and
mourning.
Where are your *pallikaria* now, your chosen warriors
sleeping,
Who fell that evil day and filled Amari's vales with
weeping?
Where are your idle afternoons, your mornings bright
with sunlight?
Your founts, your belfries in the dusk, your churches
pale with moonlight?
Where are your dove-white houses now, your soft winds
and your waters,
Your happy throngs in summer time, your golden sons
and daughters?
One fiery moment burnt them all, when roofs and walls
were riven,
And whirled them flaming to the sky and through the
gates of Heaven.
They showered their light on Crete's dark night and
kindled sparks of dawning,
They showered their light on Ida's height, pale with a
new day's dawning.
Then daybreak gleamed on Crete's dark crags, reddening
her oak-trees hoary
And Freedom's sun burst from the east and filled the
world with glory!
Gone are the bitter months and years, dark slavery's
night is over,

And now the sun of Freedom shines high in the sky for
    ever!
And you, brave village! lying there, whose holocaust still
    smoulders
Among the wreck of shattered stones and beams and
    blackened boulders,
Your life begins to stir again, to climb the path whose
    furrow
The tears of Freedom channelled there, which fell on
    Freedom's morrow.
And where your numbered children fell, where the
    barbarous bullets reaped,
Slaughtered in the flaming lanes and falling walls together
    heaped,
There, at night, a rushlight burns, its wick afloat in
    sacred oil
Pressed from the olive trees that flourish yet upon your
    holy soil.
For your children have not vanished, they shall live for
    evermore
And keep the bell of Cretan freedom echoing from shore
    to shore.
They shall be eternal martyrs who for us laid down the
    price
Of LIBERTY! For us your children bore the cruel
    sacrifice.
They are the lasting witnesses to Crete's unhappy story
Theirs are the laurels, theirs the crown of victory and
    glory!

When I finished, they all clapped a long time. But at
other feasts and celebrations I recited other verses I had
written, and, especially on New Year's Day 1945, while
the battle was raging in Athens, where civil strife had
suddenly broken out in December 1944; and when out

of the whole of Greece, the Germans only retained the small perimeter round Canea. It was before a large company gathered in the Lyceum Girls' School in Retimo that I recited the following:

Saint Basil's feast has come and gone, the New Year's
    bells are flying
Free in our Cretan belfries while our capital is sighing
Still in the chains of slavery. As brother prays for brother,
Pray that their freedom comes this year, let each one
    love the other.
And may the year bring joy to Crete's tormented
    population,
And heal the scars that fester yet from German
    occupation.
Saint Basil from whose holy hand the New Year's gifts
    are flying,
Shower down on us those precious gifts, for which all
    Crete is sighing,
Of FREEDOM and of HARMONY, and let us live
    together,
As brothers should, in peace. For now the four years
    bitter weather
Changes at last. But mothers weep still for the lost
    embraces
Of children slain, and orphans seek still for their parents'
    faces.
See, kind Saint, the village streets where walls lie burnt
    and timbers rot,
See the humble graves of thousands of our men unjustly
    shot.
Give us freedom for our brothers, grant us one more gift
    today –
Free our brothers in Canea still beneath the tyrant's
    sway.

All-Holy Virgin, great Saint Basil, listen to our litany
Fling Canea's gates wide open, lead them forth, and set
them free!
All-Holy Virgin, great Saint Basil, give us HARMONY
this year
Pluck out the tares of enmity and civil strife and hate and
fear.
Let us live in peace together, in a second age of gold,
In honour, freedom, fame and wisdom, like the famous
Greeks of old!

So the days went by, partly in idleness, partly in the
pleasures of freedom, partly on the march. But when I
went to Vaphé now, I could go by car as far as Episkopi
or Kourna, and from there on to Alikampo. All the stores
for the Service at Vaphé – our closest HQ to the German
lines – were brought from Retimo to Kourna. They were
assembled in the house of Mr Zimbragoudakis, and sent
forward by mule.

Reaching Vaphé one day, I found – sitting and drinking
and singing round a long table in the house of Uncle
Antoni Vandoulakis – Mr Tom Dunbabin, Mr Smith-
Hughes, Mr Denis Ciclitira and the high-spirited Mr
Leigh Fermor. Those were all the English I remember.
With them, too, were a lot of Cretans. They were all in
a very cheerful frame of mind, and I was received with
shouts and clapping. Before I could greet them all and
sit down, Mr Michali handed me a glassful[1] of some
reddish-brown liquid that I thought was wine. '*Po, po,
po*, Mr Michali,' I said. 'It's midday, I haven't eaten
anything today, and if I drink all that I'll be drunk.'

'But, my child,' he said, 'what is drink meant for? It's
no use for anything else. You can't rub it into your scalp

[1] About a third of an ordinary tumbler.

or clean your gun with it. You drink it for the sake of *keph*,[1] to make you happy and ready to dance and sing and to forget all your worries; in fact, to get drunk, as you say. That's just what it's meant for.'

Mr Michali was in an exceptionally happy mood for he had just returned to Crete after six months' unwilling absence since leaving Crete on the sixteenth of May with the captured General, and he had spent most of these six months in hospital with a serious illness – a kind of paralysis – caused by the hardships and exposures of his life in our mountains, from which he had fortunately recovered completely. So finding himself once more among so many of his friends in Crete, whom he loved as they did him, there was plenty of reason for him that day to drink and celebrate. I hated to spoil his fun, so I took the glass and emptied it in one gulp. It was rum. And the tragic thing was that scarcely had I drunk it before Mr Dionysios gave me another glass, Mr Tom a third, Mr Smith-Hughes a fourth, and I don't know how many others. All that I know is that, as I write now, after exactly ten years, I seem to see the world go round and round, and I feel myself drowning just as I did then, after pouring those glasses down almost without drawing breath. Outside I managed to give Mr Tom my *sakouli*, which was full of gold, then set off at a trot towards the centre of the village. Manoli Gyparis brought me back. As soon as I saw him I drew my pistol and emptied it in his direction. Fortunately he saw me in time and hid behind a rock. Then he managed to seize me just as I was trying to shoot a passing donkey through the head. But it seems there were no more bullets left inside, otherwise the innocent creature would have been killed. From there I was led off nearly unconscious to the schoolhouse, where the stores were.

1 High spirits or well-being.

Here I had an appalling pain in the stomach, and my situation for several hours was tragic.

When I got back to Retimo, I made an attempt to go to Cairo to collect my army pay, but in vain.

On the eighth of December our bands had a battle with the Germans at Vaphé, and Vasili Paterakis[1] was brought to Retimo with a bad wound in the arm. The Germans had attacked the village at dawn with an advance guard of armoured cars. The first which appeared at the turn of the road on the way into the village was wrecked by the machine-guns of the guerrillas which gave them exactly the time needed to organize themselves and fight back at the Germans until they drove off with heavy losses.[2]

1 Another member of the astonishing Paterakis family of Koustoyérako.
2 Between forty and fifty Germans were killed, and two Greeks, mostly by Vasili's Bren gun.

Trouble in Retimo

So Christmas came and the New Year. The mood of the two conflicting parties had grown considerably more acute. This was in the middle of the fighting in Athens, and the conflict was echoed in Crete by this sharpening of feelings on both sides. There was daily friction until at last the inevitable happened.

It was the dawn of the seventeenth of January 1945. ELAS units had taken up positions on various heights surrounding Retimo. They also occupied the two roads leading into the town from east and west, forbidding entry to both armed and unarmed civilians, unless they belonged to EAM. Lieutenant-Colonel Pavlo Gyparis happened to be in Retimo at the time. He was in command of the Cretan Brigade of EOK guerrillas. He sent ELAS a liaison agent with the request to raise this 'siege', and leave everybody alone. The guiding spirits of ELAS promised that this should be done, and asked to discuss the matter. I don't know what differences were discussed, all I remember is that they said they had ordered the siege to be raised. But hours passed, and it was still going on. There were new complaints, and fresh discussions. There were armed men everywhere, and threats were being bandied about on both sides.

The English, with whom we were, were informed of each new movement and situation, and gave corresponding orders. I think that it must have been after midday when Gyparis sent the EAM a message saying that either the 'siege' must be raised, or he would go with a few men and break it up. But in vain. He gave them a few minutes' grace and waited with his men, ready to attack them on the north-west side of the town. A young nephew of his in the English service, Manoli Gyparis went with another boy, called Anastasi Petrakis, to see what the Elasites were up to. But as soon as they got close, with Manoli in front gun in hand, they opened fire on him. He met their fire, and tried to jump into a suitable place from which to fire back, but he did not manage it, as other Elasites shot him dead from behind. Then the battle was engaged and, in a few minutes, Gyparis with a handful of men had mounted the slope called Evlígia and the Elasites had taken to their heels, leaving two or three dead behind them. On the EOK side, Colonel Gyparis was wounded in one hand, his nephew was killed, and two others were wounded: Vangeli Minadakis, and another whose name I forget. Another party was sent to the east side of the town, where they soon dislodged the other 'besieging' Elasites there. So by evening, only two ELAS units were left inside the town, barricaded in two buildings. Watch was mounted over them all night to keep them from breaking out, and they were to be attacked next morning. During the night, however, they got away from one of the buildings, leaving all their heavy arms behind. It seems they got away along the seashore, which had been insufficiently guarded. But from the other building, near the Unknown Soldier's memorial, they were unable to escape, so they surrendered next day, after the personal intervention of Colonel Gyparis. Another brush took place on a hill above the town, and then a chase into the Eparchy of St Basil. A few of the leaders of the ELAS were killed during all this – Lemonias, Troullinos and one or two others. The rest dispersed and went home to sit on their eggs.

In Western Crete

On the twenty-third of January, Mr Pavlo, Aleko Barbounis and I took all our stuff and climbed into one of
the cars taken over by the Service, and drove to Herakleion. From there we drove down to Ayia Galini on the
south coast. We waited a night there, and next day got
on to a caique leaving for Palaochora, over in south-west
Crete, in the Eparchy of Selino. We were to wait there
two or three days, and then head for Kastelli-Kissamou.
We went by motor-car as far as Kakópetro, where we
met one of our officers called Mr Marketaki, who supplied
us with a man to guide us to Kastelli.

There were two branches of the English in Kastelli, one
under Mr Pavlo, the other under Captain John Stanley. Mr
John had been in Kissamo some time, and had been
working in co-operation with their ELAS Kapetan,
Biblis, who had been killed by Papayannakis's security
battalion. The local people believed, wrongly, that Mr
John was a communist. Mr Pavlo found a decent house,
which belonged to Mr Koutsavtakis, in which we lived.
I stayed in the room where the wireless operator worked,
in a house nearby. Our operator was a good old friend of
ours, Hippocratis Antonakis from the village of Phourphoura in the heroic Amari. My work here was fairly
tiring, as I was the connecting-link between Kastelli and
Palaochora. But we had a very good time in Kastelli, with
a party every Saturday, plenty to eat, and lots of different

kinds of fish. But the wine poured out for us by Artemis Paterakis might have been that of the wedding at Cana of Galilee! We had a band of armed men with us, most of them Seliniots. EAM also had a small ELAS unit there, with a priest in command called Father Spyro. Often his men would sing a song about 'having written on our priest's round hat, Rule of the People, Down with the King'. This small unit, at very short notice, could be brought up to a strength of five hundred; which happened very often when there was the slightest misunderstanding, especially at the appearance in Kastelli of the reserve officer leading the Nationalist party in Kissamo, George Digridis. The surrounding hills filled with armed men thirsty for action. The situation was saved each time by Mr John, the English captain, who knew the Elasites well, was a friend of Father Spyro, and pretended to be tinged himself with leftist ideas. This situation occurred so often that each morning when we woke up, Mr Pavlo used to ask me: 'Have we taken the heights again this morning, George? Do have a look,' and then he would laugh at all our nonsense.

It was February now and carnival time was coming on. Mr Pavlo commandeered a ten-ton caique, which was to take me to Herakleion, where I was to load up with clothing and stores for the Service in Kastelli. Another soldier went with me to keep me company, and there was a crew of two. We left Kastelli in the afternoon, and, before we got out of the gulf of Kissamo, to turn eastwards, night had fallen. We passed Canea far out to sea, close to the Akrotiri, taking great care lest the engine should show any sparks and give our presence away, but it was between Asprouliáno and Petré that we were closest to the shore. There were units of the Asi Gonia band in this area, and, as we learnt later, they saw the caique and were sure it must be Germans, and were preparing to open fire. Sun rose just as we came level with Retimo. I don't remember when we got to Herakleion, only that it was Carnival Saturday, and we went to a cinema that night which was all in carnival array. A lot of people had assembled for the carnival dances and we had a fine time. Our office was in Freedom Square; there I learnt that I was to take on the stores in two or three days' time. I told Mr Alexis (Sandy Rendel) that I wanted to go to Retimo and let the other boy take the stuff back. Mr Alexis was the officer who conducted me from Cairo to Crete when I returned from the Middle East. He was a very good man indeed, and I had only seen him once in Retimo after the Liberation, although he had been in Crete a whole year. He had been working in Lasithi, the easternmost nome of Crete, to which I had then never been. He agreed that the soldier should take the things back, and put in at Retimo to pick me up, as the caique would have to stop there anyway, in order to pass the German-occupied part under cover of night.

I reached Retimo on Sunday afternoon. My reason for going there was that secret and tender feelings had taken root inside me, which perhaps I ought not to confess here. I went to the Lyceum School for Greek girls that evening, where all the smart world of Retimo had assembled. The *glendi* went on till daybreak, and I drank and sang and danced all night. I have seldom been as happy as I was that night; though it is difficult for anybody to tell if I am unhappy, because I can always disguise it under cheerfulness. I would like to expand this page into a whole volume. But it would not fit in here, and I hope I will be able to write something separate about it one day.

At least three or four days went by before the caique arrived, and I returned to Kastelli without the slightest difficulty or hindrance. Now we had plenty of food and of whatever we needed. Money was almost useless – oil was the new currency; they demanded oil for whatever we wanted to buy. Mr Pavlo condemned them as black-marketeers, but later asked if we should do the same. Nothing was easier, we told him, and started with rice, of which there was scarcely any on the market. Aleko Barbounis gave an *oka* of rice for five *okas* of oil, so we could buy anything we wanted. So the whole of February went by, and three weeks of March, with very little happening. Periodical 'seizures of the heights', *glendis* and marches to Palaochora.

Just about then Mr Pavlo took me with him to Palao-chora to await an English ship which was due. When she arrived, we embarked and sailed off to Herakleion. Mr Pavlo was leaving for Cairo by aeroplane, but he stayed several days till he finally got away. Meanwhile we stayed in the Villa Ariadne in Knossos, where the English general was staying. It was also where General Kreipe had lived.

The Changeover

A proposal had been made to the Germans, and agreed
to, about an exchange of prisoners through the Bishop of
Canea. We were to receive ten of our people from the
Service who were in Ayia Jail, and to give them thirty
German prisoners; a German officer, warrant-officer and
soldier for each of ours. Mr Dionysios summoned me to
go with him to Georgioupolis, where the German territory
began. Before dawn on the thirty-first of March, we got
into two large trucks with the thirty Germans, and set
out. At about 9 a.m. we reached Asprouliano, near
Georgioupolis, where we met the Bishop's car. Mr Dionysios got down, and conversed with the Bishop. We were
soon in front of a crowd of Germans at Georgioupolis.
The road was closed here with a large wooden beam, and
we went to the main square. The Bishop and Mr Dionysios
got out. Some German officers were waiting, and all of
'our' prisoners who were to be exchanged. Mr Dionysios
talked with a German officer, who took a list of the
prisoners' names from him. Then the Germans got down,
after the two trucks had driven inside the German area,
the beam being raised to admit them. All of the Germans
with cameras took photographs. Then came ours, each
one shouting out his name, and climbed into one of our
trucks. They were all ready to leap with delight, and quite
right they were. The one who till that moment had been
Demosthenes Palakis at once resumed his real name of

Perikles Vandoulakis . . . If they had known who he really was, quite another fate would have awaited him . . . As we left he waved his hand and shouted to the chief of the Canea Gestapo: '*Yassou*, Herr Klempin, I'm Perikles Vandoulakis, not Palakis.' Then we all drove to Retimo, and I went back to Herakleion.

The Germans, locked up now for five months in the Canea area, having lost all hope of survival or flight, determined to sue for an armistice and lay down their arms. The arrangements were made, and one day was appointed for the surrender and another when the Greek Army should enter Canea and the Greek authorities take over command of the town. But the Germans, realizing their terrible responsibility for all their tortures and executions and the destruction and ruin they had scattered throughout the island, and fearing just punishment, refused to surrender to the Greeks, and insisted on giving themselves up to the English.

On the twenty-third of May 1945, exactly four years after the fall of Crete, freedom returned to the town of Canea. We left Retimo very early with Mr Pavlo, and headed for Canea by jeep. Reaching Neo-Chorio, we encountered an endless column of vehicles and of people on foot – army and guerrilla organizations mostly. We passed them, and got ahead near Kalyves. There were arches of leaves everywhere, and flowers and placards and signs wishing us welcome by the thousand, and slogans supporting EAM or EOK here or the National Army or ELAS there, and all you could wish for. Demonstrations of joy and enthusiasm everywhere. And so it was, all the way along the road to Canea. In the capital everyone had split into two camps – one camp waiting to cheer and clap the arrival of Gyparis with the National Army, the others the arrival of ELAS. It was whispered that the two sides might come to blows. Others said: 'Only the army and gendarmerie will enter Canea'; others, 'No, the *andartes* will come too' – you heard a hundred different things. I reached the market-place, when all at once I heard shouts and music and cheers, and realizing the entry had begun, I ran towards the shouting as fast as my legs would carry me.

γ.ψ.

Index

READ MORE IN PENGUIN

In every corner of the world, on every subject under the sun, Penguin represents quality and variety – the very best in publishing today.

For complete information about books available from Penguin – including Puffins, Penguin Classics and Arkana – and how to order them, write to us at the appropriate address below. Please note that for copyright reasons the selection of books varies from country to country.

In the United Kingdom: Please write to *Dept. EP, Penguin Books Ltd, Bath Road, Harmondsworth, West Drayton, Middlesex UB7 ODA*

In the United States: Please write to *Consumer Sales, Penguin Putnam Inc., P.O. Box 999, Dept. 17109, Bergenfield, New Jersey 07621-0120.* VISA and MasterCard holders call 1-800-253-6476 to order Penguin titles

In Canada: Please write to *Penguin Books Canada Ltd, 10 Alcorn Avenue, Suite 300, Toronto, Ontario M4V 3B2*

In Australia: Please write to *Penguin Books Australia Ltd, P.O. Box 257, Ringwood, Victoria 3134*

In New Zealand: Please write to *Penguin Books (NZ) Ltd, Private Bag 102902, North Shore Mail Centre, Auckland 10*

In India: Please write to *Penguin Books India Pvt Ltd, 210 Chiranjiv Tower, 43 Nehru Place, New Delhi 110 019*

In the Netherlands: Please write to *Penguin Books Netherlands bv, Postbus 3507, NL-1001 AH Amsterdam*

In Germany: Please write to *Penguin Books Deutschland GmbH, Metzlerstrasse 26, 60594 Frankfurt am Main*

In Spain: Please write to *Penguin Books S. A., Bravo Murillo 19, 1° B, 28015 Madrid*

In Italy: Please write to *Penguin Italia s.r.l., Via Benedetto Croce 2, 20094 Corsico, Milano*

In France: Please write to *Penguin France, Le Carré Wilson, 62 rue Benjamin Baillaud, 31500 Toulouse*

In Japan: Please write to *Penguin Books Japan Ltd, Kaneko Building, 2-3-25 Koraku, Bunkyo-Ku, Tokyo 112*

In South Africa: Please write to *Penguin Books South Africa (Pty) Ltd, Private Bag X14, Parkview, 2122 Johannesburg*

READ MORE IN PENGUIN

A CHOICE OF NON-FICTION

Citizens Simon Schama

'The most marvellous book I have read about the French Revolution in the last fifty years' – *The Times*. 'He has chronicled the vicissitudes of that world with matchless understanding, wisdom, pity and truth, in the pages of this huge and marvellous book' – *Sunday Times*

1945: The World We Fought For Robert Kee

Robert Kee brings to life the events of this historic year as they unfolded, using references to contemporary newspapers, reports and broadcasts, and presenting the reader with the most vivid, immediate account of the year that changed the world. 'Enthralling ... an entirely realistic revelation about the relationship between war and peace' – *Sunday Times*

Cleared for Take-Off Dirk Bogarde

'It begins with his experiences in the Second World War as an interpreter of reconnaissance photographs ... he witnessed the liberation of Belsen – though about this he says he cannot write. But his awareness of the horrors as well as the dottiness of war is essential to the tone of this affecting and strangely beautiful book' – *Daily Telegraph*

Nine Parts of Desire Geraldine Brooks
The Hidden World of Islamic Women

'She takes us behind the veils and into the homes of women in every corner of the Middle East ... It is in her description of her meetings – like that with Khomeini's widow Khadija, who paints him as a New Man (and one for whom she dyed her hair vamp-red) – that the book excels' – *Observer*. 'Frank, engaging and captivating' – *New Yorker*

Insanely Great Steven Levy

The Apple Macintosh revolutionized the world of personal computing – yet the machinations behind its conception were nothing short of insane. 'One of the great stories of the computing industry ... a cast of astonishing characters' – *Observer*. 'Fascinating edge-of-your-seat story' – *Sunday Times*

READ MORE IN PENGUIN

A CHOICE OF NON-FICTION

African Nights Kuki Gallmann

Through a tapestry of interwoven true episodes, Kuki Gallmann here evokes the magic that touches all African life. The adventure of a moonlit picnic on a vanishing island; her son's entrancement with chameleons and the mystical visit of a king cobra to his grave; the mysterious compassion of an elephant herd – each event conveys her delight and wonder at the whole fabric of creation.

Far Flung Floyd Keith Floyd

Keith Floyd's culinary odyssey takes him to the far-flung East and the exotic flavours of Malaysia, Hong Kong, Vietnam and Thailand. The irrepressible Floyd as usual spices his recipes with witty stories, wry observation and a generous pinch of gastronomic wisdom.

The Reading Solution Paul Kropp with Wendy Cooling

The Reading Solution makes excellent suggestions for books – both fiction and non-fiction – for readers of all ages that will stimulate a love of reading. Listing hugely enjoyable books from history and humour to thrillers and poetry selections, *The Reading Solution* provides all the help you need to ensure that your child becomes – and stays – a willing, enthusiastic reader.

Lucie Duff Gordon Katherine Frank
A Passage to Egypt

'Lucie Duff Gordon's life is a rich field for a biographer, and Katherine Frank does her justice ... what stays in the mind is a portrait of an exceptional woman, funny, wry, occasionally flamboyant, always generous-spirited, and firmly rooted in the social history of her day' – *The Times Literary Supplement*

The Missing of the Somme Geoff Dyer

'A gentle, patient, loving book. It is about mourning and memory, about how the Great War has been represented – and our sense of it shaped and defined – by different artistic media ... its textures are the very rhythms of memory and consciousness' – *Guardian*

READ MORE IN PENGUIN

A CHOICE OF NON-FICTION

The Pillars of Hercules   Paul Theroux

At the gateway to the Mediterranean lie the two Pillars of Hercules. Beginning his journey in Gibraltar, Paul Theroux travels the long way round – through the ravaged developments of the Costa del Sol, into Corsica and Sicily and beyond – to Morocco's southern pillar. 'A terrific book, full of fun as well as anxiety, of vivid characters and curious experiences' – *The Times*

Where the Girls Are   Susan J. Douglas

In this brilliantly researched and hugely entertaining examination of women and popular culture, Susan J. Douglas demonstrates the ways in which music, TV, books, advertising, news and film have affected women of her generation. Essential reading for cultural critics, feminists and everyone else who has ever ironed their hair or worn a miniskirt.

Journals: 1954–1958   Allen Ginsberg

These pages open with Ginsberg at the age of twenty-eight, penniless, travelling alone and unknown in California. Yet, by July 1958 he was returning from Paris to New York as the poet who, with Jack Kerouac, led and inspired the Beats . . .

The New Spaniards   John Hooper

Spain has become a land of extraordinary paradoxes in which traditional attitudes and contemporary preoccupations exist side by side. The country attracts millions of visitors – yet few see beyond the hotels and resorts of its coastline. John Hooper's fascinating study brings to life the many faces of Spain in the 1990s.

A Tuscan Childhood   Kinta Beevor

Kinta Beevor was five when she fell in love with her parents' castle facing the Carrara mountains. 'The descriptions of the harvesting and preparation of food and wine by the locals could not be bettered . . . alive with vivid characters' – *Observer*